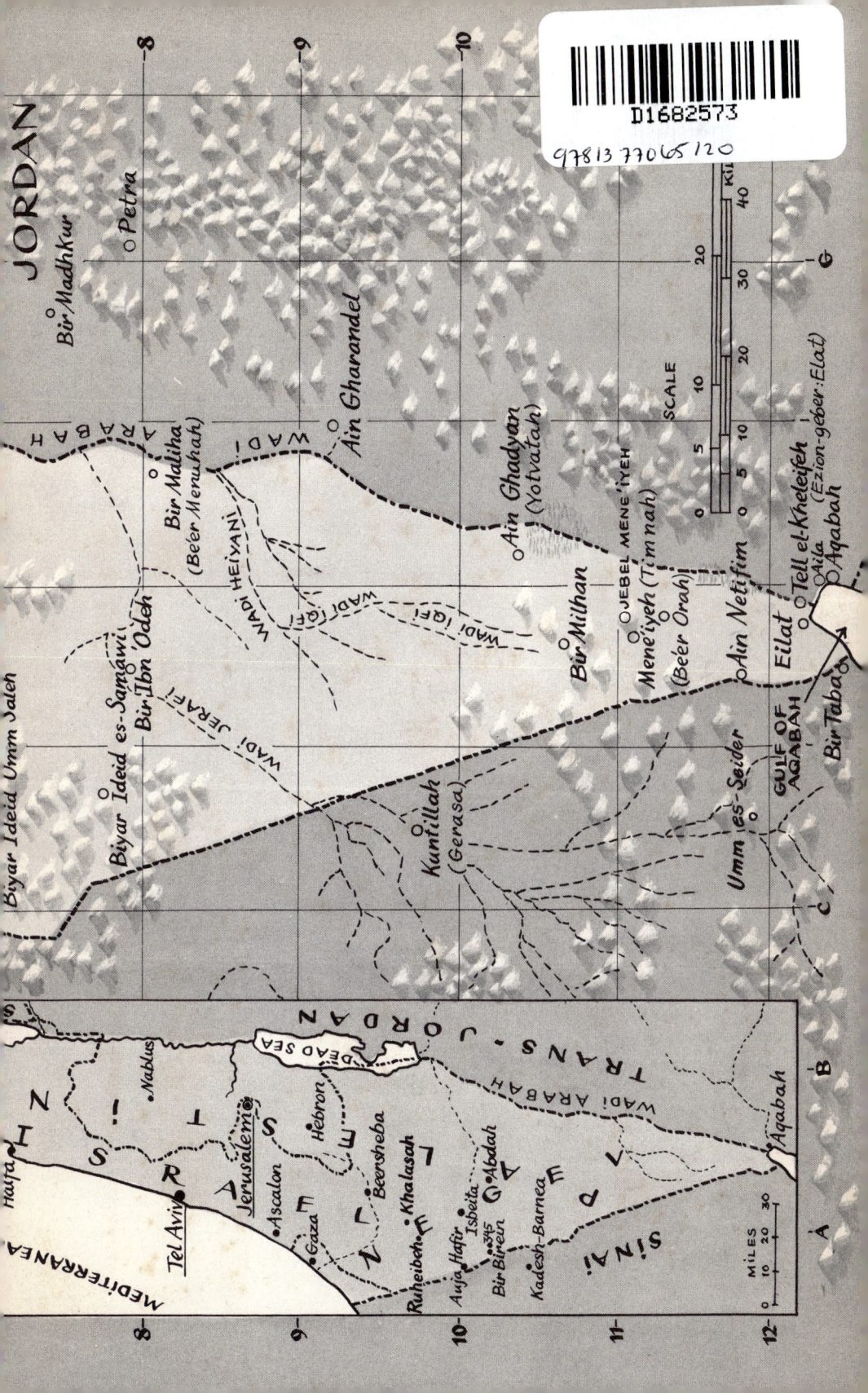

RIVERS IN THE DESERT

"Turn again, our captivity, O Jehovah,
As the streams (Afiqim) in the Negev.
They that sow in tears shall reap in joy.
He that goeth forth and weepeth,
Bearing seed for sowing,
Shall doubtless come again with joy,
Bringing his sheaves with him"

                        (Psalm 126:4-6).

RIVERS IN THE DESERT

A History of the Negev

NELSON GLUECK

Hebrew Union College—
Jewish Institute of Religion

Farrar, Straus and Cudahy
New York

Copyright © 1959 by Nelson Glueck
Library of Congress Catalog Card Number: 59-5609
Third Printing, 1959

Published simultaneously in Canada by
Ambassador Books, Ltd., Toronto

Manufactured in the United States of America
American Book-Stratford Press, Inc., New York

CONTENTS

Introduction xiv

I. "IN THE BEGINNING"

Flint Tools 1
Has the Climate Changed? 7
Response to Challenge 13
Miracles in the Desert 20
Stone Age Inhabitants 25
Is the Bible Correct? 30

II. "REMEMBER THE DAYS OF OLD"

Five Thousand Years Ago 39
Life Underground 42
A Mighty Witness 50
Distaff and Spindle 53
Places Without Names 56
An Era of Emptiness 59

III. HEARTLAND OF CONSCIENCE

The Breaker of Idols	60
"Say, Thou Art My Sister"	66
The Kings of the East	68
Pax Abrahamitica	76

IV. "THE WAY OF THE WILDERNESS"

"Is Not the Whole Land Before Thee?"	85
The Inland Road	87
Soil and Water	90
Streams in the Negev	92
The Invention of Cisterns	94
Site 345	97
The Journey of Sinuhe	101
Ebbtide	105

V. "THIS IS THE BLESSING"

Spying Out the Land	111
Old Gods and New	115
Retreat and Regeneration	118
"Thou Art the Man"	122
The Kenites of the Negev	132
Districts of the Negev	134
Editorial Favorites	136
Desert Ways	141

VI. FACING SOUTH

The First Line of Defense	146
King Solomon's Copper Mines	153
Ships to Ophir	157

CONTENTS   vii

The Unexpected 163
Reoccupation of the Negev 168
"Walls, Towers, Gates and Bars" 173
The Structure of Security 181
The Permanence of Change 186

VII. THE NABATAEANS

Out of the East 191
They Came from Arabia 193
Foundations of Empire 195
Metamorphosis of Nomads 198
Garden Cities in the Desert 201
The Scorpion Pass 205
Kurnub 207
Wonder Workers 210
A Hidden Valley 213
"Bring Forth to Them Water Out of the Rock" 215
*"He Built Towers in the Wilderness and Hewed Out
   Many Cisterns"* 222
"He Led Them Also by a Straight Path" 225
Witness Mounds 228
Then and Now 229
Pathway and Portal 232
They Drew on Rock 235
The Chain of Connection 240

VIII. THE CROSS AND THE CANDELABRA

The Turn of the Wheel 243
A New Constellation in the East 245
Renewal and Efflorescence 247

The Epicenter of Christianity	249
Old Wine in New Bottles	252
The Sign of the Cross	256
Phantom Cities	257
Aftermath	276
The Care of the Dead	277
A Passion for Worship	278
The Symbol of the Menorah	279
Index to the Text	285
Index of Biblical Citations	300

MAPS

	following page
Rainfall in Inches	20
Wanderings of Abraham	66
The Ways of Shur and the Philistines	260

ILLUSTRATIONS

	following page
Figures 1-10	46
Figures 11-19	76
Figures 20-28	140
Figures 29-37	172
Figures 38-46	204
Figures 47-55	236

INTRODUCTION

A BLANK SPACE on a historical map is a constant challenge to the explorer and archaeologist. Its emptiness disturbs him. What role, if any, did it play in the development of civilization? Where and when did its ancient inhabitants live? Was its soil rich or poor, its water plentiful or lacking, its minerals abundant or unknown, its landscape attractive or forbidding, its geographical position of great or indifferent importance?

Every area on the face of the earth, be it seemingly ever so waste and empty, has a story behind it which the inquisitive sooner or later will attempt to obtain. And when such a *terra incognita* forms a bridgehead between continents, as does that part of the Holy Land called the Negev, then the urge to explore its past becomes irresistible. I have concerned myself with that task during the last six years, under the auspices of the Hebrew Union College—Jewish Institute of Religion.

It represents the natural continuation of similar work carried out in previous years in Transjordan, which had resulted in bringing its remote and hazy past into clear focus for the first time. The discovery of more than a thousand ancient sites belonging to a whole series of advanced, agricultural civilizations existing in widely separated periods had underlined and filled out scanty references in the Bible dealing with some of them. Edom, Moab and Ammon became tangible realities, the Nabataeans were revealed as a highly civilized people, and unscientific theories of profound climatic changes in historical times had been dispelled by new and irrefutable historical facts.

It was therefore logical and alluring to extend the archaeological survey westward across the dividing rift of the Wadi Arabah, which separated Edom from the Negev. It seemed unlikely that civilization could have halted at the edge of this comparatively narrow, physical fault and tenuous boundary line which stretched from the south end of the Dead Sea to the north end of the Gulf of Aqabah. And so we plunged into the Negev and found that it was full of cultural monuments, waiting to be recognized. In the course of the last half dozen years we have been able to place on the map the locations of about four hundred sites of distant centuries, which belonged to well-developed civilizations reaching far beyond the confines of the Negev. Others too, notably Johanon Aharoni, David Alon, Emanual Anati and Jose Feldman have in recent years discovered and correctly dated some additional ancient sites there. Two of the sites mentioned in this book, namely Khirbet Gharrah and Khirbet Ghazza, were first archaeologically examined and correctly dated by Johanon Aharoni. The biographical account of man in the Negev is a long and tortuous one, with many chapters completely missing. It reaches back to early prehistoric periods, when Palestine Man first walked the face of the earth. The record of his coming and going is revealed by the changing types of skillfully made flint tools, that remained after the disappearance of his kind.

INTRODUCTION xi

History as such begins in the Negev during the latter part of the Chalcolithic period, near the end of the fourth millennium B.C., when people lived in mud-brick villages, tilled the soil, wove cloth, made fired pottery, carved ivory images and forged copper tools and weapons. The brilliant French archaeologist, Jean Perrot, has excavated one of these villages near Beersheba, and I have found others in the comparatively fertile plains of the Northern Negev. This region may be equated with the Beersheba Basin and represents the topmost and broadest section of the triangular area of the Negev.

After the Chalcolithic civilization was brought to an end by some unknown catastrophe, there ensued a long hiatus in the datable history of man in the Negev, which lasted for most of the third millennium B.C. And then, suddenly, a new civilization appeared, which can be assigned by clearcut pottery remains to the Abrahamitic Period between the twenty-first and nineteenth centuries B.C. The events in the lives of the Patriarchs, which are alluded to in the Biblical narrative as having taken place in the Negev, could have occurred only during these three centuries, if they are to be included within any historical framework at all, and if one is to rely, as I do, upon the amazing historical memory of the Bible.

These Abrahamitic Period settlements were found not only in the plains of the Northern Negev, but also among the broken highlands of the Central Negev. Indeed, in these two sections of the Negev were located most of the villages which sprang up under incredibly difficult conditions during widely separated periods of approximately four thousand years of ancient history.

The average rainfall even in these districts of the Negev, whose lands at the best must be classified as semi-marginal, ranges from less than ten to about six inches a year, as one goes from north to south. Beyond that, in the narrowing confines of the Southern Negev, the annual precipitation diminishes progressively till it measures only about an inch or less a year at Elath.

In all three parts of the Negev, we found Judaean kingdom villages and fortresses, which could be dated from the time of King Solomon at the end of the tenth century B.C. down to the beginning of the sixth century B.C., when Judah was destroyed by the Babylonians. Solomon and his successors maintained fortresses and industrial settlements even in the almost completely arid Southern Negev, to protect the trade routes through it between Jerusalem and the Judaean seaport and industrial center of Ezion-geber, and to keep the lines of communication open to and from the copper mines in the Wadi Arabah, which formed the eastern boundary of the Negev, even as Sinai bordered its western side.

The most intensive period of sedentary settlement in all of the Negev occurred during the Nabataean-Roman and Byzantine periods, extending from the second century B.C. to the seventh century A.D. This stretch of almost eight hundred years represents the longest period of continuous civilization in the entire history of the Negev. Every possible bit of ground was cultivated, and every drop of rainwater was sought. Commerce throve and the population grew as never before. As many as a hundred thousand people may have lived there then.

The long history of the rise and fall of civilizations in the Negev, with periods of sedentary occupation alternating with periods of emptiness, when Bedouins were the masters of the land, is strikingly similar to that of Transjordan. The gaps in the story must be ascribed to wars and economic blight rather than to drastic changes in the weather. As a result of these explorations, the area of the Negev no longer marks an empty space on the edge of the map of the Fertile Crescent, whose cultivable lands, extending in a great semicircle from the head of the Persian Gulf through Iraq, Syria, Lebanon and Palestine are hemmed in by the desert to the south and east, the mountains to the north and the Mediterranean to

INTRODUCTION xiii

the west. The Negev is in many ways the poorest of these lands, but far from the least important.

It is a land of sharp contrasts, of surprising fertility and extreme barrenness, of delicate flowers and fierce bushes armed with tearing spikes, of rain in scarcity and cisterns without number, of extreme dryness and heavy dew. It is a land of great heat by day and bitter cold by night, of some amazing riches and much unrelieved poverty, of cultivable plains, high and broken plateaus, deep canyons, and innumerable dry stream beds that on rare occasions are hosts to short-lived torrents. It is a strong land of wide horizons and open spaces, where divinity once made itself apparent and where sturdy pioneers seek once again to strike root.

The Biblical passages quoted are based on the Revised Version published in 1901, which happens to be the one I have had with me on my travels during the last few years, mainly because of the dictionary and concordance attached to it. I have, however, made my own insertions or translations whenever it suited my purposes.

Our work in the Negev would not have been possible without the assistance and protection of the Israeli Armed Forces. Highly to be praised are the numerous, young Israeli colonists, whose deep interest in Biblical archaeology made them gladly forego their brief annual vacations to join my expeditions in the hottest months of the year. Many thanks are due my chief assistant, Benno Rothenberg, who is responsible for all the photographs published in this book, unless otherwise specified. He has been an invaluable member of our archaeological team, and I am deeply indebted to him for his helpfulness in every possible respect. The first published description of the sanctuary in Wadi Umm es-Sedeir, which is dealt with in the last pages of this book, and the original translations of the inscriptions found there are contained in the excellent volume, *Tagliyot Sinai*, written by him and others. Jean Perrot and Dorothy Kenyon have kindly permitted the use of photographs from their excavations. Mrs. E. Philip Vogel has prepared the index.

I dedicate this book to the memory of the late Louis M. Rabinowitz, who not only supported most of my Negev expeditions with open hands and heart, but was also one of the most generous and deeply understanding patrons in modern America of arts and letters and the freedoms that go with them.

NELSON GLUECK

Cincinnati, Ohio
May 1, 1958

ARCHAEOLOGICAL PERIODS

Palaeolithic   before 8000 B.C.
(including Aurignacian and Early Mesolithic)
Natufian (Late Mesolithic)   about 8000-6000 B.C.
Neolithic   about 6000-4500 B.C.
Upper Chalcolithic   about 4500-4000 B.C.
Middle Chalcolithic   about 4000-3500 B.C.
Late Chalcolithic   about 3500-3200 B.C.
Early Bronze I-IV   32nd-21st centuries B.C.
Middle Bronze I   21st-19th centuries B.C.
Middle Bronze II   19th-16th centuries B.C.
Late Bronze I-II   16th-13th centuries B.C.
Iron I   12th-10th centuries B.C.
Iron II   9th-6th centuries B.C.
Iron III   about 550-332 B.C.
Hellenistic   332-63 B.C.
Roman   63 B.C.-323 A.D.
Nabataean   2nd century B.C.-106 A.D.
(most flourishing period)
Byzantine   323 A.D.-636 A.D.

CHAPTER I

"IN THE BEGINNING"

Flint Tools

THE KNOWN STORY of mankind in Palestine reaches back more than a hundred millennia ago. In a cave in the hills above the Lake of Galilee, in another near Nazareth, and in the cave of et-Tabun, south of Mt. Carmel at Haifa, overlooking the Mediterranean, bones or skulls or skeletons of human beings have been discovered which may be assigned to the Middle Palaeolithic period, as far back perhaps as 150,000 to 120,000 years ago.

Some of the skeletons of et-Tabun were cased in natural coffins of limestone breccia which had slowly solidified about them, as flies or beetles are sometimes entombed in coagulations of amber. The skeletons range from a Neanderthal type woman to a man with some strikingly modern characteristics. The mixture of races they represent had resulted from the meeting and interbreeding of the earliest peoples on the intercontinental bridgehead of Palestine. The vast influence Palestine has always exercised because of its geographical position affected the gradual transformation there of *homo sapiens*. A new species came into being, which has become known as Palestine Man (Palaeoanthropus Palestinensis).

The flaked flint tools this Palestine Man used have been found also at numerous places in the Negev. Palaeolithic flint hand axes of a still earlier period were found there corresponding to those discovered at the et-Tabun cave below the levels in which skeletons of Palestine Man were uncovered. The Negev, then, was within the orbit of his wanderings, as well as that of his predecessors, whose tools alone are known, but whose identity still escapes us. It is possible that the very, very great grandchildren of Palestine Man, if we assume that, somehow, there were continuous lines of succession, may include such native peoples of the Negev as the Kenites, among whom Moses found himself a wife. It is conceivable that there may be a chain of unbroken connection from the prehistoric man of the cave near Mt. Carmel to Moses, the "man of God" of Sinai and Nebo. One was dependent upon adaptability and cunning, the other upon conscience and consecration. Both of them were touched by the finger of God. Both of them, stirred by the mystery of creation, worshipped divinity in accordance with their own understanding.

Palestine Man was a mighty hunter, although the only weapons and tools at his command were those he learned early in his career to shape out of flint and basalt. He acquired this skill apparently not long after crossing the immense chasm that yawns between beast and man. With such simple means and the intelligence that enabled him to contrive traps of various kinds, he managed to keep alive and perpetuate his kind in the savage conflict for existence.

Monstrous rhinoceroses, hippopotami, elephants and cave oxen were common in his age. Their bones have been dug up all over the country from the Mediterranean coast to the Jordan river valley and in the mountain ranges between. In the ancient bed of the Jordan, which lies considerably below the present one, there was found an elephant's tusk six feet long. Bones and teeth of these great beasts have been discovered also in the hills of Bethlehem.

In those days tropical conditions prevailed. The land was raw and damp and hot. Then a series of radical changes followed during approximately the next 100,000 years, until a dry, warm climate developed at the beginning of the Mesolithic Natufian period, about the eighth millennium B.C. By then the original types of animals had vanished, and deer and gazelles became abundant. The climate has remained much the same to this very day!

During the passage of these eons of time radical alterations in the face of the earth were taking place. Seas withdrew, lakes dwindled, swamps dried up and the courses of streams were diverted or blocked. As the result of a great upthrust of land, the southward flow of the Jordan was locked in a thirteen-hundred-foot-deep pit to form the leaden mixture known variously as the Asphalt Lake, the Sea of Salt, the Sea of Lot or the Dead Sea.

Throughout these countless years, the Beni Adam (the Children of Man) did not lose ground but strengthened and improved their lot. Some fauna and flora disappeared completely, but mankind surged forward, succumbing neither to cataclysms of nature nor to catastrophes of its own making. Ingenious, inventive, indomitable, the Children of Man rapidly achieved dominion over all other living creatures. "And God said, Let us make man in our image, after our likeness: and let them have dominion over the fish of the sea, and over the birds of the heavens, and over the cattle, and over all the earth, and over every creeping thing that creepeth upon the earth" (Genesis 1:26).

With the advent of the Natufian period, some ten thousand years ago, there came a revolutionary development. The inhabitants of the land began to practice a primitive kind of agriculture. They used flint tools to break up the ground for planting, harvested wheat with sickles of fine flint blades embedded in bone handles and crushed the grain with pestles in mortars of limestone and basalt. With these first halting steps to produce their own food, instead of relying exclusively upon hunting and the gathering of wild fruits, they left the world of the savage and entered the Modern Era. Flocks began to be raised, baskets made, sculpture attempted. Bone pins and awls came into use. Pendants and beads appeared as ornaments. A sickle handle of bone found at et-Tabun was carved to represent a fawn. The inhabitants of Natufian Jericho commenced living in houses of their own construction, instead of in caves. By the beginning of the Neolithic period, about 6000 B.C., Jericho already had experienced several millennia of what by all counts must be considered civilized history.

Man was on the march and he would establish cities and kingdoms and cultures. The quest for knowledge and power would become a conscious and growing concern. He would learn how to bake pottery, smelt ores, weave cloth, reckon time by the stars in their courses, create languages with alphabets to express his thoughts, build towers which reached arrogantly toward the skies and bend the forces of nature ever more to his will. And then disaster would strike. Deserts would appear where irrigated fields had flourished, entire states collapse with their cities literally disintegrating into dust, whole populations melt away where multitudes had thrived. Instead of laughter and song and the bustle of creativity, there would be the silence of emptiness and the stillness of death. But then, after a time, all of this would start all over again, with sometimes the embers of previous gains serving to kindle the new developments.

Thus for long years, or even centuries, various parts of the earth would lie waste and void, until newcomers often of a different culture and speech and sometimes of a different race took possession of the land. They would erect new dwellings and sometimes protective walls around them over the debris of the old, the sameness of location determined by unchanging factors of topography, water, defense and economics. As a result of the frequent repetition of this process in the lengthening calendar of civilization, there would arise in time over the original knoll an artificial city-hill, which would finally be abandoned forever for one reason or another.

It was not uncommon for the debris of these ruins piled on top of one another, as one superimposed city after another was destroyed, to rise as much as a hundred feet or even more. Some of these *tells,* as they are known in Arabic and Hebrew, or *tillu* (ruin-heap) in Babylonian, conceal the ruins of as many as twenty cities, encompassing almost the total span of history. Later, during the Hellenistic-Roman period especially, new cities were built on previously unoccupied sites because of their very large and heavy foundations and structures and because it was no longer necessary for each one to be strongly fortified and located on an easily defendable position.

Whole landscapes in large parts of the Fertile Crescent, which are bare of population and cultivation today, are strewn with these tells, testifying both to the creative genius and the nihilistic tendencies of mankind. Excavations undertaken among some of them indicate the existence of temples and houses and of arts and letters of exciting excellence in early ages. Many of the achievements in such countries as ancient Assyria, Babylonia and Egypt have rarely been surpassed. From an airplane one can see lines of ancient canals, now silted over, which once extended between the Tigris and the Euphrates. They testify to the existence of widespread and intensive irrigation agriculture in what was, it is thought, formerly the Garden of Eden. In our time a fine start has already been made to restore all this country to its former fertility. With tranquility, vigor and vision, the glories of Assurbanipal, Nebuchadnezzar and Artaxerxes could be equaled again in the same lands.

There are some countries, however, such as Transjordan and the Negev, where these multilayered mounds of former civilizations are rare. If you travel through the one you will be convinced from casual observation that large sections of it were from very early times, if not always, beyond the limits of settlement. If you travel through the other, it will seem obvious that it was, on the whole, never anything but an uninhabited and uninhabitable wilderness. It has indeed been thought, and little wonder, that "no great route now leads or ever has led through this district of the Negev." It has always appeared as a blank on every Biblical map because of the familiar and generally accepted dictum of high authority that "[the Holy Land] practically extended from Dan to Beersheba, where, during the greater part of history, the means of settled cultivation came to an end" (George Adam Smith, *The Historical Geography of the Holy Land*, p. 280).

These judgments are not correct for either of these lands. In each of them, for many reasons, periods of urban settlement were hundreds and sometimes thousands of years apart. The extreme desolation created repeatedly by merciless invaders resulted often in the total disappearance of civilizations. "And he took the city, and slew the people that were therein; and he beat down the city, and sowed it with salt" (Judges 9:45).

In the fallow periods that followed, there was no law nor order, and Bedouins roamed the countryside. Their depredations, along with the forces of natural deterioration, resulted frequently in the remaining ruins being leveled to the ground. When new settlers arrived, sometimes after prolonged intervals of time, they would neither know nor be able to recognize the locations of the previous town sites and would build their houses of stone or of mud brick on virgin soil. No firmly rooted people of the land would be left who had retained and could transmit from historical memory the heritage of unbroken tradition. Only by chance would they build exactly where perhaps a thousand years earlier another village had once stood.

Has the Climate Changed?

The easy and unsubstantiated explanation frequently given for the absence or for the downfall and disappearance of whole kingdoms and cultures in the ancient Near East is to assume climatic changes of such severity as to make the establishment or continuation of civilized life impossible. Yet the horrifying tendency of man, wearily repeated throughout the centuries, to take his neighbor's goods or country, or to "scorch" the land for his own protection and his enemies' hurt, is all too adequate a reason. It certainly makes understandable why scores of cities have been reduced to piles of faceless rubble, rich countrysides transformed almost overnight into wildernesses, and why dark ages have followed times of cultural enlightenment.

I could show you a thousand or more sites of antiquity in Transjordan which existed during and after the time the land was supposed no longer to be able to sustain them because of radical, pronounced and permanent climatic changes. The settlements on them flourished in spite of currently popular theories of a steady diminution of rainfall that made permanent, sedentary, agricultural occupation progressively impossible. Their imagined absence in many apparently vacant regions had to be accounted for, and this theory of climatic change seemed to furnish the answer. The fault lay perhaps in the fact that most of the ruins which barely fleck the surface could not be discovered without mastery of the modern techniques and tools of archaeological investigation. These were developed and perfected in the first half and particularly in the second quarter of the twentieth century A.D. in Palestine by such scholars as Sir Flinders Petrie, Père Hugo Vincent, Clarence S. Fisher and William F. Albright, among others. Only then was it possible to recognize the locations and determine the dates of such ancient sites as were marked by often little more than surface scraps of pottery.

The science of pottery identification has now developed to such a degree that from broken fragments alone, which are almost invariably found on the surface of every ancient site, the competent student can determine the spans of civilized occupation they represent with less of an error than a hundred years in a thousand. Pottery, made of clay mixed with a binding material of tiny stones or shells and thoroughly baked in a kiln, is perhaps the most durable substance that man has ever created.

Pottery can be shattered, but the pieces will remain, indeed have remained intact for thousands of years. Stone crumbles. The limestone fortification walls of ancient Biblical cities were regularly breached by the enemy's building huge brush fires against them and literally burning them down. Copper and iron, unless specially treated, corrode and decompose. Glass decays and flakes away. Wood, leather, papyrus, paper and cloth disappear unless properly protected or buried in absolutely dry places where no moisture can penetrate. Pottery alone is impervious to such chemical changes and has endured since it was first invented, as an exceedingly important handmaid of history. Man's discovery of how to make and bake earthenware vessels in which water could be carried and food prepared and stored, ranks in importance not far behind his learning the kindly uses of fire for his internal and external comfort.

As a result of empirical experience, gained from numerous scientifically controlled excavations of ancient sites, it has become possible to fix the dates of widely distributed pottery vessels, whether found in context or not. At first, complete pieces of pottery, or even fragments from a distinctive level of a tell, could be dated by all kinds of associated criteria, ranging, for instance, from previously well known types which may have been imported from abroad to scarabs or coins or inscriptions. In time, through the extension of this process, it became possible to utilize just potsherds, found on the top or slopes of a tell or on a completely razed site, as keys to open gates in what previously may have appeared to be blank walls of history. These artifacts were familiar to the ancients and were referred to frequently: "Woe unto him that striveth with his Maker! a potsherd among the potsherds of the earth! Shall the clay say to him that fashioneth it, what makest thou?" (Isaiah 45:9).

The forces of erosion cutting away constantly at the sides of every layered tell expose to sight pottery and potsherds usually of every period of its occupation. If hundreds of ancient sites in a given area are examined only in this one fashion, the margin of error in fixing the periods of sedentary occupation is either nil or is reduced to negligible proportions. Dates arrived at from such surface finds have been regularly corroborated by subsequent excavation. Years ago, William Foxwell Albright, the most outstanding scholar and archaeologist of the ancient Near East, examined the potsherds on Tell Beit Mirsim (Biblical Debir or Qiriath-sefer) in southwestern Palestine and decided that it had been inhabited from 2000 to 600 B.C. Four years of excavations followed. On the basis of the huge quantity of materials excavated, he came to the conclusion that his previous figures were wrong. Instead of from 2000 to 600 B.C., the proper dating, he said, should have been from 2200 to 586 B.C.!

I have gathered fragments of pottery from the surfaces of one or another ancient site which fairly shout out the periods of history they belong to. It is as if they had been waiting for ages for someone to come along and notice them and pick them up, so that they could describe with eloquent pride the time and quality of their kingdoms. I can assure you that the archaeologist regards each artifact with feelings akin to personal affection.

With the "open sesame" that such surface sherds afforded our expeditions, we worked our way, square mile by square mile, through Transjordan and later on the Negev, prospecting for the treasures of antiquity. It was not easy in this fashion to glean the stuff of history from large areas repeatedly scythed bare of flourishing communities. As a result, whole civilizations came to the fore whose real nature had either been insufficiently comprehended from scanty Biblical references or whose very existence had escaped recognition. In Transjordan, the Biblical kingdoms of Edom and Moab, among others, assumed the substance of tangible reality. Mesha, king of Moab, consequently became a person of flesh and blood and not just a shadowy figure in the Scriptural account, as did also Balaam of Ammon, who refused at the behest of Balak of Moab to curse Israel, and Job of Edom who refused to curse God. The famous stele, on which was incised the account of how Mesha regained his country's independence from Ahab of Israel, became more understandable in the light of the numerous fine cities and stout fortresses we discovered that belonged to the highly developed kingdom over which he ruled. And the kingdom of Edom was found to be just as strong.

It became clear too, why, being denied permission to travel via the King's Highway through the center of Edom and Moab, in spite of their specific promise to deviate neither to the right nor left of it, the Israelites of the Exodus had no choice but to heed the refusal. Their enfeebled forces would have been overwhelmed by the armies of these entrenched kingdoms. They therefore took the desert route northward around the east borders of Edom and Moab before turning westward to cross over the Jordan and enter the Promised Land at Gilgal and Jericho. The Exodus through easternmost Transjordan could thus not have taken place before the thirteenth century B.C. If it had occurred earlier, the wanderers would have found neither Edomites nor Moabites with sufficient strength to say them yea or nay with regard to anything.

The onslaught of Babylonia and not any cataclysms of nature finally brought about the downfall of Edom and Moab and their contemporaries on both sides of the Jordan in the first part of the sixth century B.C. Considerable numbers of their populations were dispersed to other countries. Thousands of Judaeans were exiled to the banks of the Euphrates, whence later on with Persian aid some hundreds returned. In Edom and Moab, to speak of those countries alone, civilized life ceased to function for a long time. Uninhabited houses collapsed, ungarrisoned fortresses caved in, cisterns became filled with sediment and untilled acres assumed the appearance of barren desert. Only the climate remained the same.

Centuries earlier, another civilization of high achievement had flourished between the twenty-first and nineteenth centuries B.C. till it was savagely liquidated by the Kings of the East. According to Biblical statements, which have been borne out by archaeological evidence, they gutted every city and village at the end of that period from Ashtaroth-Karnaim in southern Syria through all of Transjordan and the Negev to Kadesh(-barnea) in Sinai (Genesis 14:1-7). From then on, for hundreds of years, till the establishment of the kingdoms of Edom and Moab and Ammon in the thirteenth century B.C., there was a great gap in the history of permanent, sedentary settlement. Bedouins roamed freely throughout the length and breadth of most of Transjordan. With a few notable exceptions in the area of Ammon, the central and southern parts of the land knew the sound of the carpenter's hammer and the ring of the stonemason's chisel no more. Systematic agriculture became a thing of the past. Commerce ceased. There are no pottery remains of this period other than at several isolated places to testify to civilized activity, which continued uninterruptedly in Canaan on the west side of the Jordan. And, again, all these changes can be ascribed not to radical shifts in climate, but rather to the vagaries of human character.

The phenomenon of the rise and fall of civilizations in Transjordan, the Negev and Sinai seems to be governed by a tidal regularity of building up and breaking down, with a slow gathering of strength for renewed effort in between. Unrestrained by governmental authority, which halted them normally at the edge of the desert, Bedouins were always prepared to seize the lands of the Sown. A miracle of transformation would then gradually take place as the Bedouins became in their own right tillers of the soil and architects of new cities and civilizations. But then, apparently inevitably, some centuries later, new invaders from afar or other nomads from nearby would dispossess them in turn.

After the fall of Edom and Moab, hordes of Nabataean nomads infiltrated into the vacuum to dominate for a while the ever changing scene. Many Edomites were pushed into southern Judah, where they became known as Idumaeans, and from among whom came the ancestors of Herod the Great. Gradually the Nabataeans built up a remarkable civilization of their own, learning much from the remaining Edomites and Moabites whom they absorbed. The kingdom they created included southern Transjordan, as well as the Negev and Sinai and northern Arabia. At the height of its development between the second century B.C. and the second century A.D., it extended from Syria to Arabia and to the borders of Egypt. Their rule was short lived. The fate which had overcome all of their predecessors overtook them. They, too, succumbed to conquest by arms and not to uncontrollable forces of nature. The resulting diversion of trade to other regions and routes drained away their economic lifeblood, and not the drying up of their lands because of a sudden lack of water.

The conclusion seems inescapable, wherever it has been possible to check, that the major factors affecting the course of human history certainly in the Near East, and probably elsewhere, during the last ten thousand years, are those over which in general there is a large measure of human control.

Response To Challenge

It was because of the challenge which the Negev as a conspicuous *tabula rasa* among the historical maps of the ancient Near East presented that we found ourselves journeying through it, with the determination to examine archaeologically every square mile of its entire area. A similar undertaking in Transjordan had resulted in the curtain of its past being raised, so that the wonder of its history stood out for all to behold like a statue recovered from the sea. Why not the same for the contiguous territory of the Negev, we asked ourselves? Could this isosceles triangle of the Southland have been as empty of civilization and untouched by animal husbandry and agriculture and permanent places of inhabitation as it was generally made out to be?

Part of the misapprehension with regard to the Negev, as I have already said, is the "from Dan to Beersheba" statement which stems from Judges 20:1 and reads: "Then all the children of Israel went out, and the congregation was assembled as one man, from Dan even to Beersheba, together with the inhabitants of the land of Gilead, unto Jehovah at Mizpah." In I Samuel 3:20, there is a similar reference to "all Israel from Dan to Beersheba. . . . " The phrase "from Dan . . . to Beersheeba" became a household word. It is supposed to have been quoted by the Bible-bred Welshman, Lloyd George, at the Versailles Conference in 1919, after the end of the First World War. The victors were engaged in carving up old states, dishing out new ones, allocating spheres of interest to one another and drawing new maps. When a proposed new sketch map of Palestine, which had been placed under British mandate, was handed him, it showed, so the story goes, that the ancient site of Biblical Dan was not included in it. With a sweeping stroke of a large red crayon, Lloyd George redrew the boundary line so that it was north of Dan, bellowing out that every idiot knew that the Holy Land stretched from Dan to Beersheba.

Assuming that this account is not apocryphal, and that Lloyd George was unaware of the Talmudic injunction not to use the Bible "as a spade wherewith to dig," he might have cited as warrant for further expansion of mandatory territory still other passages in Sacred Writ, indicating that the kingdom of Israel extended from "the entrance of Hamath unto the Brook of Egypt," with all of Palestine and the Negev in between (I Kings 8:65; II Kings 14:25; Joshua 15:1-4). That would have given him everything from Syria to Sinai.

Ancient Hamath is to be identified with modern Hama on the Orontes River, which cleaves the length of most of Syria before turning sharply west to pour into the Mediterranean. The Brook of Egypt, known today as the Wadi el-Arish, bisects the peninsula of Sinai from south to north, and empties into the Mediterranean at el-Arish. The prime minister may simply have overlooked this portrayal of the extreme reaches of Solomonic suzerainty. He may also have been conscious of a prior agreement, that Syria was to be guided to independence by France and that the destiny of Sinai was to be supervised by Great Britain. In all events, the Negev was and has remained until recently a largely unknown quantity so far as both its physical and historical properties are concerned.

The more I thought about the Negev, the more my curiosity about it was aroused. Was it a real desert or only seemingly so? Was it actually as bare and barren and inhospitable to sedentary occupation as had for so many centuries been taken for granted? And even if apparent poverty of natural resources and the marginal nature of much of its soil made an absence of permanent settlements seem plausible, it was obvious that from earliest historic and even prehistoric times important travel and trade routes had passed through it. Where were the camps and fortresses and guard posts and sources of water supply which must have existed along their lengths? Which were the tracks that Abram (Abraham) and his retinue had followed on their journey from Canaan to Egypt and back again? Was it possible to figure out from the topography of the country, together with Biblical descriptions, the lines of march that the Israelites of the Exodus had wearily pursued through the Negev en route from Sinai to the Promised Land?

How did Solomon and the kings of Judah after him manage the logistics of conquest and defense and commerce between their capital in Jerusalem and their distant port of Ezion-geber on the north shore of the east arm of the Red Sea, if the Negev in between were an uncontrolled and lawless wilderness? At what stations and by which cisterns or wells or springs did the caravan of the Queen of Sheba halt at nighttime and for rest periods during the day while crossing the Negev in the course of the very long and necessarily arduous trip from her mystery-shrouded kingdom in Arabia to the mountain throne of Solomon in Jerusalem? Did the Biblical name of the Wilderness of Zin apply to the entirety of this Southland, or just to one of its parts? Could indeed the Negev ever have been a forlorn no man's land of history, being completely encircled as it was by Egypt, Sinai, the Aegean cultural area, Canaan, Edom and Arabia?

Bare landscapes, bold colors and fiercely bright light stand out in the picture of the Negev. The picture is one of strength and simplicity. Hunger and thirst are its patrimony, but there are great treasures of ore and oil concealed in its most desolate wastes. Its hills are gaunt and there are lunar-like craters and massive depressions imprisoned below almost sheer cliffs. It has some fertile plains and innumerable patches of good soil in carefully terraced creek beds. Wide stretches of *hamada* desert are covered with flint and slate and sandstone pebbles as if the earth in abject mourning had strewn itself with sackcloth and ashes. A few springs and infrequent wells accentuate the general poverty. It is a land ravaged by drought, but where on rare occasion freshets tear through normally dry stream beds.

It is indeed difficult for the newcomer facing the blazing desolateness of most of the Negev, especially during the summer and autumn months, to believe that it ever was or ever could be anything but a completely barren desert. Some of it is just that and always has been. To conjure up in it, however, verdant crops, fat flocks of sheep and goats and herds of cattle, hundreds of camping sites, strongholds and thriving villages would seem to require a wildly uninhibited imagination.

If one looks at its soil during the unlidded hours of unrestrained sunlight, then the earth is stripped of all sculpturing shadows and bleached of the hues that make parts of it appear at other times like a painter's palette. Surely, you say to yourself, this is nought but a nether world of "hissing and howling." The massive heat of the midday hours is intensified in the shelterless open during the silent fury of the breathless *hamsin*. One shivers under the penetrating cold which comes with the quick darkness. Pity those who must cross its expanse eastward to Edom, or turn off from the south to Arabia or Egypt, or strike northward to Palestine and Syria.

Was it not natural, then, in accordance with normal human weakness, that the people of the Exodus should yearn to return to the lush fields and plentiful water of the Nile Delta lands, quickly forgetting the slavery they had chosen to escape? We can read with sympathy the outpourings of their hearts: "And the Children of Israel, even the whole congregation, came into the Wilderness of Zin . . . and . . . abode in Kadesh. . . . And there was no water for the congregation; and they assembled themselves together against Moses and Aaron. And the people strove with Moses, and spake, saying, Would that we had died when our brethren died before the Lord! And why have ye brought the assembly of the Lord into this wilderness, that we should die there, we and our beasts? And wherefore have ye made us to come up out of Egypt, to bring us unto this evil place? It is no place of seed or of figs or of vines or of pomegranates; neither is there any water to drink" (Numbers 20:1-5).

And so, in despair and ingratitude, the Israelites raised their voices in rebellion. Thus they turned against the leaders who had guided them through perilous difficulties, and demonstrated their lack of faith in the God of freedom and humanity, without whose illumination they were lost. They were to pay grievously. They would wander till the end of their days. It would take a generation with stronger moral fiber and firmer adherence to God than they possessed to reach the goal of their vision.

Had they moved on, they would have found the bareness and grimness of the Negev far less formidable than first sight or report made it appear to be. Even in late summer, during the early morning hours, low-lying mist frequently blankets the gouged earth so completely as to efface all landmarks and blot out visibility. This moisture alone suffices for the few vineyards and gardens, which can be found in the most unexpected places. They grace the severe landscape, normally burned out and bare at this season, with rare greenness.

Almost every afternoon, even during the hottest months of the year, refreshing breezes blow. I have been able to stave off the exhaustion that threatened me on more than one occasion while searching out the past in the Negev only because I knew that around four o'clock these gentle winds would come to revive my spirits. In the softer light of this temperate interval, as also at the beginning of the day, the soil sheds its aspect of whitefaced hostility. The subtle richness of its reddish browns and saffron grays becomes perceptible. The rainbow hues of multicolored sandstone formations are seen most vividly when the sun is well removed from its zenith. The values of the Negev must be sensed and sought out in order to be appreciated. Patience and imagination are required to understand its moods, skill and strength and courage to surmount its rigors.

The Negev has always played an epic role in the annals of Israel and of mankind. It represents an amazing phenomenon which cannot be made completely understandable by any sum of rational factors. The actual size of this triangularly shaped Southland of the Bible, measuring some seventy by one hundred and twenty miles at its greatest dimensions, bears no relationship to its limitless and continuing importance. Neither its geographical position nor its physical characteristics can, by themselves, adequately explain the uniqueness of its influence. Of all the places which figured in its ancient past, the names of only a few stand out. The others are lost in deep obscurity. Even these few would not be known were it not for the highly selective records of Sacred Writ. As a result, the Negev has long appeared to be an empty wilderness which people crossed with all possible speed and in which only nomads were really at home.

Its boundaries are indicated by four points which box the compass. They are Kadesh-barnea near the eastern edge of Sinai, Hormah between Beersheba and Arad at the entrance to Canaan, Elath by Ezion-geber on the Gulf of Aqabah, and Punon in the Arabah on the way up to Edom. I have never traveled along the time-rutted trails that tie them together without feeling a sense of excitement. I have never walked in the footsteps of the Patriarchs and the Prophets without wondering what new view of the miraculous past might be unrolled before me. I have never wandered over the Negev or Sinai without realizing that here God's will was revealed to mortal men, giving them a status little lower than the angels.

As we traveled with frequent halts at many places in the Negev, the lines of demarcation between periods of time seemed to disappear. The panoramas of the past merged in our consciousness with the scenes of our own day. The events that had taken place there were part of the substance of our own selves. This was not a far country that we were visiting as casual tourists. We were back in the land of our spiritual belonging. It was as if our own grandfather were leading us by the hand and showing us the scenes we seemed to remember from the stories of his youth he had so often told us.

As we thought and talked of Abraham and Moses, of King Solomon and the Queen of Sheba and of many others in the long annals of the history of the Negev, and as we looked for the paths they followed, and found by the hundreds the places they had halted at or sojourned in, comparing what we saw and experienced and discovered with what we knew had gone before, it frequently became difficult to distinguish between present reality and past happenings. A kaleidoscopic parade of many peoples and eras and tongues filed before us, with the line reaching back much farther than we could ever possibly see.

One day we searched out and established firmly the dates of the Judaean fortresses guarding the little-known Way of Shur of Biblical fame, which crossed through the Negev and central Sinai to the Egyptian border (Genesis 16:7; 20:1; 25:18; Exodus 15:22; Numbers 33:8). Abraham and Isaac and Jacob had used it (Genesis 24:62; 26:22), and hosts of others, too.

At one point there, a caravan was approaching us! It could have belonged to the Midianites who sold Joseph to Potiphar, the captain of Pharaoh's guard. Many centuries later yet another Joseph, together with his little family, probably traveled the same route the Midianites must have followed through the Negev and Sinai to Egypt. It is told that he heeded the warning of an angel of the Lord, who appeared to him in a dream saying: "Arise and take the young child and his mother and flee unto Egypt and be thou there until I tell thee: for Herod will seek the young child to destroy him. And he arose and took the young child and his mother by night and departed unto Egypt; and was there until the death of Herod" (Matthew 2:13-15).

The route of Joseph's journey could have been little different from the one Jeremiah is supposed to have taken when he escaped from Judah after its conquest by Babylonia (Jeremiah 43:6-12). And earlier still, Hadad the Edomite had been taken to Egypt by his father's servants when he was "yet a little child," returning only after David's death to become "an adversary to Solomon" (I Kings 11:14.17.21-22).

The small band now appearing above the skyline might be Joshua and Caleb and their companions sent out by Moses to make their way from Sinai to spy out Canaan. There is a raggedly dressed man standing on the side of the road and motioning to us with cupped hands for a drink of water! Give him the full canteen! Of striking appearance, he is obviously someone of quality, with his wise and deeply furrowed countenance. He could, indeed, be taken for the Prophet Elijah, fleeing from the fierce anger of the Phoenician princess, Jezebel, whose misrule in Samaria he had fearlessly condemned. Far removed from her and Ahab's rich and corrupt court, he sought in the great stillness and sanctity of this region to hear the voice of God.

Miracles in the Desert

The question of water clamorously raised by the Israelites at Kadesh-barnea has always stood in the forefront of human concern in the Negev and Sinai. Only about eight inches of rain fall in the most favored Beersheba region in an average year, with the amount being progressively reduced, until it is little more and frequently less than an inch a year at Eilat. And more often than not, most of it comes in a few torrential storms. Men and tribes will fight bitterly over wells or cisterns. Bedouins shot at my party last summer when we suddenly appeared without previous announcement at one of their watering holes on the border of Sinai. They feared that we had come to preempt it and deprive them and their animals of its life sustaining supply. Understanding their feelings, we did not fire back but shouted explanations and soon made friends with them.

I have experienced the thickness of tongue, the salty crust of drying spittle, the flaking and cracking of swollen lips and the leaden faltering of limbs that attend prolonged thirst in

RAINFALL IN INCHES

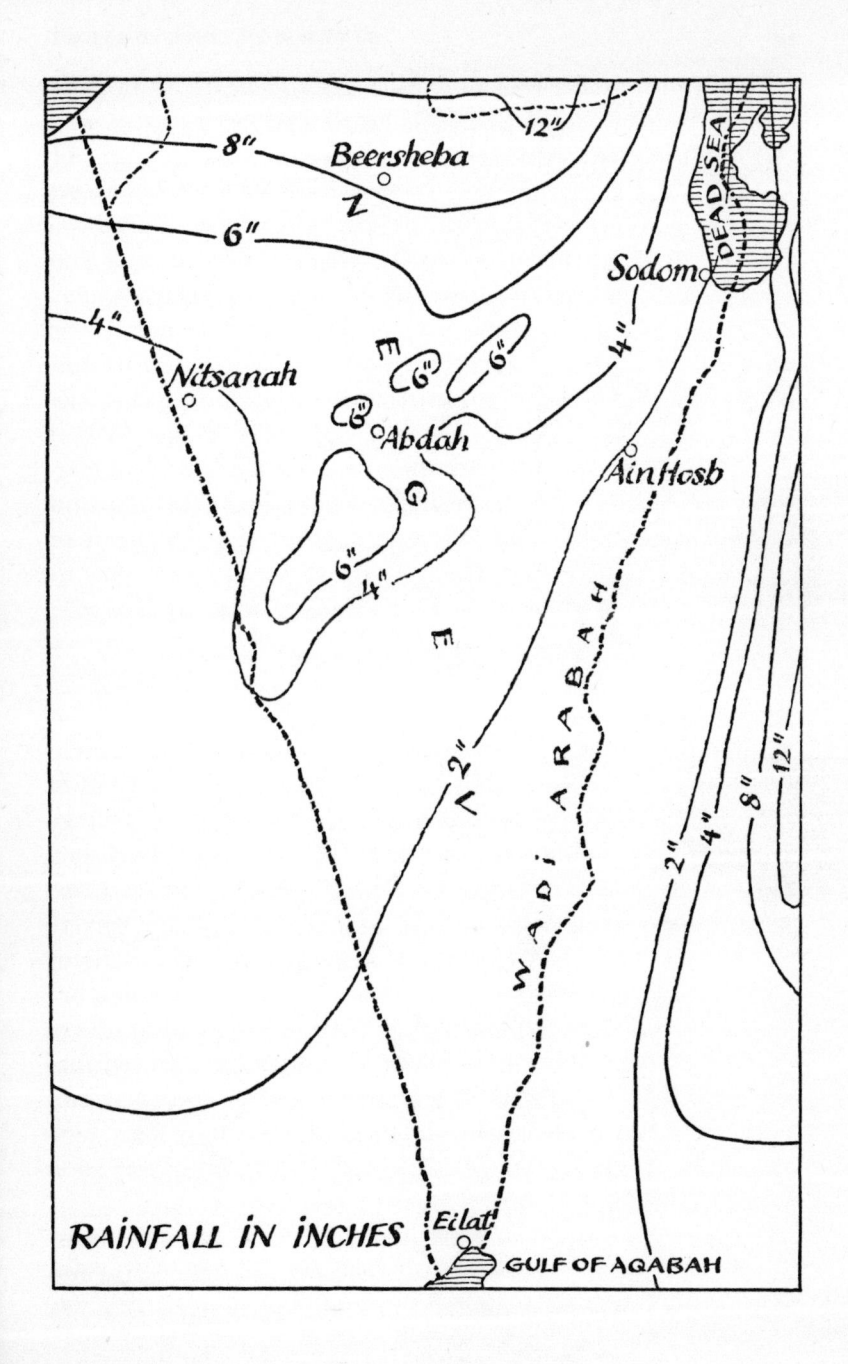

the desert. I have never stumbled across water in Moab or Edom or in the Wilderness of Zin or Paran, without uttering a prayer of thanksgiving. Not to have water in the Negev or to know where to find it can spell disaster and even death.

The simple Biblical account of Hagar and her infant son tells of such a near tragedy:

"And Abraham rose up early in the morning, and took bread and a bottle of water, and gave it unto Hagar, putting it on her shoulder; and gave her the child and sent her away. And she departed and wandered about in the wilderness (south) of Beersheba. And the water in the bottle was spent, and she cast the child under one of the shrubs. And she . . . sat over against him and lifted up her voice and wept. And God heard the voice of the lad; and the angel of God called to Hagar out of heaven and said unto her: What aileth thee, Hagar. Fear not, for God hath heard the voice of the lad where he is. Arise, lift up the lad, and hold him in thy hand, for I will make him into a great nation. And God opened her eyes and she saw a well of water; and she went and filled the bottle with water and gave the lad to drink. And God was with the lad, and he grew and dwelt in the wilderness, and became, as he grew up, an archer. And he dwelt in the Wilderness of Paran (in Sinai) . . ." (Genesis 21:14-21).

It is hard to understand at first sight how life of almost any kind can exist in many wild stretches of the Negev. We were talking about this fact while looking about us from the top of a rock-ribbed hill overlooking the Wadi Hafir. It is a long, fairly wide, cruelly bare little valley, scarred by a shallow, twisting, dry stream bed braided with heaps of stones. There was no hint of cultivation, nor any sign of man or beast. In the changing light of the late afternoon, however, the surrounding foothills began to assume distinctive character. Suddenly, there was life after all!

Coming out from the clefts and slopes of the hills were irregular blurs of movement that seemed to be converging toward a central point in the valley. As they came closer to us, we could make out that they were straggling lines of sheep and goats. The two figures, looking like scarecrows, that glided ahead of them were shepherdesses, almost completely muffled in long black garments trailing the ground. We learned that they were headed for the low-lying well of Bir Hafir.

Age-old tradition and hard experience have taught the Bedouins that water can be found in even the most inhospitable reaches of the Negev. "And the servants of Isaac dug in the *nahal* (the wadi or dry stream bed), and found a well of living water" (Genesis 26:19). In numerous places, *thamileh* holes need be sunk only to a shallow depth until a moderate amount of underground water is reached.

The discovery of water in these regions can frequently only be described in the language of religious experience: "Thus saith the Lord: dig numerous holes in this *nahal* . . . Ye will see neither wind nor rain, yet the torrent-bed shall be filled with water, that ye may drink, ye and your cattle and your beasts. And this is but a light thing in the eyes of the Lord . . ." (II Kings 3:16-18). A well in this part of the world is a continuous miracle, evoking joy and song: "Spring up, O well! Sing to it. The well which the princes dug, which the nobles of the people sunk with scepters, with their staffs" (Numbers 21:18).

I have often joined throngs of Bedouins at wells such as Bir Hafir to exchange greetings and news with them, while they filled and refilled the adjacent stone troughs until the thirst of their animals had been slaked. They would always gladly interrupt the rhythm of drawing up brimming bucketfuls, with ropes sliding smoothly along grooves cut by long usage in the stone facing of the well's mouth, to give me a cooling drink or pour water over my head and hands to wash off the dust and sweat of the way.

"And it came to pass . . . that behold Rebekkah came out . . . with a pitcher on her shoulder . . . and she went down to the fountain and filled her pitcher and came up. And the servant ran to meet her and said, Give me to drink, I pray thee, a little water from thy pitcher. And she said, drink, my lord, and she hasted and let down her pitcher upon her hand and gave him to drink. And when she had done giving him drink, she said, I will draw for thy camels also, until they have done drinking. And she hasted and emptied her pitcher into the trough, and ran again unto the well to draw, and she drew water for all his camels" (Genesis 24:15-20).

The well of Bir Hafir has recently been deepened and strengthened with cement walls. There can be little question, however, but that a cruder predecessor or others like it served earlier inhabitants of this area. In more propitious centuries of political security and peace, there had been stone villages alongside and overlooking the Wadi Hafir. Their occupants dry-farmed some of it with occasional success, but their herds and flocks of domestic animals were their main concern. They engaged in trade, too, because a very important travel route led through the valley, connecting the Abdah area with Sinai. Their lives always revolved around their wells and later on also around their cisterns, as do those of the modern Bedouins. It is axiomatic that wherever there is or once was water in the Negev or elsewhere in the Fertile Crescent, it is possible to find remains of ancient settlements. Many of them antedated by millennia the beginnings of historical times, which are marked by man's invention of fire-baked pottery.

On another trip, we arrived one day at the green-tinged pool of Ain Yerka. It is hidden in a muddy hollow at the base of a semicircle of sheer walls which slant upward and inward to a small skylight opening at the top. It reminded me of a font in a dimly lit cathedral, whose dome is pierced with a small window letting in the sun's rays for a few minutes each day. The rare rain waters of the entire depression of the Machtesh Gadol (Wadi Hathirah) fling themselves in their united volume through this narrow, purse-lipped aperture to form for a while a thunderous waterfall twenty-five feet high.

Its flood is funneled then through the canyon of the Yerka to plunge down to the Wadi Arabah. Imagine the ecstasy of the ancients at the sight of this boisterous torrent, however short-lived its violent passage might be. Pools of water, remaining at various places along its length for weeks at a time, were utilized to the last drop. And enough seeped underground farther back to keep the modest spring of Ain Yerka alive throughout the entire year. Completely dependent upon it in former times were several villages, whose sad remains we discovered on the neighboring hills.

The importance of this spring and of the transient spate with which its waters are occasionally mingled may be judged from evidence of the considerable effort undertaken in antiquity to afford easy access to it. Out of the rock face of the cliff on the steep north side of the canyon were cut flights of steps. With low, carefully calculated risers and landings, they follow the contours of the hillside down to the bed of the wadi. Turn to the left then, and behold the precious spring! The vaulting cavern which houses it has been hollowed out by the seasonal waterfall.

There is absolutely nothing to indicate when the steps were first built or by whom. It must have taken well-tempered tools to hew them out of the hard, gleaming white limestone. This was not the handiwork of unskilled laborers but of highly trained craftsmen. The height of each riser had correctly to be figured and the space of each tread exactly measured. Each step had to be chiseled out carefully along previously drawn chalk lines. Where did the artisans come from? What language did they speak? When and why did they and their community disappear, without leaving a single trace of their identity behind them?

As I stood wondering about these matters, there suddenly appeared a herd of goats, which came skipping down the steps. Behind them were several Bedouins who, with judiciously thrown pebbles, directed their course. Watching them, I seemed to recall other figures like them descending the staircase to the spring, and thought I heard snatches of song. The wind was blowing in the wrong direction, and it was hard to make out the words. Were they in Nabataean Aramaic or in the soft-spoken Hebrew of southern Judah? But then these were in vogue two and three millennia ago, and surely my imagination was playing me false. Yet these steps must have been made and used in one or both of these periods and perhaps still earlier too. The song I was listening to came clear to me now. It was in a quavering, nasal Arabic to the thin tune of a high-pitched flute. Music of this kind must have been heard frequently before at this place, with its melody penetrating the recesses of shadowy beginnings and its beat harking back across the centuries to the mallet blows of master masons. In admiration of their handiwork, we salute their memory, however veiled in mystery their tribe and tongue and time may be.

Any source of water, however small and brackish, as long as it is at all drinkable, is accounted precious in the Negev. Even chance pools collected in hollows or wadi beds after the brief winter rains are not neglected. I have seen modern Bedouins pitch their tents by them till nothing was left but a rapidly drying patch of mud. They would then depart leaving behind them few traces of their stay which time would not surely efface. This practice was followed as far back as prehistoric periods, with the difference that worked flint tools were extensively employed then. They were commonly abandoned as it became necessary to move from site to site, it being easy enough to fashion new ones wherever a long halt was made. They are enduring records of the passage of early peoples across the face of the land, with each age putting the imprint of unique characteristics upon its artifacts.

Stone Age Inhabitants

On the surface of a Stone Age site alongside the Wadi Nitsanah was much evidence that people had once lived there.

The ground was thickly strewn with fine stone implements shaped by the hands of men. An extensive flint-tool industry had flourished here. Wherever we turned were pestles and mortars of stone, and flint cores from which blades, picks, axes, adzes and arrowheads had been skillfully flaked. Much of the raw material had been struck from blocks of flint dug out of the ground so that in their "green" state they could more easily be worked, being less brittle than when long exposed to the elements on the surface. Admire the delicacy of stroke necessary to produce, for instance, these fine blades and spear- and arrowheads, some with barbed or serrated sides! They bear with remarkable fidelity the stamp of the Neolithic period of their origin. It hails back, approximately, from 6000 to 4500 B.C. That was long before written documents of any kind could have come into existence.

This particular center of Neolithic tool industry was only several miles northwest of Auja Hafir or Nessana (Nitsanah), as it was known in classical times. An age-old travel route passes by it that led from Palestine through the Negev to Sinai. A clear Bedouin trail follows the same path to this very day. There are scores of similar and also earlier prehistoric sites in the Negev. Is a wisp of cloudy memory about the Neolithic peoples who lived there and in Canaan to be found in the names of the mysterious Refa'im and Zamzumim (Deuteronomy 2:20) who get such scanty mention in the pages of the Bible?

However, the Neolithic peoples of the Negev or of the ancient Near East in general were not merely primitive nomads distinguished only by the ability to make excellent tools out of ordinary stones. There were already in this age in Canaan highly developed urban communities of sophisticated civilization, to judge particularly from discoveries at ancient Jericho. Some twenty successive phases of superimposed houses of the Neolithic period, resulting in the accumulation of forty-five feet of debris, as one house was built on top of the ruins of the preceding one, have been opened

"IN THE BEGINNING" 27

up there. In the excavations, each stratum or level of occupation was separately removed, starting from the top down, as if they were successive floors of a multi-storied building that was being wrecked. In a scientific excavation, every possible detail is noted, recorded, measured, drawn and photographed, with many individual objects being carefully preserved. The remarkably advanced architecture of Neolithic Jericho was characterized by well-proportioned rectangular rooms, solid walls built of bricks of a distinctive, flattened cigar-shaped style, and by carefully laid, lime-surfaced, painted and burnished clay floors with walls to match. Flint tools, polished stone bowls, grinding querns and pestles were common, and in the middle of the period the use of pottery was introduced.

Deeply concerned with the mysteries of life and creation and reproduction, the Neolithic Jerichoans were devoted to a pronounced fertility cult and to a highly developed ancestor worship. That their sheep, goats, cattle and pigs might reproduce and increase in number, diminutive clay replicas of them were placed in a shrine as freewill gifts of thanksgiving and supplication. Phallic objects expressed their concern for the perpetuation of their own kind.

Such offerings and symbols were not new in early Jericho. They had played a central role in the religious expression of human beings for millennia preceding the Neolithic age and were to be employed for long periods following it there and in the Negev and throughout all of the ancient Near East. The children of Israel were to fashion a golden calf in the plain below Mt. Sinai at the very moment of Moses' confrontation by the deity, whose Being could not be imprisoned in corporeal form. Prophets and priests were to inveigh against the making of idols and images designed to ward off barrenness and ensure fecundity, but it was to take many lifetimes before the sense of their message became part of the innermost consciousness of their people.

Especially remarkable in Neolithic Jericho are sculptures of gods or humans which reveal high artistic achievement.

Several groups were found there, each representing an early triad of god, goddess and offspring. Each figure was built up, about two-thirds life size, on a skeleton framework of reeds over which lime marl was placed and molded into shape. One head of astonishing sensitivity and power has been preserved almost intact, being formed to show the full face. It is very thin in profile, having only sufficient depth to support the features. Deeply impressed shell eyes, ridged eyebrows, aquiline nose, prominent cheeks, thin mouth above protruding lips, high forehead crowned with raised coiffure and lines of paint representing tattooing or hair or both make this sculpture appear like the death mask of someone who had been of outstanding character and rank in actual life. The artist has captured in the attractive and ageless feminine face a reflection of deep wisdom and strength and serenity that indeed make a goddess out of a mortal queen.

In another form of sculpture commonly employed in this sophisticated city, which may first have been founded ten thousand years ago, actual human skulls were employed. Over their bone structure, the features of the dead were faithfully reproduced in plaster, with detailed representation of nostrils, ears, eyelids and mouth. The eyeballs were formed in some cases by rounded shells in two segments, with a vertical or horizontal slit to represent the pupil. In another type, the eyeballs were formed by cowrie shells, with their horizontal openings giving the effect of eyes nearly closed in sleep or death. There is evidence that the plaster features were flesh-tinted with paint. In one instance, in order to complete the realism, a mustache was painted on. Horizontal bands of blackish paint decorated the top of one of the skulls, which were usually left bare. Thus the departed chieftain or king and heads of households were made ever-present gods. They could be worshipped, and their favorable intervention in the lives and fortunes of their families regularly implored.

Neolithic and still earlier Natufian Jericho could not have been an isolated phenomenon. It must have had widespread connections with other Natufian sites, whose history extended from the eighth down to about the middle of the fifth millennium B.C. Other towns of equal antiquity are bound to be excavated sooner or later in Palestine, and will be found to be sisters in culture and accomplishment to this sourcespring of civilization in the Jordan Valley. The tool makers of the Neolithic site near Auja Hafir were embraced within the general civilization which early Jericho so amazingly represented. Their skills in fashioning flint implements seem less surprising in view of the advanced attainments of their urban brothers.

It is hard for us who measure periods of time by the span of our own life expectancy to appreciate the reality of people who lived so long ago. Yet they were graced with all the native endowments which enabled them, in spite of frequent setbacks, to expand the frontiers of knowledge. In retracing the steps which have led us to our present state of civilization, we are constantly astounded by the kind and quality of human achievements, which frequently have been completely forgotten and buried in the oblivion of the past. The lure of archaeology is in reaching back to the realms of our physical and spiritual ancestors and walking with them through both the darkness and light of their days toward a future, which has become part of our own present.

We have learned through detailed and comparative studies, which concern themselves with everything from climate to geology to pottery to literature, to find our way back with much certainty to very distant reaches of human history. Now we resort also to the new science of Carbon-14 dating to help determine the general correctness or errors of our conclusions with regard to the time limits of periods of antiquity. To be sure, in this kind of dating it is necessary to allow a leeway of several hundred years each way. By this method, through the measurement of the surviving radioactivity of charcoal from Neolithic Jericho, a date of about 6250 B.C. was obtained for the first two-thirds of the series of houses with plastered floors. Earlier levels precede them, which probably bring the beginnings of Jericho to the eighth millennium B.C. Indeed, history was at home in this fabulous town. Its very name, like that of ancient Beth Yerah (the Temple of the Moon), which is located on the south shore of the Lake of Galilee at the point where its waters funnel into the Jordan, indicates the worship of the lunar deity there. The story of civilization might well start with the words: "And in the beginning, there was Jericho."

It is difficult to realize, in view of the remoteness from us of the Neolithic peasants of Jericho and of the nomads of the Negev who were embraced within the outer limits of their culture, that all of them would have been considered upstarts in any genealogical Blue Book of human society of the ancient Near East. They were latecomers on the scene, with little or nothing being known of their origins. If aristocracy is determined by the questionable standards of mere longevity and continuity of background, then they must be judged to have been extremely plebeian in comparison with their Paleolithic predecessors.

Is the Bible Correct?

Here, then, was the Negev, like an unscaled mountain, unknown but not unknowable. Our methods and techniques of penetrating its secrets were the same as those we had used in our archaeological mapping of all of Transjordan and the Jordan Valley. They had been perfected in modern times especially by William F. Albright. The first task was to assemble and examine the literary evidence. The chief source of information was the Bible itself. Its historical memories and descriptions and sometimes exact references to particular places are of inestimable value to the scholar.

The purpose of the Biblical historian and archaeologist is, however, not to "prove" the correctness of the Bible. It is primarily a theological document, which can never be "proved," because it is based on belief in God, whose Being can be scientifically suggested but never scientifically demonstrated. Sacred Writ was concerned in its entirety with setting forth and underscoring the uniqueness and universality of God as the Source of all being and the Father of all mankind, whose wisdom was supreme, whose word was law, and whose imperatives were the moral mandates of human conduct. Saga and song, legend and myth, fact and folklore were woven into the text to illustrate and emphasize this central theme.

Those people are essentially of little faith who seek through archaeological corroboration of historical source materials in the Bible to validate its religious teachings and spiritual insights. The archaeological explorer in Bible lands must be aware of the fact that as important as the Bible is for historical information, it is definitely not primarily a chronicle of history, as we understand that term today. It is above all concerned with true religion and only secondarily with illustrative records. Even if the latter had suffered through faulty transmission or embellishments, the purity and primacy of the Bible's innermost message would not thereby be diminished.

As a matter of fact, however, it may be stated categorically that no archaeological discovery has ever controverted a Biblical reference. Scores of archaeological findings have been made which confirm in clear outline or in exact detail historical statements in the Bible. And, by the same token, proper evaluation of Biblical descriptions has often led to amazing discoveries. They form tesserae in the vast mosaic of the Bible's almost incredibly correct historical memory.

The whereabouts of Solomon's long-lost port city of Eziongeber was for centuries an unfathomable mystery, because no one paid attention to the Biblical statement that it was located "beside Eloth, on the shore of the Red Sea, in the land of Edom" (I Kings 9:26; 10:22). And that is exactly where we found it, in the form of the small, sanded-over mound of

Tell el-Kheleifeh on the north shore of the Gulf of Aqabah, which is the eastern arm of the Red Sea. Memory of its location had been snuffed out like the flame of a gutted candle.

Assuming, however, as we did, that the Biblical statement was literally correct, it was not too difficult to rediscover it. Previous explorations had convinced us that the line of the present seashore had changed but little since Biblical times, and that the land of Edom did indeed reach that far south, and also that the Nabataean-Byzantine site of Aila near Aqabah must be on or close to the site of ancient Elath. From that point on, there was little more to do than to stroll along the seashore and examine the only little tell there, which, shortly before our arrival, had been visited by another explorer, Fritz Frank. He, however, had not been trained in pottery identification.

Surface pottery finds and the results subsequently of three seasons of excavations there enabled us to identify Tell el-Kheleifeh with Solomon's fabled seaport. His ships, made and manned by Phoenicians, used to sail from there to distant Ophir and back (I Kings 9:26-28). In a similar manner, our discovery of Solomon's copper and iron mines in the Arabah rift north of Ezion-geber verified completely the sometimes questioned description of the Promised Land as being in part a land "whose stones are iron and out of whose hills you can dig copper" (Deuteronomy 8:9). On the basis of that information, whose reliability we accepted as a matter of course, and acting on a "hunch" as to where to look, we were able to locate the ancient mines and furnaces and slag heaps and establish their dates by pottery finds.

Our task was to spy out the Negev. It was necessary first of all to examine the geography and topography of the land and become acquainted with its physical nature. The lay of the land has throughout the ages determined the location of the roads. We soon discovered that if we followed modern Bedouin trails we would find ourselves on ancient highways. A firmly trodden track used by nomads today passes along the middle of a Roman road in the desert depression of the Wadi Raman, as if it were a painted line separating lanes of traffic on a modern thoroughfare. Clumps of fallen and broken Roman milestones accentuate its antiquity and past unchangeability. We were able to establish that it had been used in Judaean and earlier times too. The modern Israeli road parallels part of its course. Its counterpart in Transjordan is called the *Tariq es-Sultani* (the "Road of the Sultan"). In many places it runs next to or directly over the road built by Trajan from Damascus to Aila, which, in turn, superseded the *Derekh ha-Melekh* (the "King's Way") of the Bible.

Soil and natural resources had to be studied too, to see what use, if any, had been made of them in the past, even though present neglect seemed to belie that possibility. Furthermore, every spring, however small, and every well, however insignificant, had to be visited, every means of securing and saving water examined. There is a cardinal rule in archaeological exploration which bears frequent repetition, namely, that people will have built houses wherever there is good water. I have on occasion visited an area around a spring or well and failed at first to find the ancient site that must have existed in its vicinity, but I have almost always discovered it sooner or later if I persisted in the search.

Ours was not the first venture of its kind in the Negev. In the fall of 1913, two young English archaeologists undertook the exploration of parts of Sinai and the Negev. They tried through surface reconnaissance to determine more about the ancient history of this area than had previously been known. Each of them was subsequently to achieve international renown. The one, Sir Leonard Woolley, as the excavator of Ur of the Chaldees and other sites of absorbing interest. The other, T. E. Lawrence, as a redoubtable desert warrior and as the greatly gifted author of *The Seven Pillars of Wisdom*. They published the results of their investigations in a book called *The Wilderness of Zin,* which appeared in 1915.

The Wilderness of Zin refers loosely to the region between the camping place of Moses and his people at Kadesh-barnea in northeastern Sinai and the Ascent of Aqrabbim (Scorpion Pass), which marks the steep rise from the Arabah into the broken hill-country of the Negev (Numbers 13:21; Joshua 15:1-4). Within this expanse are contained some of the most important parts of the Negev.

The investigations of Woolley and Lawrence dealt with a few of the comparatively small number of tells to be found in the northern part of the Negev and with the small Judaean kingdom fortress located at Kadesh-barnea. Also described are several of the springs and wells and cisterns and ancient burial tumuli they came across. Their special concern was with the easily recognizable ruins of half a dozen towns of amazing size and still recognizable grandeur, whose greatest development and final collapse occurred during the Byzantine period.

The vaulting walls of excellent masonry of magnificent churches, which are among the earliest in Christendom, can still be seen at some of these sites. Those at Isbeita are particularly striking. They give a vivid impression of the brilliant Christian civilization which flourished in the Negev particularly during the fifth and sixth centuries A.D. The main Byzantine sites discussed in *The Wilderness of Zin,* in addition to Isbeita, are Mishrefeh, Abdah, Khalasah, Ruheibeh, Nitsanah and Kurnub. They were all built over the ruins of earlier Nabataean and Roman cities, whose beginnings may be traced back to the second and first centuries B.C. The antecedents of some of them reach farther back into still earlier historical times.

Through no fault of their own, neither Woolley nor Lawrence nor anyone else of their time could conduct a proper archaeological exploration of the Negev or Sinai or Transjordan, because they lacked the simple but indispensable tool of pottery identification. That tool was not really developed and sufficiently refined for scientific use until almost a generation after their archaeological venture in Sinai and in the Negev. It provides the modern archaeological explorer, as I have already said, with the equivalent of an almost infallible divining rod.

Even a single potsherd can sometimes be of considerable significance. A number of years ago, some of us were walking along the top of the ancient city wall which still surrounds the magnificent remains of Roman Gerasa (modern Jerash) in Transjordan. Some Roman sherds were visible in the debris on top of the wall. They had been washed down from the adjacent hill slope, whose soil, through forces of erosion, was now flush with the top of the wall. The ancient stone terraces which had once kept the soil in place had through centuries of neglect almost completely disappeared. Suddenly, we saw among them a single fragment of pottery which could be clearly dated to about 2000 B.C. This was a source of pleased amazement to us, because it indicated the possibility of the existence of a pre-Roman and pre-Hellenistic site at Gerasa, for which we had long been searching. However, one swallow does not make a summer, and one potsherd does not make an ancient settlement. For all we knew, some modern Job might have brought it from elsewhere to scratch his boils (Job 2:8).

Looking about then very carefully, we saw a low, flat-topped, completely isolated hill nearby. A painstaking search of its slopes was undertaken, and it soon became apparent that the single sherd was not a lonely waif strayed far from home. It was one of many, which increased in number as we reached the hilltop. Flush with the ground were the foundation remains of the stone fortification wall that had once surrounded it. We had found the Bronze Age city of Gerasa, which had flourished about four thousand years ago. We had simply overlooked it previously, even though it occupied a classical position. Almost directly below it was the powerful spring around which the Roman city was built two millennia later on.

In a somewhat similar fashion, our expedition recently discovered a striking Solomonic fortress on a Gibraltarlike hilltop above the extremely powerful spring and rich garden lands of Ain Ghadyan in the southwest part of the Wadi Arabah. It guarded access to some of the most important copper and iron mines there, which had been intensively exploited by King Solomon, and it commanded the main highway on the west side of the Arabah rift to and from his chief seaport, Ezion-geber:Elath, on the Red Sea.

The blossoming Israeli settlement of Yotvatah is now located at Ain Ghadyan. Newly planted groves of date palms and orchards of other fruit trees and widespread, irrigated fields yielding abundant harvest of various crops testify to the creative labors of its young pioneers. They are blessed with an abundance of water both from the spring and from as many wells as they care to dig through earth and several feet of rock to reach a plentiful supply of underground water in the Arabah proper. Much of the water of the spring is piped about eight miles south-southwest to the Arabah site of Timnah, known to the Arabs as Mene'iyeh. The mining operations extensively carried on in former times at Timnah by Solomon's men are being repeated on a much larger scale today. A modern smelter has been erected there to process the ore. We had found its equivalent in Ezion-geber, where Solomon's engineers had, about 3000 years ago, erected an elaborate smelter. It utilized the principle of the Bessemer blast furnace system. Flues were provided in its walls through which the strong and constant winds from the north were admitted to furnish the draft necessary for the charcoal-fueled flames in the furnace rooms.

On a previous occasion, we had discovered the remains of a Nabataean caravanserai at Ain Ghadyan, together with some fragments of the beautiful pottery of this gifted people. There were also some pieces of slag, indicating that copper ores which had been mined somewhere in the vicinity had been given a preliminary "roasting" before being brought to the Solomonic smelter at Ezion-geber for further refining. Slag heaps scattered throughout much of Arabah and in many of its lateral approaches testify to the extensiveness of these early mining operations.

When we arrived at Ain Ghadyan this time, we heard that pieces of pottery and slag had been found on the rectangular, sheer hill overlooking the spring. We immediately ascended the very steep trail leading to its top, to discover that it was another of the fortresses that Solomon had built, and that some of his successors had rebuilt in the Wadi Arabah and throughout the Negev to guard the mines and to protect the avenues of communication and commerce so vital to the safety and economy of Israel and Judah. Without the surface sherds which dated this stronghold to the time of Solomon about three millennia ago and also to later periods of occupation, we could have guessed at, but never firmly fixed, its place in history.

Pottery, literary references, topography and geography, soil and minerals and water and climate, varying economic, religious and cultural factors of local or foreign origin, shifting populations, public security and the impact of personalities like Moses and Solomon—all these and more too must be considered by the archaeological explorer, as by the historian, in order to find and intelligently put together the pieces of the puzzles which lost civilizations represent. Experience counts for much, and driving curiosity accounts for more.

After a while, the archaeological explorer begins to understand the genius and moods of a country, to gain an insight into the alchemy of influences which conditioned its development. He becomes familiar with the backgrounds and complexities of its ancient civilizations, and conscious of the inclinations and aptitudes of its former inhabitants. He relives their past, learning to plan and build with them, to share their fights and fears, their triumphs and defeats. He begins to recognize from far away the places of their lodging and to know in advance the circumstances of their living and the forms of their self-expression.

In one age, the people of the land would prefer to build their villages on long, fairly gentle slopes, open to the breezes, close to the fields they tilled and within a reasonable distance of the water they required for themselves and their animals. In another, they would pick strategically located hilltops which they would strongly fortify and provide with cisterns they had learned how to dig and make watertight. In yet a later period of immense skills in soil and water conservation, they would establish settlements in inhospitable areas where none before them and few after them were able to strike root and survive. Each age obviously had its own peculiarities, and each segment of the earth's surface possesses unique characteristics which make it different from any other. This applies certainly to the story of the Negev.

CHAPTER II

"REMEMBER THE DAYS OF OLD"

Five Thousand Years Ago

THE ATTEMPT to unravel the story of civilization in the Negev gave rise to innumerable questions and problems. Was this *terra incognita,* as had been generally assumed, in truth a kind of Paradise Lost situated between the granaries of plenty known as Egypt and the country "flowing with milk and honey" called Canaan? Could it indeed be dismissed as being merely a grim and gray and nearly waterless desert link between these totally dissimilar parts of separate continental masses, whose fortunes were bound up respectively with the flood of the Nile and the flow of the Jordan?

The easiest and most natural point of departure for the history, archaeology and geopolitical significance of the Negev is from the city called the Well of Seven or the Well of Oath, which are the Biblical explanations for the Hebrew name of Beersheba (Genesis 21:30-31). Age-old renown and geographical location have conspired to make and keep it famous as a meeting and market place and administrative center. Excellent farm and grazing lands surround it. They are part of the elongated valley which rises imperceptibly eastward from the Mediterranean coast to the plain of Arad, beyond which a weird confusion of dessicated gullies plunges swiftly down to the Dead Sea. A single dry stream bed of many names and multiple branches but of undisturbed continuity is drawn through its entire length like a shining thread through a drab sash.

This band of good earth is bordered on the north by the abruptly rising Mountains of Judah and dissolves in the south into the broken hill-country of the continuation of the Negev, which is deeply pockmarked in places with lunarlike craters. This northernmost district was blessed with approximately eight to six inches of rain annually. However meager that quantity is, it sufficed, together with the natural fertility of the loess soil of this basin, to support a chain of rich cities reaching eastward from Beersheba to Arad, not to speak of those extending westward from Beersheba to the sea.

Like Megiddo and Taanach and Bethshan in the somewhat similar valley of Jezreel and Esdraelon, memorial monuments in the form of a few massive tells testify to the rise and repeated reconstruction and final abandonment of some of the northernmost cities of the Negev in the course of the millennia. There were others, however, of no less antiquity or importance, whose graves were not marked by tiered mausoleums of their skeletal remains heaped up hill high. One of them was Khirbet Samra, whose character was completely obscure until recently. Another was Beersheba itself, whose name has remained faithful to its present position through all the ups and downs of good and ill fortune.

It has generally been thought that the name of Beersheba came from a nearby ancient mound, about three miles to the east-northeast, called Tell Sab'a. One of the main periods of occupation there was from the nineteenth to the sixteenth centuries B.C., when permanent sedentary settlement seems to have been absent in the Negev. While it is very close to the border, it appears that Tell Sab'a should be regarded as one of the southernmost cities of Judah rather than as belonging to the Negev. Its strategic position was, to be sure, incomparably better than that of Beersheba, which has always been in the defenseless open, and in centuries of danger it may have served as its protective fortress. However, there were many cities of early periods in the Negev which were built without protective walls. To regard Tell Sab'a therefore as the founder of the older city of Beersheba is unwarranted and unfair. It makes an imposter out of an honest tell, which deserves the dignity of its own identity—whatever that may originally have been. It is more likely that it was named after Beersheba, rather than the reverse.

Paths from all directions and people of most diverse backgrounds and cultures have met in Beersheba from the start of the story of civilization. Its position, wells, soil and constantly renewed population have given it a deserved preeminence in the memories and annals of history. It was natural and perhaps inevitable that the census figures of its citizenry should have leaped from less than five hundred to approximately forty thousand within the first decade of the existence of the modern state of Israel.

The most direct route from Kadesh-barnea in Sinai led directly to it and to nearby Hormah. Travelers from Eziongeber or from the oases of Arabia who were headed to the coastal cities of the Philistine Plain or to Jerusalem had perforce to pass through it. There must always have been heavy traffic from it to Beth-eglayim (Tell el-Ajjul), near the Mediterranean and on the north side of the Wadi Ghazzeh, and constant intercourse with the cities in between them such as Gerar (Tell Abu Hureireh) and Sharuhen (Tell el-Far'ah).

If you look at the map, you will see that the position of Kir-haresheth, the capital of Moab, is almost exactly parallel to that of Beersheba. The road eastward from Beersheba leads to the dominating mound of Tell Arad. It then descends the severe slopes beyond it to the shore of the Dead

Sea, which is nearly thirteen hundred feet below sea level. A ford, still passable at the beginning of the twentieth century A.D., led to the peninsula of the Lisan on its east side. From there, you can still follow the clearly defined Roman road which climbs up to the massively fortified crag of Kerak (Biblical Qir-haresheth), on top of the high, broken, Moabite plateau. Or, leaving Tell Arad, you can journey southeast past the Judaean stronghold of Khirbet Ghazza, descend to the Dead Sea plain, skirt its south end, and then, after crossing the Wadi Arabah, ascend to the great mound of Edomite Bozrah or find your way to the fantastic mountain metropolis of Nabataean Petra. The spokes of many travel routes have always led to Beersheba.

Life Underground

Fairly early in the fourth millennium B.C., not long after people had learned how to store and cook food and carry water in pottery containers, a full-blown civilization was transplanted bodily to Beersheba and its surroundings. Whence it came, we do not know, at least not for certain. We may never find out why it came just then, although we can hazard an explanation. It has to do, as usual, more with conquest than with climate, with increase in population rather than with decrease in rain. It was based on agricultural persistence, not nomadic happenstance, on the spread and skills of arts and crafts in urban centers in contrast to the limiting sameness and insufficiency and constant vagaries of an exclusively pastoral economy.

This civilization was called Chalcolithic, and nowhere does the term apply more aptly than to Beersheba and its daughter towns. It designates the cultural epoch when copper and bronze were employed, preceding the use of iron. To quote the dictionary, the first part of the word is derived from the Greek *chalkos,* meaning copper, and the second part from the Greek *lithikos,* pertaining to stones. The brilliant excavations of Jean Perrot at one of several Chalcolithic suburbs of earliest Beersheba revealed the presence there of an advanced copper industry. This particular suburb is called Tell Abu Matar, and is located about a mile southeast of the old city of Beersheba, on the west or right bank of a bend of the Wadi Sab'a. It is reasonable to assume that if excavations were undertaken in Beersheba proper, where Chalcolithic pottery has been found, corresponding evidence of this Copper Age would be obtained.

The catalogue of copper objects recovered at Tell Abu Matar is an impressive one, including some of the inevitable weapons with which every generation girds itself. In this instance, they consisted of pear-shaped, perforated maceheads, well designed for the breaking of skulls. The metal, out of which the finished products were fashioned, was comparatively unalloyed, although not of the almost absolute purity of the Lake Superior nuggets which the American Indians sought out. It resulted apparently from the utilization of ores of high mineral content. They were crushed on large flint anvils, and, after a preliminary "roasting," were smelted in specially constructed clay furnaces and further refined in small pottery crucibles. The molten ore was poured then, apparently, into earthen moulds. It was a process handed down from age to age. The Bible suggests a similar one executed about twenty-five centuries later by Hiram of Tyre, who was Solomon's master coppersmith. "All the vessels which Hiram made for king Solomon in the temple of the Lord were of burnished copper. In the plain of the Jordan did the king have them cast, in thickened earthen molds, between Succoth and Zarethan" (I Kings 7:45-46; II Chronicles 4:17).

Tell Abu Matar obviously did not obtain its ores from the thick loess soil of the Beersheba basin, in which there are no mineral deposits, nor from Sinai, which would seem to have been too far away. The most likely source was the "land whose stones are iron and out of whose hills you can dig copper"

(Deuteronomy 8:9), which is to be identified with the great rift of the Arabah. It may well be the same as the mysterious Valley of the Smiths with its City of Copper, which are glancingly referred to in I Chronicles 4:12-14.

The first copper mine of King Solomon which we discovered on the northeast side of the Wadi Arabah, being attracted to it in part by its name, was called, in Arabic, Khirbet Nahas, which means the Ruin of the Copper City. There, and at nearby Feinan, which is the Punon of Biblical fame, and at similar sites between and beyond them on the way to the Red Sea, we picked up numerous pieces of malachite which analyzed from 10% to more than 50% pure. It seems likely that only the richest chunks of ore were gathered and transported to Chalcolithic Beersheba and its satellite towns to supply the small copper industry which flourished there. All this happened very long before Israel was even a gleam in the eye of history and the gigantic figure of Solomon had emerged to exploit anew in his day the mineral wealth of this Valley of the Smiths.

Some sixty-three miles separate Beersheba in the northernmost Negev from Punon to the southeast of it, far below in the Arabah. It is clear that they were both contained, as early as the fourth millennium B.C., within a widespread civilization which embraced both sides of the Arabah rift and its copper mining sites. Punon was not only a source of precious metal, but perhaps more importantly was an oasis watered by a perennial stream from one of the branches of the Wadi Dana which rises in the highlands of Edom. It provided a welcome camping place for the Israelites of the Exodus during their trek to the Promised Land (Numbers 33:42). Its modern Arabic name of Feinan is almost exactly the same as the Biblical name of Punon, it being necessary to remember that in Arabic speech every "p" becomes either a "b" or an "f."

It seems reasonable to assume a relationship, tenuous as it may be, between the inhabitants of Chalcolithic Beersheba and Tell Abu Matar of the fourth millennium B.C. on the one hand and the Israelites of the thirteenth century B.C. and Solomon and his kingdom of the tenth century B.C. on the other. One should remember in this connection that the Kenites, whose name is a synonym for coppersmiths, were native to the southern Negev and neighboring Edom, and that from the time Moses took a Kenite woman to wife, Israel retained the closest relationships with them. It is written that the cousins of the Kenites, called the Kenizzites, lived in the Valley of the Smiths (the Wadi Arabah), and, furthermore, that Tubal-cain, the latter part of whose name is just a different English spelling for Kenite, was the first forger of copper and iron instruments (I Chronicles 4:12-14; Genesis 4:22). It may well have been in Punon that Moses, with the help of his Kenite-smith relatives, made the copper serpent that he set on his standard, before leading his people from there to the next station of the Exodus at Oboth, farther north on the same east side of the Arabah (Numbers 21:8-10; 33:43). I am inclined to think that there is a link of hereditary and industrial union, which binds the Kenite and Judaean miners and craftsmen of the Wadi Arabah with their very distant Chalcolithic predecessors at Tell Abu Matar, even as its primitive copper crucibles, unchanged in style throughout the centuries, may have served as models for those in Solomon's intricate smelter at Ezion-geber.

In the fourth millennium B.C. Tell Abu Matar was, indeed, an extraordinary place. The actual site was spread over a gently rolling landscape, some distance above the flood plain of the Wadi Sab'a. It was surrounded in season with fields of grain, barley and lentils. Although it had some stone huts and rectangular mud-brick houses with stone foundations, and silos and hearths visible on the surface, it was largely an underground village, with groups of dwellings and storerooms joined together by connecting galleries. Access was gained either by approximately six feet deep vertical shafts, provided with hand- and footholds, or by tunnels sloping in from the sides of the rise on which it was located. Both forms of entrance permitted a certain amount of light to enter the rooms nearest to them. The ventilation was surprisingly good.

Not all the rooms had been carved out at one time, nor on the same level. Some of the earliest of them measured roughly twenty by ten feet and others about fifteen by ten feet. Smaller ones of apparently later date were circular or oval in shape, with some of them faced with stone in whole or in part. The ceilings were so low that the occupants had either to be very short or move about in a perpetual crouch. Storage pits were dug along the sides of the walls or in the center of the rooms or in the passages giving access to them. There were large flint anvils on which the smiths of this village practiced their handicraft. The fiery god, Vulcan, would have felt very much at home.

Among the fine pottery vessels and stone dishes found at Tell Abu Matar were some excellently shaped basalt bowls and chalices, in which food and drink were served. Basalt is a hard stone to work, yet some of the utensils of this material were very smoothly cut and only two-fifths of an inch thick. The inside and outside of the basalt rims were decorated with triangular hatchings. One of the larger bowls was ornamented on the outer surface with incised bands of herringbone design, alternating with bands of horizontal lines. This was a typical and widespread type of ornamentation of the period. These basalt vessels may have been imported from Egypt or perhaps obtained from the Wadi Arabah, where basalt stone is found. They could also well have been shaped in Tell Abu Matar, as undoubtedly was the very good, largely handmade Chalcolithic pottery found there.

Particularly striking were the fourth millennium B.C. ivory sculptures at Tell Abu Matar. Among them was a tiny, long-necked, small-breasted ivory amulet of a fertility goddess. Her aristocratic face reflected an expression of deep inner repose. There seemed to be a look both of remoteness and

Fig. 1. Modern Midianities in the Negev (see page 19).

Fig. 2. The flooded basin of the spring of Ain Yerka at the base of the torren hewn dome above it (see pages 23-24).

Fig. 3. Nabataean-Roman road in the Wadi Raman (Machtesh Ramon), still used by Negev Bedouins (see pages 33, 226-227).

Fig. 4. Goatskins are used for water containers by Bedouins in the Negev today, instead of the graceful pottery

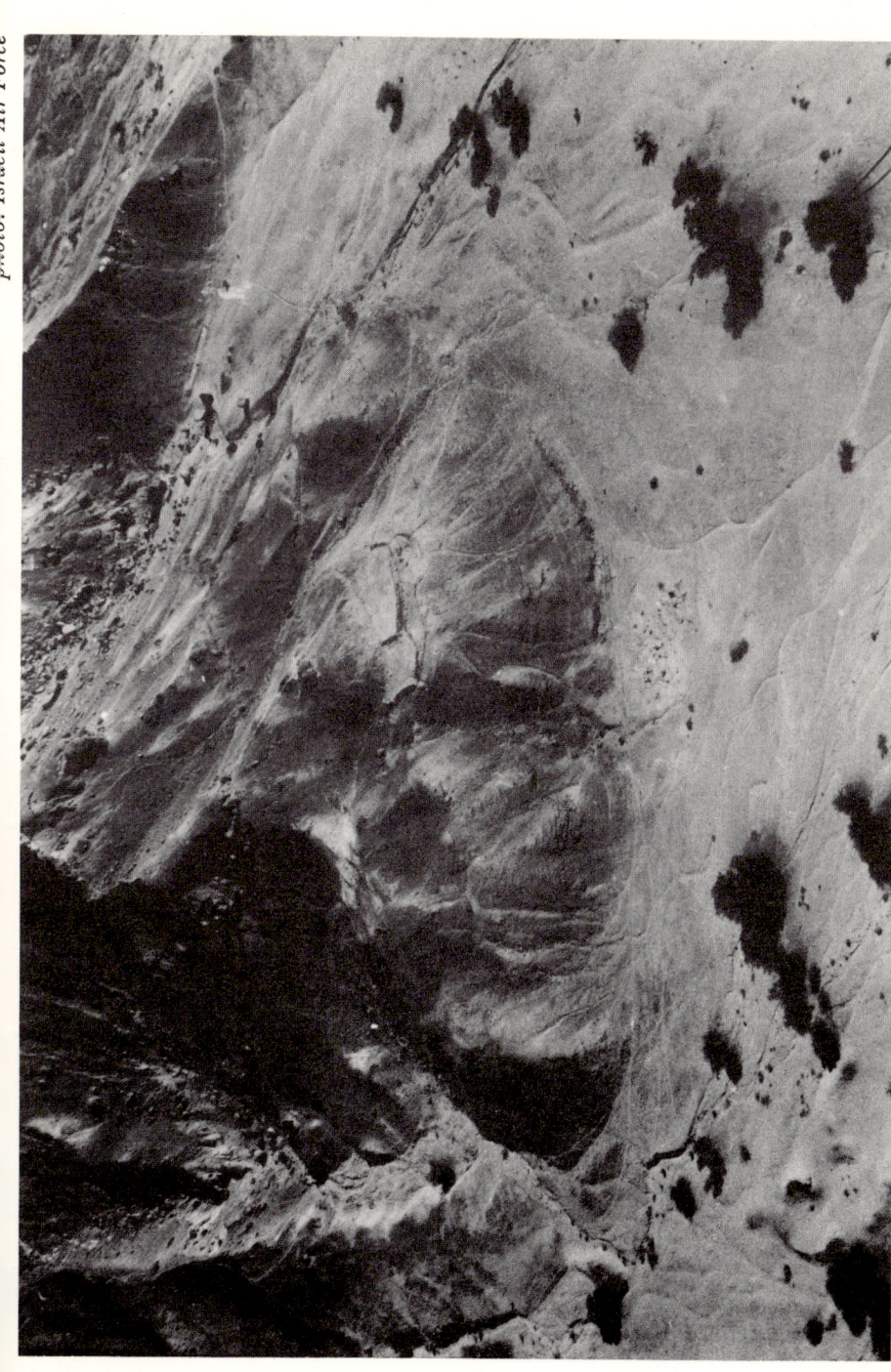

Fig. 5. Walled, Judaean hilltop fortress in the Wadi Arabah, guarding spring of Ain Ghadyan and nearby Solomonic copper mines (see pages 36-37).

Left: Fig. 6. Ivory ladle handle, carved in form of bearded male figure, from fourth millennium B. C. Tell Abu Matar, outside Beersheba (see pages 46-47).

Right: Figs. 7 (a) and (b). Ivory figurines, much enlarged, from Chalcolithic Tell Abu Matar (see page 47).

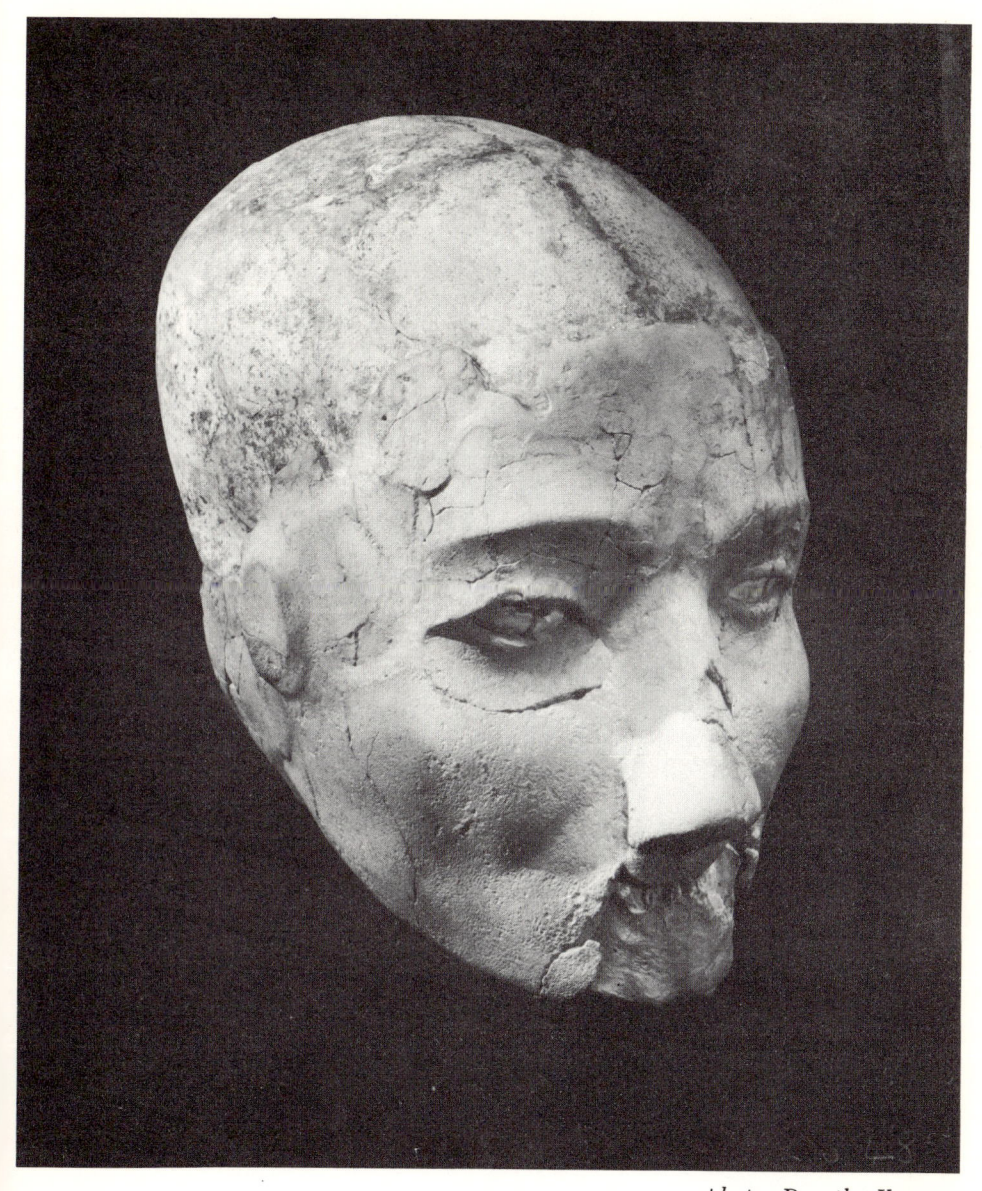

photo: Dorothy Kenyon

FIG. 8. Portrait bust of a man from Neolithic Jericho (approximately 5000 B. C.), made of plaster over a human skull, with segmented shells for eyes (see page 28).

photos on opposite page: Jean Perrot

photo: Jean Perrot

FIG. 9. Fourth millennium B. C. basalt vessels from Tell Abu Matar (see page 46).

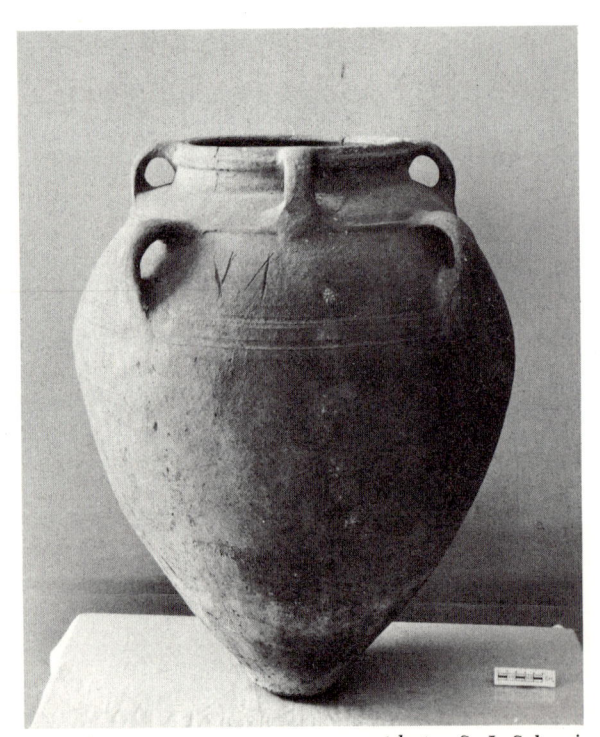

photo: S. J. Schweig

FIG. 10. Judaean kingdom period storage jar from Ezion-geber, with potters' marks on its shoulder (see page 162).

serenity in her eyes, which had been formed by inlaid plugs of ivory. Her ears were indicated by two circular cavities. Two round holes in her high forehead were paralleled by two others in the back, with one each on the right and left sides, and all of them at the same level. She appeared delicate yet forceful. She was mother and mistress; she was budding life and flowering future.

Some of the ivory sculptures formed parts of household implements. The features of one feminine head, distinguished by an extraordinary coiffure, verged almost on those of a caricature. Of arresting charm was a skillfully portrayed pelican, which formed the top of a bone toggle pin. The wealth and fine taste to be encountered at Tell Abu Matar were revealed also through an ivory ladle handle, which was carved in the form of a bearded man of contemplative mien and freely stylized posture. Another handle was decorated with a tiny female head of ivory, which, too, revealed workmanship of high quality.

Chalcolithic Tell Abu Matar was obviously occupied by highly civilized human beings. It was one of a series of similar settlements of the same period on both sides of the Wadi Sab'a, centering about Beersheba. There is no reason to believe that their inhabitants burrowed into the loess soil of their new habitat in imitation of previous cave-dwelling habits. Nor was it because of implacable enemies who left them no peace on the face of the earth that they took refuge beneath its surface. Convenience was their motivation and comfort of their criterion.

Whatever the cause of their final downfall about the thirty-second century B.C. may have been, it was shared by all of their more normally housed contemporaries on both sides of the Jordan and of the Arabah rift. Incidentally, the collapse then of the Chalcolithic civilization may also not be attributed to the catchall excuse of climatic change. That this did not occur is evidenced by the discovery in the excavations at Tell Abu Matar of burned shells of a terrestrial mollusc which is very sensitive to variations of humidity, and which still thrives in the Beersheba region, as Jean Perrot points out.

Subterranean dwellings, astonishingly similar to those of Tell Abu Matar, are still used by Bedouins of the central Negev. This of course can hardly prove that the residents of Tell Abu Matar were primarily nomadic in character, although it is probable that they used their village mainly during the planting and harvesting seasons of the year. It is noteworthy that in later periods numerous villages were cut into chalky hillsides. A classic example of that is the great Nabataean-Byzantine hillsite of Abdah, which was honeycombed with underground houses. In all of these periods, from the remote historical past to the present, the *raison d'être* of this particular type of housing seems to lie in simplicity of construction and ease of protection both from burning heat by day and biting cold by night.

Tell Abu Matar was not a mean village lacking in comfort and culture. Among its residents were farmers, shepherds, potters, weavers, smiths and other artisans of high attainments. They stored their grain in pits made moistureproof with plaster linings. The furniture of their households and the tools of their trades were fashioned out of flint, basalt, limestone, ivory and bone. Distinctive pottery was shaped by hand with partial or occasional use of the tournette, and fired so well in kilns that some of it has survived the passage of six millennia. Men and women adorned themselves with stone and ivory bracelets, copper rings, pendants of mother of pearl and amulets sometimes of striking beauty. Multiples of the number seven, repeated in patterns of forty-nine squares incised on stones, testify to the early preoccupation of mankind with this magical figure. Clay figurines of sheep symbolized the prayers for increase of flocks. Children's lives were sacrificed to secure from insatiable gods the currency of abundance. In many respects, the Chalcolithic civilization of Tell Abu Matar was indistinguishable from that of sites of the same period elsewhere. It obviously did not exist in a vacuum.

The radius of interrelationship extended northward to the rich lowlands and to parts of the fertile highlands of Palestine and Transjordan, and southward as far as Egypt. The predynastic Amratian culture of Egypt knew the use of copper, and it possessed art forms to which the ivory and bone sculptures of Tell Abu Matar bear haunting resemblance. The succeeding Gerzean period produced pear-shaped maceheads which call to mind those found in the Beersheba suburb, as well as types of wavy-handled jars which find their reflection in Late Chalcolithic and Early Bronze Age pottery of the ancient Near East. That there was contact between Egypt and Canaan via the Negev as early as the fourth millennium period of Tell Abu Matar seems certain. It is much more difficult to gauge the degree of influence which the cultural expressions of the one exercised upon the other.

A more direct chain of connection with Tell Abu Matar reached westward and eastward from sea to sea, from the Middle Sea, better known as the Mediterranean, to the Dead Sea, described by Josephus as the Asphalt Lake. There is a whole series of civilized settlements which flourished and fell in concert with it on both sides of the Wadi Sab'a and its continuation to the western edge of the coastal plain. Among them are such famous sites as Sharuhen and Beth-eglayim, which to be sure figured but little in Biblical history, and whose tells bear the modern names of Far'ah and Ajjul.

Together with other centers of agricultural settlement, they indicate the natural geographical boundary line of the Wadi Sab'a-Ghazzeh. It runs through the northernmost part of the Negev and separates the comparatively fertile and well watered coastal lands encompassed by ancient Philistia from the sandy wastes of northwestern Sinai. The hegemony of the kingdom of Israel once extended over this latter area as far south as the Brook of Egypt, which meets the Mediterranean at the small oasis of el-Arish. Except for the coastal route which parallels its shoreline, and long ago was part of the Way of the Land of the Philistines (Exodus 13:17), this stretch of Sinai seems to have been little touched by the forces of history.

A Mighty Witness

Eastward of Beersheba too, the fertile loess fields of the northernmost Negev supported important Chalcolithic communities. Striking tells stand as sentinels over most of them, having mounted in height through accretions of later periods. Shreds of stone foundation and scraps of pottery scattered over the surface are all that are left of others. The most imposing site of them all is the great mount of Tell Arad, which shoulders itself mightily above the surrounding landscape. It is about 22½ miles east-northeast of Beersheba.

It was a proud site, whose tremendous repute is reflected in its massive appearance. Throughout eras of renown and ages of neglect, it has preserved its Scriptural identity. Not even during Hellenistic to Byzantine times, when name changes were common, did that of Tell Arad fade away into obscurity. Fine old names were frequently discarded in favor of fancy new ones, in order to keep up with the current style. Thus Rabbath Ammon became Philadelphia and Bethshan yielded to Scythopolis, although both were in time to revert to their original nomenclature. But Arad remained unchangeably Arad, with only the addition of the title of tell to indicate its retirement from history.

How one wishes that all other ancient sites in the Negev had followed Tell Arad's example in this respect and not merely an additional few. There is Khirbet Ar'areh, which is Biblical Aroer (I Samuel 30:28), and Feinan in the Wadi Arabah, which can be recognized as Biblical Punon (Numbers 33:42), and Tell Ajjul, identified with Beth-eglayim, which is not mentioned in Sacred Writ, and we are done. Intensive archaeological inquiry has enabled us, as pointed out above, to identify Tell el-Kheleifeh on the north shore of the Gulf of Aqabah with the Solomonic port city and industrial town of Ezion-geber:Elath. The original nomenclature of the hundreds of other ancient sites we have discovered in the Negev has disappeared like dew under the desert sun. Indeed, their individualities have been so completely effaced that, lacking any designation whatsoever, it has been necessary to treat them like common criminals rather than ambassadors of antiquity and give them numbers instead of names. Among those cloaked in this way with seemingly impregnable anonymity must be the twenty-nine "uttermost cities . . . and their villages of the tribe of the children of Judah toward the border of Edom in the Negev" (Joshua 15:21-32).

Flying above Tell Arad in an airplane, one can see better than from the ground why it waxed mighty beyond its fellows in the northern Negev. A good agricultural area, dry-farmed today with the frequent result of bumper crops, contributed to its growth and prominence. Anchored securely on a rise in the center of a wide, slightly rolling plain, its robust mound has withstood the violence of the elements and the vandalism of man. A network of paths and dirt roads encompasses it. Several of them wind northward on the east and west sides of Tell Arad to disappear among the foothills of the abruptly rising mountains of Hebron. Fortified further by the Canaanites, these high ranges proved to be an impenetrable barrier to the Israelites seeking the most direct route from Sinai to the Promised Land. Lunging northward through the Negev, they were unable to penetrate them by frontal assault. In blocking the attack of the invaders and beating them back, the King of Arad and his allies played a leading role.

Groups of black tents of semisedentary Arab cultivators can be seen sprouting along the edges of the Arad lands and climbing the slopes rising northward to the hills beyond. Like patches of dark purplish iris which spring up magically in the farthest reaches of the desert in springtime, and whose beauty entranced the Crusaders, clusters of houses of haircloth and of stone have risen in the Negev whenever and wherever it was safe to plow and plant and to graze their domesticated animals. The strong-armed security established there by the present government enables the inhabitants of the Arad area, for instance, to till their spacious lands and tend their numerous herds and flocks with the assurance that they will be able to enjoy the yield of their labor. Firm public authority has always been the prerequisite of a viable economy, particularly in the very difficult terrain of the Negev, whose frontiers are wide open to forays from the desert. Civilization in this Southland depends more than elsewhere in comparatively favorable climes of the Fertile Crescent upon the undisturbed exercise of industriousness and ingenuity.

The prosperity of Tell Arad has always been advanced by the excellent strategic position it occupies in the northeastern Negev. The knoll on which it stands is the apex of a gently sloping watershed, which separates two groups of wadis of unequal size. A short distance to the east of it commence the outrunners of several of them, that increase speedily in size and depth. Reinforced with growing branches, they soon rip their way down abrupt terraces and steep hillsides to empty at separate places into the dead-end trough of the Sea of Salt. To the west are visible the threadlike beginnings of what soon becomes a major stream bed, which is joined by numerous side creek beds. It slopes down very gradually toward yet another sea.

The different sections of its trunk length are all separately named. They are like marathon runners over a single course, passing the torch from one to the other at successive points, till the last one delivers it to the final goal. From below Tell Arad to the vicinity of Beersheba, it is known as the Wadi Mishash, and after that, successively, as the Wadi Sab'a, Wadi Shellaleh, and finally as the Wadi Ghazzeh, under which name it reaches the Mediterranean. A major highway has paralleled the entire length of this wadi in every period of history. With all its various names, it forms a natural boundary line between the richer and better watered lands of Canaan to the north and the climatically less favored and more or less marginal lands of the Negev to the south. Actually, the lands of the Negev may be said to reach to the foothills of the Mountains of Hebron.

Distaff and Spindle

The earliest of the innumerable artifacts scattered over the shroud of soil covering the multitiered ruins of many pre-Biblical and Biblical cities buried within Tell Arad, reach back well over five thousand years to the Chalcolithic period. Not far from it, less than four miles to the south-southwest, are the exceedingly inconspicuous and almost unrecognizable remains of Khirbet Samra, the Ruin of Samra, which belong to the same remote age. It has not previously been accorded even the dubious attention of being regarded as a poor relative of its powerful neighbor. Aside from the ignominy of having been designated as an ancient rubbish heap marked by a dot on the map, it has been completely ignored.

Were it not for its name, which conveys some sense of antiquity, we might well have missed the site. In the grain growing season, it is covered with stands of wheat. At the time of our visit, camels and donkeys in the unequal yokes forbidden by the Bible were treading sheaves spread out on a threshing floor, which once was part of the townsite proper. Khirbet Samra was originally located on two long and gentle slopes opposite each other. Between them was a small, shallow wadi, which was divided into a series of descending rectangles by low, well-built stone terraces. These terraces are probably no earlier than Roman or Byzantine, and may be related to foundation ruins of large buildings which can be seen near the top of the west slope. Otherwise, with the exception of some rude burial circles and piles of field stones, called *rujum,* there is nothing to be seen above the surface. The devastation purposely wrought in dim history by vengeful enemies has unintentionally been completed throughout the ages by the industry of plowmen.

In the terraced wadi bed and particularly along the lower parts of the slopes above it, we found very large numbers of Middle to Late Chalcolithic potsherds, dating back to the fourth millennium B.C. Dug up and buried and re-exposed countless times, booted about, bruised and broken, over and over again, these fragments of pottery have survived the vicissitudes of centuries. They spell out the chapters of history of which they are part. Their easily recognizable characteristics make it possible to assign them to their proper shelves in the library of civilization, as if they were stamped with the places of their manufacture and the date of their issue. Many of them belonged to the common, almost completely handmade, wet-smoothed, Chalcolithic pithos type with everted rim, thick walls, pierced ear-handles and flat base. Others were parts of hole-mouth jars of various sizes, some so large that an Ali Baba could easily have concealed himself in one of them. There were also pieces of coarse bowls with notched ledge-handles and sherds of fine bowls too. The edges and tops of rims were often notched. Variegated bands and daubs of reddish-brown paint were used as decorations, as were raised, indented bands. Among the surface finds were numerous rounded sherds which undoubtedly were once used as game pieces. There were also flint tools typical of the Chalcolithic period.

I explained the significance of the potsherds to the Arab inhabitants of the site, who had clustered around us as we combed the ground for these ceramic gems. They had hardly ever noticed them before, regarding them as little more than pebbles underfoot. They too began to collect them for us from the fields and look at them really for the first time, while listening with a certain amount of incredulity to our tales about them. With the *w'allahis* and *ya b'illahs* of expressions of wonderment, they examined the vestiges of the handiwork of *fellahin* like themselves, who more than fifty centuries before them had worked the very same land and harvested its crops in much the same fashion they did, but who excelled them greatly in the art of pottery making. Waterskins are commonly used by the Arabs of the Negev today, when empty five-gallon gasoline tins and stouter receptacles introduced by modern armies are not available. Such pottery as is in use consists of the rather fragile, black, ribbed ware which comes from the kilns of Gaza.

The friendly people of Khirbet Samra were particularly interested in what might have appeared to be an ordinary, dirt-encrusted stone when we first saw it, but which turned out to be an oval, limestone loom weight. It attracted our attention because it looked as if it had been worked. Carefully shaped and laboriously perforated by someone whose dust had long previously merged with the soil that covered it, it was meaningful to the onlookers because of its similarity to the kind used by their own womenfolk in weaving cloth. In that process, the threads of the warp, which are fastened to the top or end beam of the loom, have loom weights tied to their lower ends to hold them straight and taut.

It is the fashion among shepherdesses to be engaged in spinning while walking about or seated with their flocks. Holding in the left hand a distaff onto which is hooked a mass of wool or goat hair, wisps are drawn from it and attached to a spindle weighted with a stone or pottery whorl which they rotate in the other hand, producing spools of coarse thread. "A worthy woman, who can find? . . . She seeketh wool and flax and worketh willingly with her hands. . . . She layeth her hands to the distaff and . . . the spindle. . . . She is not afraid of the snow for her household, for all her household are clothed with scarlet. She maketh for herself carpets of tapestry. . . . She maketh linen garments and selleth them. . . . Strength and dignity are her clothing

... and let her works praise her in the gates" (Proverbs 31:10-25).

On the way to Khirbet Samra, we watched a Bedouin woman working on a horizontal loom, which rested on stones on the ground. Either one of its sturdy side beams could have served as the staff of the spear of Goliath of Gath which was "like a weaver's beam" (I Samuel 17:7). She was completing a long section of heavy, goat hair fabric, into which she had woven traditional designs. It would in time become part of a new tent, replacing the badly tattered, open-ended one which still shielded her labor from the burning sun. Goats and chickens and a nursing child hovered about and occasionally had to be swept off the textile, which was taking slow shape under her deft hands. The shuttle flew, as effortlessly, almost automatically, she passed it through the warp threads from one side to the other. It was a scene such as this that Job must have had in mind when he said: "My days are swifter than a weaver's shuttle, and are spent without hope" (Job 7:6).

Places Without Names

It is clear that this village of Khirbet Samra at the eastern end of the plains of the northernmost Negev was economically and culturally part of a widespread and well advanced Chalcolithic civilization. The road it is on joins the ancient and modern route connecting Tell Abu Matar and Beersheba with Tell Arad. Between them, going from west to east, was a whole series of ancient sites such as Khirbet Medhbeh, Khirbet Mishash and Tell Milh, whose earliest periods of occupation belonged, like the first settlement of Tell Arad, to the fourth millennium B.C. There were also some places among them like Khirbet Samra, leveled to the ground like ruthlessly felled forests, with little but flints and pottery fragments left on the surface. These sufficed, however, at least to determine their day in history, if not to establish their individual identities. To one of these sites, which lacks even a modern Arabic name, we have given the number 308 in the sequence of our discoveries in the Negev. It is several miles south of a point about midway between Beersheba and Khirbet Samra.

This large, completely destroyed farming community overlooks the west side of the Wadi Ar'areh, which is one of the southern branches of the main wadi leading from Tell Arad, past Beersheba, to the Mediterranean Sea. Below it, in the Wadi Ar'areh, are numerous bushes which remain green even in summertime, indicating the presence of underground water fairly close to the surface. Indeed, a little over a mile to the south of it, is the imposing mound of Khirbet Ar'areh, the seat of a succession of flourishing cities in the time of the Judaean kingdom, although it was inhabited both earlier and later too. Close by are the shallow wells of Biyar Ar'areh, which are still much used by the Arabs of the district. They find it easy enough now to dig new wells, when old ones cave in.

Little is left on the surface of Site 308 except broken millstones, numerous flint tools and large quantities of broken pottery. Most of it was indistinguishable from the Middle and Late Chalcolithic wares of Khirbet Samra, Tell Arad and Tell Abu Matar. Of especial interest was a fragment of a pottery beaker with a tapering cone or cornet shaped base, which could be held in one's hand or stuck into the ground. This kind of a cup or beaker was standard equipment of almost every household in the fourth millennium B.C. agricultural settlement of Teleilat Ghassul, located at the northeast end of the Dead Sea in the Plains of Moab. Extensive excavations there by the Jesuit Fathers Alexis Mallon and Robert Koeppel have contributed much to our knowledge of the nature of the Chalcolithic civilization.

Our excitement mounted as it gradually became evident that the existence and radius of permanent settlement based on an agricultural and pastoral economy established so long ago was not limited to a narrow belt of land on both sides of the Wadi Mishash-Sab'a-Ghazzeh. Its stream bed was definitely not the boundary between the Desert and the Sown even as far back as the earliest millennia in the calendar of remembered or recorded or reconstructed history. The idea of the emptiness of the Negev began increasingly to be dispelled as we proceeded farther with our explorations.

About thirteen miles due south of Site 308, we came across another Chalcolithic site, as empty of distinctive features as a toothless skull. Fortunately, there was a wealth of flints and sherds on the surface. They made it possible to issue the appropriate historical license tag indicating date of origin, periods of rebuilding and total distance traversed not in miles but in millennia. About a mile to the west-northwest of it is another site of equal anonymity and similar decrepitude, whose first blossoming likewise took place in the copper-minded centuries of the fourth millennium B.C. To each of them we assigned a number, 307 and 310, coldly impersonal, not remotely related to the pulse beats of the flesh and blood men and women and children who called these places home. Both of them are located in the extreme southern part of the Northern Negev, which includes the Beersheba Basin. The name of the Near Negev has been given to it by some, to distinguish it from the rest of the Southland, which then is referred to as the Far Negev, on the assumption, now proved baseless, that advanced agricultural civilization was unlikely or impossible there.

The Chalcolithic farming communities in the Northern Negev belonged to an advanced agricultural civilization, which extended throughout the Fertile Crescent. Evidence of it may yet be found farther south in the Negev and in Sinai too, en route to Egypt where it was firmly established. It is known to have existed in Palestine and Transjordan. Excavations at Khirbet Samra or related places could yield discoveries rivaling those already made of ivory and bone statuettes and a copper industry at Tell Abu Matar on the outskirts of

Beersheba, or the remarkable frescoes in brilliant colors on lime-surfaced walls of gods and birds and a great eight-pointed star at Teleilat Ghassul in the Plains of Moab.

An Era of Emptiness

The exact causes of the downfall of the Chalcolithic civilization in the ancient Near East in general and the Negev in particular may never be ascertained, although they were probably political and economic in nature. In the Negev as in Transjordan, in contrast to Canaan immediately adjacent to both, there ensued a fallow era which lasted for about a thousand years. This was the millennium of the Early Bronze Age, during which flourishing civilizations graced most of the countries of the Fertile Crescent. There is some evidence indicating sporadic attempts at civilized settlement in the Negev during the first centuries of this age, but they were short-lived. On the whole, it was an interval of emptiness, with nomads becoming the undisputed lords of the country. Such caravan traffic as continued through the Negev from Arabia and Egypt to Canaan must necessarily have been protected by large and well-armed escorts.

After each historical gap due to destruction and disorder, it took time in such lands as the Negev and Transjordan until civilized forces in sufficient strength could again be assembled to push back and keep in check the flood of nomadic encroachment and depredation behind a dike of governmental authority. Given the prerequisite of public security and firmly established peace, seeming deserts in the ancient and modern Near East have in considerable part been transformed time and time again through steadfast endeavor and ingenuity into life-sustaining agricultural lands.

CHAPTER III

HEARTLAND OF CONSCIENCE

The Breaker of Idols

IT WAS NOT UNTIL near the end of the third millennium B.C. that a clear change occurred widely in the Negev, as indeed it did also in Transjordan. Numerous, more or less uniform stone villages sprang up, with many of them, as in the distantly removed Chalcolithic period, being occupied only several months a year. They were not the result of an isolated mushroom growth, but were part of an economic and cultural renaissance in the Fertile Crescent which took place in the so-called Middle Bronze I Age between the twenty-first and nineteenth centuries B.C. All of them can be linked to contemporary settlements in Canaan by the accurate criterion of pottery of amazing uniformity. A firmly based and productive peace was established and generally maintained throughout this age, which enabled dynamic people to create flourishing civilizations from Mesopotamia on the one hand to Egypt on the other. Both the regional divergencies and likenesses of these widely separated regions and of the lands in between, which included greater Syria, Canaan, the Negev and Sinai, are dramatized in the Bible through the person and peregrinations and experiences and through the places of sojourn and settlement of the heroic figure of Abram, who became known as Abraham (Genesis 17:4-5). His association with the Negev was a singularly striking one.

When Abraham and his people traveled through the Negev, they probably did not recognize the sorry remains of the Chalcolithic villages that had been destroyed many centuries earlier. But the fashion of child sacrifice, which was in vogue in the Chalcolithic period, prevailed also in his time and for long thereafter. The pottery and sculptures and copper maceheads and loom weights of such Chalcolithic sites as Tell Abu Matar, Khirbet Samra and Teleilat Ghassul revealed only part of the story of their culture and period. Even more revealing is the skeleton of a newborn babe found under a fireplace at Tell Abu Matar and of a child buried as a foundation offering under a stone wall there, and of an infant stuffed into a jar that had been placed under a threshold at Teleilat Ghassul.

The firstborn of man and woman were offered to the gods so that the hearth might be full, the women conceive easily and bear many sons, the tilled acres yield their crops in unfailing abundance, the herds and flocks increase with numberless calves and lambs and kids, the newly built house be full of blessing. Such gifts were intended to placate their wrath or elicit their favor. Generation after generation throughout centuries and millennia repeated this pitiful rite. Then somehow in the midst of the remote fastness of Sinai, a still small voice penetrated the innermost consciousness of man.

Out of the blue there had come to Abraham the insistent admonition: "Lay not thy hand upon the lad" (Genesis 22:12). He heeded it in time to stay the sacrifice of his son, Isaac. The sanction of such a hideous ceremony was swept away forever. In his youth, Abraham had broken idols. In his maturity, he continued to attack idolatry. His act of substituting a burnt offering for a human life showed Israel the way of the future. God's word was henceforth ever more explicitly to be spelled out. Not death but life, not sacrifice but service, not ritual but righteousness, and, above all, love and knowledge of God were His demands (Hosea 6:6; Isaiah 1:16.17). An endlessly new idea had emerged, which can be traced back to the dawning of conscience. The idea of the oneness, universality and omnipotence of God and of the relationship between Him and mankind and all creation, first came alight in the events that transpired in Sinai and in the Negev. In the language of religious experience, it was the revelation of God's will to His children.

What anguish the three-day journey had been for Abraham! Distractedly, he had listened to his beloved son's chattering and answered the child's torrent of questions. The last one had been the hardest of all: "And Isaac spake unto Abraham his father and said, My father, and he answered, Here am I, my son. And he said, Behold the fire and the wood, but where is the lamb for a burnt offering? And Abraham said, God will himself provide the lamb for a burnt offering, my son . . ." (Genesis 22:7.8). What father would not endure all possible pain to spare his child suffering! Abraham had been tried far beyond the boundaries of normal endurance, yet his faith was unshakable. God, Himself, had provided the answer and humanity had been given a new direction. "And Abraham called the name of that place *Jehovah-yir'eh* (the God-Who-Seeth), as it is said to this day, In the Mount of Jehovah, it shall be seen" (Genesis 22:14).

Is there truth in this story? I believe there is! Does this place exist? I believe it does. The locale is referred to in the Biblical account: "And it came to pass . . . that God did prove Abraham . . . and said, Take now thy son, thine only son, whom thou lovest, even Isaac, and get thee into the land of Moriah and offer him there for a burnt offering upon one of the mountains which I will tell thee of" (Genesis 22:2). This "Land of Moriah" has been identified mistakenly by some with the Mount Moriah of Jerusalem on which Solomon erected the temple. It is an impossible identification, bringing together two widely removed places bearing the same name (cf. II Chronicles 3:1). It would not have been necessary for Abraham for days on end to drag a supply of kindling with him for the altar fire had his mission been to the wooded hills of Judah. God's revelation, which is a free translation of what Moriah means, is pictured on the contrary as having taken place in the severe and treeless ranges of Sinai. The new horizon glimpsed by Abraham was seen in the loneliness and austerity of the wilderness.

On his way between Canaan and Egypt and back again, Abraham and his retinue had traveled through the wilderness of the Negev and Sinai and had long sojourned there. He knew it well. The pregnant Hagar had sought refuge in it from the burning wrath of her barren mistress, Sarai (Sarah), who had previously given her to Abram's (Abraham's) bosom. "And the angel of Jehovah found her by a fountain on the Way to Shur. And he said, Hagar, . . . return to thy mistress . . . Behold thou are with child and shalt bear a son, whose name shall be Ishmael (God-Listeneth), because Jehovah hath heard thy affliction . . . And she called the name of Jehovah that spake unto her, Thou art a God-That-Seeth . . . Wherefore the well was called *Be'er-la-hai-ro'i* (the Well-Of-The-Living-One-Who-Seeth). Behold it is between Kadesh and Bered" (Genesis 16:7-14). The location of Bered is uncertain, but that of Kadesh is fixed. It is to be identified with the fertile gardens of Wadi Qudeirat watered by the powerful spring of Ain el-Qudeirat in Sinai.

Abraham was at home in the Negev and Sinai. "And Abraham journeyed toward the Land of the Negev and dwelt between Kadesh and Shur . . ." (Genesis 20:1). Somewhere in the neighborhood of Kadesh-barnea was this spot to become hallowed, which was called *Jehovah Yir'eh,* The

God-Who-Seeth (Genesis 22:14). There Abraham had found the inner strength to break the chains of rigid religious tradition. A frightful superstition compounded of primitive faith and fear was shattered. In the rejection of savagery in the name of the gods, Abraham saved his beloved son and his people in the name of God. As a result of his revolutionary comprehension of God's will, he received the promise: "And in thy seed shall all the nations of the earth be blessed, because thou hast hearkened to my voice" (Genesis 22:18).

It is more than possible that this sanctuary of the God-Who-Seeth was close to the Well-Of-The-Living-One-Who-Seeth, by which Hagar cowered in despair. The remarkable historical memory of the Bible seems to indicate this. From the scene of the rejection of human sacrifice, "Abraham turned back to the young men (whom he had left behind when he and Isaac went on by themselves to meet God), and they arose and went together to Beersheba, where Abraham took up his abode" (Genesis 22:19). The place where God's voice had penetrated his heart was therefore located somewhere between Kadesh-barnea and Beersheba, perhaps at Bir Birein near the Sinai border. The geographical unit of the Negev and Sinai thus became early in history what it has always remained since—a center of divine revelation. It was there that the basic character of Israel as a people covenanted with God was hammered out on the anvil of suffering.

The place of Hagar's further tribulations was in the same general area. Expelled from Abraham's household by Sarah, who was wildly jealous for the son she herself had finally borne, Hagar, with her infant child slung on her back, was compelled to wander about helplessly in an unfamiliar desert. But once again an angel of God addressed her, this time saving her and the lad from thirsting to death by pointing out to her the location of a well (Genesis 21:19). Once again, God had intervened to preserve a life. The Biblical narrators repeated this theme over and over again, until it became a **leitmotif** of Israel's religious philosophy. They never tired of emphasizing that the relationship of God to all human beings was of a father to his children, and of His desire for them to live, and to worship Him in accordance with His moral law: "I call heaven and earth to witness against you this day, that I have set before thee life and death, the blessing and the curse. Therefore, choose life . . ." (Deuteronomy 30:19).

Hagar's son, Ishmael, was also to be blessed as the progenitor of a great nation (Genesis 21:18). Grown to manhood, he and his Egyptian wife dwelt, together with his mother, in the Wilderness of Paran, between Kadesh (-barnea) and Elath (Genesis 21:21). Hagar and her kin became deeply rooted in Sinai, with which her very name became synonymous: "For it is written that Abraham had two sons, one by the handmaid and one by the freewoman. Howbeit, . . . these women are two covenants; one from Mount Sinai . . . which is Hagar. Now this Hagar is Mount Sinai in Arabia . . ." (Galatians 4:22-25).

Abraham's perceptions in Sinai inaugurated a new era in human history. They were strengthened by the revelations subsequently made there to Moses on God's sacred mountain and transmitted by him to the Children of Israel and through them to all mankind. The lessons once learned were not, however, always remembered and immediately followed. Constant exhortation and insistence were required before the rite of human sacrifice whether by knife or fire was eradicated. It took a long time before absolute abhorrence of the pagan practice of passing "through the fire all that openeth the womb" (Ezekiel 20:26) entered the soul of Israel.

Abraham commenced the journey. Moses climbed to the summit of God's mountain. Others after them extended the horizons of their vision. Amos demanded in the name of God: "let justice roll down as waters and righteousness as a mighty stream" (Amos 5:24). Isaiah, voicing God's wishes, exclaimed: "What is to me the multitude of your sacrifices? . . . Cease to do evil, learn to do good, seek justice, relieve the oppressed, protect the fatherless, plead for the widow . . ." (Isaiah 1:11.16.17). And Hillel and Jesus underscored the Levitical injunction: "Thou shalt love thy neighbor as thyself" (Leviticus 19:18; Aboth II:4; Shabbath 31a; Matthew 7:12; Luke 10:25-27.36.37). Thus, and thus only, they taught, could the love of God be expressed (Deuteronomy 6:15; Luke 10:17).

This was a miraculous development of the human spirit. The sight of the ruins of cities and villages that litter the face of the earth as a result of mankind's savagery is more than counterbalanced by the pilgrim's progress, however painful and slow, through the march of history. Nowhere has the manifestation of the divine and man's approach to it been more marked than in Sinai and the Negev and the Holy Land, which form the physical and spiritual heartland of the world.

"Say, Thou Art My Sister"

The epic of Abraham's journey from Ur of the Chaldees to Canaan and from Canaan to Egypt through the Southland of the Negev is briefly outlined in the Book of Genesis. This occurred at about the beginning of the twentieth century B.C. After he has been pictured as having erected an altar to God near Bethel, we find him, many unwritten chapters later and without a single break or pause in the story, described in Genesis 12:9, and following chapters, as journeying resolutely southward to and through the Negev. His goal was Egypt and its fat fields and full granaries, whose grain he sought for his people to alleviate the severe famine which had scourged his newly found homeland. Time and trouble are surmounted with scarcely a look backward in this highly abbreviated record of Abraham's Egyptian sojourn. That he obtained all the food and fodder he and his followers and their animals required is taken for granted. There is some humor in the narrator's report of how Abraham deceived the

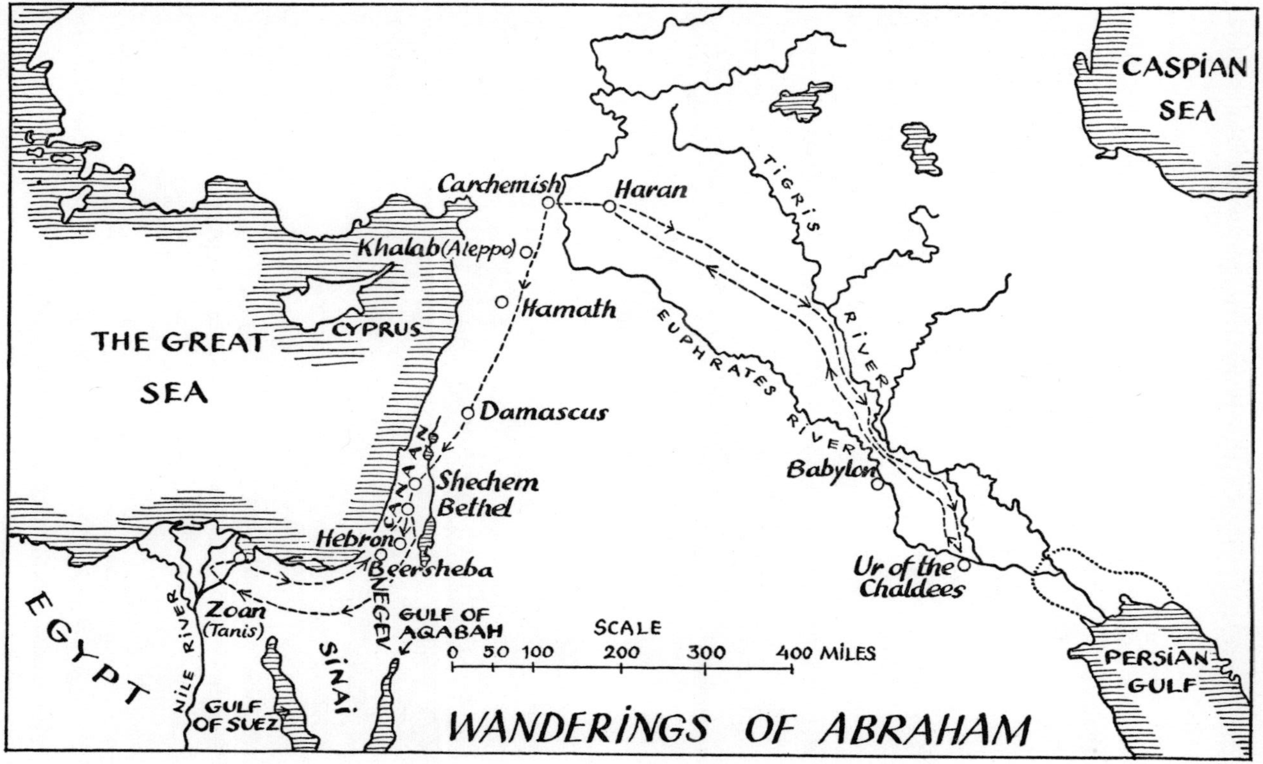

WANDERINGS OF ABRAHAM

Egyptian Pharaoh with the truth, and how he amassed great wealth of sheep and cattle and male servants and female servants and asses and camels and silver and gold. Then, abruptly, we find that Abraham and his following and their sizeable caravan, heavily laden with new possessions, have moved northward from Egypt and back into the Negev for what must have been an extended stay. And finally "he resumed his journey from the Negev to Bethel," back to his starting point (Genesis 13:3).

The entire account of this formidable trip is compressed within twenty-five exceedingly short verses (Genesis 12:1-20; 13:1-5). The actual length of time from Canaan to Egypt and back again may easily have taken many weeks or months, if indeed not longer, for even swift and unencumbered travelers cannot cross the length of the Negev except in many strenuous days. How could a large company of many families with all their burden of unequally strong members and all their baggage, however slender, and all their trailing animals, however few, sustain itself for more than the briefest interval in the Negev, if indeed it were the fierce desert it has been considered? Even more, how could a caravan, as large and laden as Abraham's was, to judge from the definitely credible Biblical description, survive for more than a few days in the Negev if the minimum requirements of survival could not be found there, if there were no water for man or beast, no grazing for flocks, no shelter at night, no security from attack, no clear trodden paths to follow?

It seems to me that all of these are taken for granted in the Biblical account of Abraham's Negevite odyssey, unless indeed we are prepared to dismiss the whole episode as being from a storyteller's imagination, which we are by no means prepared to do. On the contrary, implicit in the entire tale is the background of the Negev as a land where Abraham and his people could and did sojourn and find means of livelihood for fairly long periods of time, where domesticated beasts could find forage and both men and animals obtain water. These conclusions are of course influenced by the hindsight of our archaeological discoveries in the Negev, but contemplation of the meaning of the large silences between the short sentences of the brief story might have helped us arrive at them anyway. It is a fact, certainly, that the natural conditions in the Negev and the historical data discovered there are in complete harmony with the Biblical exposition.

The Kings of the East

The Negev of the Age of Abraham was indeed far from being an empty and forlorn wilderness. It was dotted with villages which were founded at or near the beginning of the Middle Bronze I period in the twenty-first century B.C. and were destroyed at its end in the nineteenth century B.C. The evidence of their existence has a great deal of bearing upon fixing the dates of Abraham, or at least of the period with which the Biblical writers associate him. This is a moot question for many, but not for those of us who rely heavily upon the almost incredibly accurate historical memory of the Bible, and particularly so when it is fortified by archaeological fact. Either the Age of Abraham coincides with the Middle Bronze I period between the twenty-first and nineteenth centuries B.C. or the entire saga dealing with the Patriarch must be dismissed, so far as its historical value is concerned, from scientific consideration. This would of course have no bearing upon the validity of the religious message which the Biblical writers sought to convey through the description of the fortunes and above all of the faith of Abraham. The flesh and blood personage of Abraham—if indeed he did live, which we have no reason to doubt—could not have existed later than the nineteenth century B.C., at the end of Middle Bronze I, for otherwise there would have been no historical framework into which his life could have been set. We have been able to establish through archaeological exploration that that period was preceded and followed, respectively, both in the Negev and in Transjordan, by an extended break in the history of permanent, sedentary, agricultural civilization.

Abraham's experiences in the Negev and Sinai did not occur in a vacuum. An Abraham of the eighteenth to the eleventh centuries B.C. would have found the Negev to be an almost unrelievedly harsh and uncultivated wasteland. His heavily laden, slowly moving and unarmed caravan would have fallen speedy prey to vulturelike nomads; nor could he have sojourned there, as we are told he did (Genesis 20:1), without incurring the danger of being cut off and destroyed by them.

The background of the Biblical narrative implies on the contrary the existence in the Negev during the Age of Abraham of villages and camps, and, above all, of conditions of general peace. It assumes the presence of a friendly population that received him and his retinue with hospitality and passed him on from place to place until he reached his journey's goal. It takes for granted that he found among them a common language, common customs and in general a common way of life. The very earthenware dishes in which the food of hospitality must have been extended to him in the Negev and Sinai were exactly the same kind of pottery familiar to him from Beersheba to Bethel and beyond.

We found the pottery evidence of the Age of Abraham in the Negev startling and exciting. At every one of the numerous settlements there, which were destroyed in the nineteenth century B.C. and which for the most part were never again reoccupied, we found fragments of the easily recognizable and strikingly unique types of pottery which are characteristic of this period. They are absolutely indistinguishable from those found, for instance, in great abundance at contemporary sites in Eastern and Western Palestine on both sides of the Jordan. There is no mistaking this pottery, which has its own peculiar hallmarks. It fixes without words or letters or numerals the extreme limits of the Middle Bronze

I occupation of the Negev and conclusively demonstrates its integral relationship with the cultural world round about it. The typical envelope- and ear-handles, the well known fashions of face combing and of indented bands of raised, rope-like ornamentation, the texture of the clay with its frequently tiny binding materials, the familiar flat bases and handmade walls and wheel-made rims of many of the vessels, the common caliciform shape, the degree of firing, the general coloring of grayish-buff to dark reddish-brown, and still other criteria of shape and substance make it easily possible for the initiated to pick up pieces of pottery from the surface and with certainty identify them.

The amazing uniformity of this pottery, whether found in the heart of the Negev or in the fertile fields of Gilead in northern Transjordan, was the result of the free interplay in wide areas of common cultural and economic forces during the several hundred years of the Middle Bronze I civilization. This does not mean that all the Middle Bronze I pottery found in the Negev was imported, although some of it may have been. It emphasizes that the Negev was then, what it had been previously in the Chalcolithic period and what its geography compelled it endlessly to remain, a crossroads of trade and travel between continents, facilitating, among other things, the widespread use of these common types of pottery. The benefits that the Negev enjoyed in this respect were a mixed blessing. The same routes which opened the cultivable areas of the Negev to civilized settlement in times of peace were also the ones invariably followed periodically by invading armies. What these armies could not consume or carry away they would burn or break. The land would be strewn with the skeletons of villages. The nomads who would lurk just beyond the rim of control would sooner or later pitch their flimsy tents on or near them. They were always the only ultimate victors, who had only to bide their time in order to win every war.

The battle for domination of the Near East, with the

greatest world powers choosing opposite sides, has been an endless one. Yesterday the contestants were the Egyptians and the Hapiru, the Ptolemies and the Seleucids, to mention some of the long list. One of the main invasion routes between them led through Sinai, the Negev and Transjordan to Syria, or the other way round. The Bible recounts a savage incursion in the time of Abraham which extended from Syria southward through the length of Transjordan and westward through the Negev to Sinai and back. It may be regarded as a sideshow of a major upheaval which resulted in the complete collapse and disappearance of the Middle Bronze I civilization throughout the Fertile Crescent. If through archaeological fact we can corroborate the description both of the general background and of many of the details of the Biblical narrative, as indeed we can, it follows naturally that we can establish the approximate date of the political circumstances described and broadly determine the time limits of the Age of Abraham, or at least of the period to which his name has been attached.

There is a clear reflection in Biblical literature of this early war. It is in the fourteenth chapter of the Book of Genesis. The wonder of the accuracy of historical memory in the Bible is again evident when one remembers, in accordance with the evidence of pottery remains, that this episode occurred near the very beginning of the second millennium B.C. That was many centuries before the Biblical record could possibly have been compiled. Somehow or other, by word of mouth from father to son and by recitals of wandering minstrels in the living tradition of unwritten lore, the story of the catastrophic conflict was transmitted from generation to generation until it achieved immortality in the pages of the Bible. Even the names of the dramatis personae and places they appeared in were repeated year in and year out in what became in effect the form of a sacred and unchanging liturgical ritual.

Among the chief protagonists listed in Genesis 14 are Amraphel, Aryoch, Chedorlaomer and Tid'al, described as the Kings of the East. Under the leadership of Chedorlaomer, they spread havoc wherever they went in this early version of the Four Horsemen of the Apocalypse (Revelation 6:2-8). Mentioned too are Bera, Birsha, Shinab, Shemeber and one other whose name was not remembered. They ruled over the Dead Sea cities of Sodom, Gomorrah, Admah, Zeboyim and Zoar, and sought to shake off their servitude to Chedorlaomer and his confederates. A battle took place in the vale of Siddim which was "full of bitumen pits" (Genesis 14:10), when the might of the four was being pitted against the strength of the five, to the discomfiture of the latter. Many fell, others fled, and some were taken captive. "And they took Lot, Abram's brother's son, who dwelt in Sodom, and his goods, and they departed" (Genesis 14:12).

No sooner was the news of the disaster conveyed to Abram, tenting at Hebron, than, gathering together all those capable of bearing arms, he sped to rescue and revenge. The harm of any member of the family or tribe was the hurt of all. The bonds of brotherhood united them, scattered as they might be. "And when Abram heard that his brother was taken captive, he led forth his trained men, born in his house, three hundred and eighteen, and pursued as far as Dan. And he divided himself against them at night, he and his servants, and smote them and pursued them unto Hobah, which is on the left hand of Damascus. And he brought back his brother Lot and his goods and the women also and the people" (Genesis 14:14-16).

The rebellion of the small kings of the cities on the east side of the Dead Sea against what must have been the extortionate rule of absentee suzerains was brutally crushed. This comparatively minor insurrection was thereupon utilized as a pretext to settle old scores and to raid and ravage with unleashed ferocity for as much booty as could possibly be won. An old order was crumbling. From southern Syria to central Sinai, their fury raged. A punitive expedition developed into an orgy of annihilation. I found that every village in their path had been plundered and left in ruins, and the countryside laid waste. The population had been wiped out or led away into captivity. For hundreds of years thereafter, the entire area was like an abandoned cemetery, hideously unkempt, with all its monuments shattered and strewn in pieces on the ground.

The sorry tale is compressed in the Bible into a few bald sentences: "And it came to pass in the days of Amraphel king of Shinar, Aryoch king of Ellasar, Chedorlaomer king of Elam and Tid'al king of Goiim, that they made war with Bera king of Sodom, and with Birsha king of Gomorrah, Shinab king of Admah and Shemeber king of Zeboyim, and the king of Bela (the same is Zoar). All of these joined together in the vale of Siddim (the same is the Salt Sea). Twelve years they served Chedorlaomer, and in the thirteenth year they rebelled. And in the fourteenth year came Chedorlaomer and the kings that were with him and smote the Refaim in Ashtaroth-karnaim, and the Zuzim in Ham, and the Emim in Shaveh Kiriathaim, and the Horites in their mountains of Seir unto El-paran which is by the Wilderness. And on their way back they came to En-mishpat, (the same is Kadesh), and they smote all the country of the Amalekites and also the Amorites that dwelt in Hazazontamar" (Genesis 14:1-7).

It is not yet possible to identify exactly every one of the sites mentioned in these passages. The first and last of the long line of cities listed as having been destroyed by the Kings of the East are, however, of particular interest to us, being Ashtaroth Karnaim and Ain Mishpat or Kadesh. Ashtaroth Karnaim, apparently a composite of two names, can be identified with two sites very close to each other in southern Syria, namely Tell Ashtarah and Sheikh Sa'ad. The latter was called Carnaim in New Testament times. Ain Mishpat or Kadesh (-barnea) has been identified with the powerful spring of Ain el-Qudeirat in the lush little valley of the Wadi el-Qudeirat in Sinai, where a Judaean fortress was discovered by Lawrence. Further proof of the reliability of the historical memory of Genesis 14:5-7 has been furnished now by the discovery of a twenty-first to nineteenth century B.C. agricultural settlement on the hill immediately overlooking the spring. Between Ashtaroth Karnaim and Kadesh-barnea lay the ancient route of march, whose line has not deviated to this very day. From Ashtaroth Karnaim it leads across the Syrian border to Ham in northern Transjordan and then continues southward through that country and westward across the Negev to Kadesh-barnea and thence to El-paran, of still unknown location in Sinai.

Archaeological discovery has thus buttressed the accuracy of the Biblical account of the existence and destruction of this long line of Middle Bronze I cities by the Kings of the East. Particularly remarkable and worthy of special emphasis is the fact that all of them were destroyed at the end of that period in the nineteenth century B.C., with only a few of them having ever again been reoccupied. Yet, as I have already said, the knowledge of their existence and destruction was faithfully preserved by word of mouth until, many centuries later, it was incorporated into the Biblical account in outline form.

The incident of the war undertaken by the Kings of the East and the names of some of the sites destroyed were selected by the Biblical editors to illustrate the workings of divine will. The role of Abram or Abraham was the concern of the compilers of the religious charter of their people; the sketching of his figure as the father and hero of Israel, as the servant and champion of God, was their objective. For them the Bible was an anthology of revelation.

Its scope was so great and its concept so profound that they limited themselves to materials they considered most pertinent. What determined the inclusion of historical facts was whether or not they helped clarify the nature and commandments of Jehovah and His relationship to Israel and mankind. The purpose was neither to write history nor to compile legends, which were always recast into new forms, but to translate the intangible into significant terms and to clothe concepts of divinely based ethics with the wrappings of familiar language and examples.

The power of Scriptural portrayal rests upon its simplicity and honesty. God's protagonists are presented with all their human foibles. Abraham embraced Hagar who bore him a son, yet he abandoned her and their child to possible death in the desert at Sarah's bidding. But the genius of even this account lies in the opportunity it presents to delineate Jehovah as the protector of the weak and innocent and to portray Him furthermore as being also the God of Ishmael, the son of Hagar, as well as the God of Isaac, the son of Sarah. Themes such as these were common in the Biblical writings, with the result that it is frequently difficult to distinguish between the authors of some of the prophetic books and the editors of such didactic tales as are contained for instance in the Book of Genesis.

The peaceful journeys of Abraham from Canaan to Egypt and back again and the predatory incursion of the Kings of the East from southern Syria to westernmost Sinai alone suffice to emphasize the importance of the Negev between the end of the third and the first part of the second millennium B.C. Its character as a land providing possibilities for settlement and that of Kadesh-barnea (Kadesh) as a well-known dwelling and camping place and as a junction of important roads and, furthermore, the connection of Abraham with them are neatly capsuled in Genesis 20:1, which reads:

"Thereupon Abraham journeyed from thence (Zoar of the Cities of the Plain) to the land of the South (the Negev) and dwelt there between Kadesh and Shur (east of the Nahal Mizraim), and he sojourned at Gerar (Tell Abu Hureireh on the northern border of the Negev)."

The picture commonly evoked by the account of Abraham's stay in the Negev is one of Bedouins and camels and billowing sands, of tent encampments and simple tribal life.

Imaginative tales and romantic drawings and simple lack of knowledge have contributed to the prevailing misconceptions about the physical nature and cultural history of the Negev. To the untrained eye, there are few areas or places in the Negev which could support an agricultural economy, yet our archaeological explorations have revealed in the time of Abraham alone the existence of numerous farming communities there. The Age of Abraham was a flourishing period of peace and of cultural expansion, of energetic and seemingly undisturbed cultivation of the soil for about three hundred years, of growing population which pushed even into marginal lands such as the Negev and made careful use of every available acre in dry creek beds and along the slopes leading down to them and in the valleys hidden between hills. It was an age made lustrous by the experiences and insights of the "Father of a Multitude of Nations," as Abraham was called in the Bible.

Pax Abrahamitica

It might be said that a Pax Abrahamitica prevailed in the Negev. With very few exceptions, the villages and towns were not fortified. No strong surrounding walls fenced them off from vengeful enemies or famished nomads. Bound together apparently only in the loosest kind of confederation, they succumbed with terrifying ease to the savage attack of the Kings of the East, who swept like a tornado over much of the Fertile Crescent, leaving behind a swath of destruction.

The Negev was rich then in civilized communities of advanced attainments. Stone houses, however crude many of them may have been, were common. Agriculture was practiced and animals were raised for meat and milk and to carry burdens and pull plows. A sophisticated kind of pottery was manufactured of exactly the same types as were in general use throughout other Bible lands. Trade with neighboring countries was carried on, and travelers like Abraham and his

Fig. 11. Partly artificial city-hill of Tell Arad, which still retains its Biblical name (see pages 50-52).

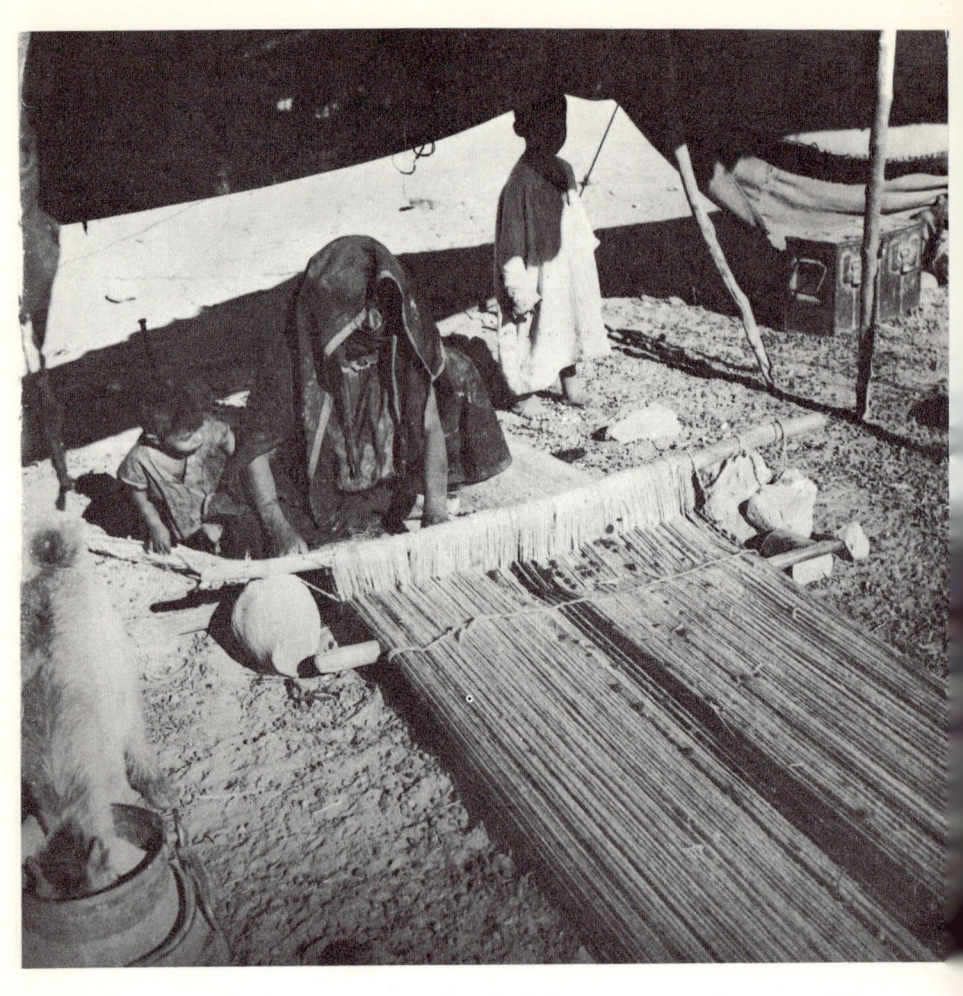

FIG. 12. Bedouin woman weaving cloth for a new tent (see page 56).

FIG. 13. Circular foundation of conical stone house in the Negev, dating to the beginning of the second millennium B. C. (see pages 77, 81-82).

Fig. 14. Nabataean-Byzantine dam at Kurnub (Mampsis) (see pages 80, 209).

Fig. 15. Modern Israeli dam, near the new village of Kfar Yeruham in the Negev (see pages 80-81).

FIG. 16. Ancient "cup-hole" in which grain was ground, found in connection with Abrahamitic period farming villages (see pages 77, 83-84).

FIG. 17. Terraced field of ripened barley in Wadi Raviv, with ruins of Judaean kingdom fortress on hilltop in left background (see pages 214-215).

Fig. 18. Head of pottery Astarte figurine of Judaean kingdom period, from Beersheba (see page 117).

Fig. 19. Crude Astarte figurine found in northern Transjordan (see page 117).

retinue must have been a fairly common sight. When Abraham and his people journeyed through the Negev, therefore, they found themselves in a familiar world whose towns, people, language, pottery and general way of life were in most, if perhaps in not all ways similar to their own. A common community of culture embraced them all. In the steadfastness of his faith which enabled him to surmount the fierceness of his trial, Abraham was to be the first of the giants of heart and mind who found their way in the bleakness of the Negev and Sinai to an increased understanding of God.

Throughout the entire Negev, with the exception of its raw and riven and almost hopelessly arid southernmost part, which receives about an inch or less of rainfall a year on the average, there is an amazing number of Middle Bronze I settlements dating between the twenty-first and nineteenth centuries B.C. Their characteristic locations, generally on hilltops and on long slopes open to the breezes, overlooking cultivable fields and near some source of water, the distinctive circular and oval foundations of their crude stone houses, the frequent cup marks on flat rock surfaces close to them, and above all the unmistakable fragments of pottery which can be found particularly on the slopes below them, date them as clearly as if there had been signposts with words and numbers.

Pick up a map of almost any one of the sections of the Central and Northern Negev and note the areas designated "cultivated" or "cultivated in patches." The mapmakers indicate in this way the stretches which in past years were cultivated by the semi-Bedouins in the Negev, who scratched the soil with their light plows pulled by camels or donkeys or both, scattered the seed and then returned in due season to harvest the grain, if perchance Allah had favored its growth. Experience has taught us to examine such areas carefully, because what can be cultivated sporadically in modern times was almost always cultivated methodically in ancient times and frequently as early as the Middle Bronze I period of Abraham or even as early as the Chalcolithic period which came to an end a thousand years before. The obverse of the coin is also important. The discovery of hundreds of ancient settlements in the Negev is absolute warrant of the possibility of rebuilding new ones there in greater numbers in modern times.

If, in addition, in such a region or district there was a rare spring or well, or if water could be found by digging several feet into the bed of a wadi, the chances were very good that we would find one or more ancient sites spanning, with long interruptions, the entire gamut of ancient history. Add to these factors the examination of travel routes ancient and modern, with especial attention to the clear trails grooved indelibly over the terrain by continuous Bedouin passage, and the network of clues begins to be drawn tightly around likely positions of ancient sites which once flourished there and which have been rendered practically unrecognizable by tragedy and time. It became almost a matter of routine thereafter, based to be sure upon some knowledge of the characteristics of past ages, to rediscover the villages which existed in the time of Abraham or the Judaean fortresses and agricultural and industrial centers which Solomon and Uzziah of Judah constructed, or the numerous farming and trading communities which dotted the Negev and Sinai in Nabataean to Byzantine times.

Such a district is the broad, hill-ringed Basin of Rekhmeh (Biq'at Yeruham), which looks irretrievably barren, but is essentially fertile and in former times was intensively cultivated. It measures about nine by three and a half miles from northeast to southwest. The valleys of Wadi Sab'a and Wadi Rekhmeh form the northern and southern boundaries of the Northern Negev. This geographical division is separated from the adjacent one of the Central Negev (the Mountains of the Negev) by a long watershed, which twists across the entire country roughly from northeast to southwest.

Below this watershed, all the creek beds bend either eastward to the Dead Sea fault or to the Ghor Basin south of it or southeastward to the Arabah Rift. Above it, they cleave north and northwestward to find new designations and final destiny in union with the east-west course of the Wadi Sab'a-Ghazzeh, whose terminus is the Mediterranean. Otherwise, the slopes and drainage system are westward, with the Wadi Abyad (Nahal Lavan) and the Wadi Auja (Nahal Nitsanah) joining the Sinaitic Wadi el-Arish (Nahal Mizraim), which also empties into the Mediterranean.

There could hardly be a more desolate looking region than the Rekhmeh Valley, particularly during the summer and autumn months. Its most outstanding landmark is the gleaming, Sphinxlike bulk of the grayish-white, completely natural, chalk hill of Tell Rekhmeh, which is about seventeen miles south-southwest of Beersheba. The name it bears is a complete misnomer. No village or houses of any kind were ever built on it and there are practically no sherds whatsoever to be found on its surfaces. The distinction of its appearance is the sole explanation of its holding the degree, *honoris causa*, of tell, which carries with it the connotation of being manmade and a monument of history.

Less than ten miles to the east of Tell Rekhmeh and almost parallel with it is another famous landmark, set apart by the striking character of its location, the grandeur of its history and the sad glory of its ruins. Known as Kurnub today, it was called Mampsis in Roman-Byzantine times. It has sometimes, probably incorrectly, been identified with the Judaean kingdom administrative center of Mamshat. That name occurs on royal seals, which were stamped on jar handles of large pottery amphorae by fiscal agents of the kingdom of Judah, perhaps in the time of Hezekiah. Byzantines, Romans, Nabataeans, Judaeans, Canaanites and Chalcolithic peoples, to follow their order backward in time, have left the impress of their occupancy on or near this site.

Far below it, at the bottom of the steep walled Wadi

Kurnub, which has sliced its way through high hills, is an excellent stone dam of great age. Built perhaps by the Nabataeans about two thousand years ago, it was kept intact by the Byzantines and repaired in modern times by the British. It has withstood the battering of centuries of brief but violent floods and has dammed up waters behind it for provident use in prolonged months of drought. Some fifty-six yards farther upstream is another dam, which too is well preserved. Still higher up the wadi are several other dams of similar history, which, however, have suffered from attrition and neglect. All of them served the additional purpose of preventing the soil in the wadi bed from being washed away.

Between Tell or Bir Rekhmeh and Kurnub there runs an ancient track which connects the Chalcolithic sites of 307 and 310, and is still followed by modern Bedouins who hew to unchanging lines. It parallels the one about sixteen miles to the north of it near the top of the Basin of Beersheba, where the Chalcolithic settlements of Tell Abu Matar and Khirbet Samra were located. The many hundreds of square miles of cultivable lands between these two parallel roads were studded in the past with thriving villages, the oldest of which belonged to the Chalcolithic period in the fourth millennium B.C. Whether any of this vintage will be found farther south in the Central Negev, as we believe they will, remains to be seen.

A whole series of roads converged at Bir Rekhmeh, making it an important hub of traffic between Beersheba to the north, and Abdah and Eilat to the south, and various points in Sinai to the west and southwest, and Sodom at the lower end of the Dead Sea and Ain Hosb in the Wadi Arabah to the east and southeast. The Rekhmeh Valley narrows considerably near Bir Rekhmeh and even more so just beyond it to the west, where it becomes known as the Daiqa. Just at that point, a modern dam of considerable size has been built. The result is that for the first time since the Kurnub dams were thrust across their canyon about two thousand years ago, a large body of water can be seen in the Negev. The volume impounded each year from a few rains is so great that it has backed up into numerous side channels. Eye-soothing greenery has sprung up along their sides, all the more startling because of the contrast with the burned-out dreariness of the abandoned lands beyond. When we first came across this desert lake, we could hardly believe our eyes.

It was natural for us to be cautious. On a previous occasion, some years back, we had been driving at top speed across the pool-table smooth mud flats near Mudowerah in southeasternmost Transjordan, when suddenly not very far ahead of us we saw a beautiful expanse of water ringed with palm trees. Automatically we stepped on the brakes, in order not to be plunged into it at the speed we were going, till we realized we were looking at a magnificent mirage.

This Rekhmeh lake before us now was very real, however. It was a wonderful sight for weary explorers, and it was natural for us all to yield to a common impulse. We stripped and went in swimming—during the torrid August heat in the middle of the Negev!

In retrospect, it should have come as no particular surprise to us to find the remains of ancient settlements in the Wadi Rekhmeh and on the slopes and hilltops above it. A few of them dated back more than five thousand years, as I have pointed out, to the Chalcolithic period. Others belonged to the Abrahamitic Age or to the time of the Kingdom of Judah and still more of them to the later Nabataean to Byzantine periods. The prerequisites for the agricultural civilizations they belonged to existed there in the form of water, arable soil and commerce from many directions. Of particular interest was a whole chain of ruins of Abrahamitic period on the slopes and heights overlooking Bir Rekhmeh.

What appeared to be little more than accidental piles of stones turned out upon examination to be roughly circular or oval foundations of houses, to which walled courtyards were attached. When the sun is high and there are few or no shadows to create distinguishing contrasts, it is easy to overlook these ruins from only a short distance away. The typical house of this period, as we were to learn from many hundreds of examples, was beehive-shaped. It had almost exactly the same type of construction as the circular, dry-stone dwellings with thatched roofs that exist in modern Basutoland in South Africa. This architectural style was so characteristic of the Abrahamitic Age that even without the telltale fragments of pottery it could be properly dated.

But the age-revealing sherds themselves were not lacking. Everywhere among the ruins, in cracks and crannies, behind walls and along slopes, hundreds of them were found belonging unmistakably to the twenty-first to nineteenth centuries B.C. One piece from the neck and shoulder of a jar bore a decoration of diagonal incisions, another a horizontal band of face combing, with a wavy band of similar decoration below it. A third piece was part of a small, pierced ear-handle, while a fourth consisted of a smallish, envelope ledge-handle, so called because the ends had been folded over and pressed down while the clay was still pliable. There were many additional ones, too, which were classroom examples of this Middle Bronze I period.

We were particularly interested in two walled hilltop sites, which belonged to the extensive group of this era, overlooking Bir Rekhmeh. The higher one was roughly triangular in shape, being more than one hundred and ten yards in length and narrowing in width from north to south from about one hundred and fifty to twenty-five yards. The encompassing wall had been strongly built of large, crudely shaped stones. It was about a yard wide and in some places still three to four courses high. None of the other Middle Bronze I settlements in the Negev which we have discovered was similarly fortified. The area inside the wall was crowded with foundation remains of various structures. Among them were several aggregations of cup holes, looking like hollowed-out cones, cut into the flat surfaces of limestone rock.

The wall around the lower hilltop was too poorly constructed ever to have served defensive purposes. At the most, it could have helped set it off as a particularly important place. In the center of the enclosed area was a bare, rock surface which was pitted with seven cup holes. Surrounding it were the oval and circular foundations of houses which had access to it. It reminds one of the crude rock altar in the Mosque of Omar in Jerusalem, whose sanctity hails back to earliest antiquity, preceding both Solomonic and Jebusite times.

This hilltop seems to have been no ordinary site, and may well have served as a central sanctuary for the inhabitants of the area and the members of the passing caravans that halted below it at night by the side of the well of Bir Rekhmeh. It is easily possible that Abraham and his company may have camped there. Water and food and fellowship were available and an altar upon which to bring offerings of thanksgiving for the blessings of the way that lay behind and of supplication for assistance against the difficulties and dangers that loomed ahead. The culture of the Bir Rekhmeh region was part of Abraham's own background, the farmers and shepherds dwelling there of his own relationship, the language they spoke being little different from his own, and the gods they worshipped familiar to him from his iconoclastic youth.

Had he indeed halted at Bir Rekhmeh, or at one or more of the other wells on his way from Canaan to Egypt and back again, such as Ain Mureifiq, Bir Hafir, Bir Reseisiyeh (Resisim) or Bir Birein, he would have found villages to receive him hospitably, where he would have felt very much at home. There is little doubt in my mind but that that is exactly what happened. They are along the best route he could have taken, and, considering the size and nature of his caravan, the only possible route. How else could he have traveled later on with his son and servants through the wilderness of the Negev south of Beersheba?

The great number of cup holes or cup marks in the face of

the surface rock of the lower hilltop site may possibly have some connection with religious ceremonies conducted there and at such related sites as Bab edh-Dhra, which was discovered by William F. Albright on the east side of the Dead Sea and properly connected by him with the Cities of the Plain (Genesis 13:12). A more prosaic explanation seems in order for the others we have found at almost every Abrahamitic site in the Negev. It is most unlikely that they were all employed for ritualistic purposes.

We are convinced that their most common use was as rock-bound receptacles or mortars in which grain was pounded to flour with stone pestles. Their like is in current use in Basutoland, whose primitive agricultural civilization parallels in important respects the Middle Bronze I civilization of the Age of Abraham. Cup holes occurred with such frequency at these twenty-first to nineteenth century B.C. sites in the Negev that they may be regarded as being characteristic of the period, although not exclusive to it. The discovery of sherds or foundations of circular houses of this period came to lead us to search for cup holes and vice versa, and almost invariably the one led to the other. The fact that we found one of them with a stone lid covering it raises the question whether many of them were not similarly equipped.

CHAPTER IV

"THE WAY OF THE WILDERNESS"

"Is Not the Whole Land Before Thee?"

THE PIONEERS who settled in the Negev were called upon to exercise all the skills at their command to make reluctant nature tributary to their needs. The press of population in more clement regions, commercial considerations and military compulsions were the individual or collective factors which made them plant their households in this marginal land. In spite of the difficulties of the terrain and the scarcity of water, they built cities and civilizations there which left discernible marks on the face of the earth and made lasting impressions on the course of history.

Travelers needing to pass through Sinai and the Negev naturally obtained as much advance information as possible about them before starting out. They would inform themselves about the main routes of travel, the important geographical features, the directions and depths of the wadis, the location of water, the possibilities of food for themselves and forage for their animals and the nature of the people they might meet.

Having wandered much in Arab countries, I can testify that after a courtesy call of some length in the tent of a tribal chieftain, I would not only receive permission to explore his territory, but much valuable information as to where to go and how. Maps would be drawn for me in the sand showing wadis, wells, water holes, tracks, ruins and contours of the land. More often than not, the sheikh's son or cousin or someone else would be sent along to act as guide and general assistant.

When Joshua and Caleb and their companions traveled from Kadesh-barnea in Sinai to spy out the Promised Land, they probably had been given so much information about what lay ahead of them that they could have journeyed through the Negev at nighttime, had concealment by day been necessary. The road they took was the one followed somewhat later by the main body of the Israelites, whose hearts were set upon entering Canaan from the south. It was the shortest, easiest and best watered way. Bitter experience, however, was to teach them the frequent correctness of the truism, that the longest way around is often the shortest way home. Their attempt to enter Canaan from the south was severely defeated at Hormah.

The Negev may be divided roughly into three parts, Northern, Central and Southern. The Israelites must have known about them and weighed the various possibilities of reaching their goal before they failed in one direction and succeeded in another. There can be little question but that the related and friendly Kenites had drawn maps for them in the sand. The Northern Negev could have been shown as extending between the Wadi Mishash-Sab'a to the north and a line to the south composed of the Wadi Fiqreh on the east side and the Wadi Abyad on the west, with the eastern wadi emptying into the Arabah and the western joining the Wadi el-Arish in Sinai. Below it, a single line drawn eastward from

Sinai to the Arabah would have denoted the Wadi Jerafi, which separates the Central from the Southern Negev. Another scraggle still farther south would have represented the west-east Wadi Heiyani, whose farthest removed outrunner reached the mud flats of the Wadi Iqfi in the narrowing end of the Negev triangle.

Other features of the Negev must have been portrayed for the Israelites before they set off on that hazardous and unsuccessful venture to Hormah. They must have known that a diagonal, northeast to southwest watershed undulated across the land, deflecting the courses of the wadi systems either eastward to the great trough of the Dead Sea and its Wadi Arabah extension or westward to the Mediterranean. It must further have been brought to their attention that the various wadis of the Jerafi-Heiyani-Iqfi drainage area pass through what are, on the whole, the worst lands of the entire Negev, being extremely poverty stricken both in sweet water and arable soil.

They could not fail to have heard much talk about the fearsome and desolate and strategically important Wadi Raman (Machtesh Ramon). Looking like a gigantic footprint stamped deeply at the time of creation into the crust of the earth, it straddles much of the width of the scarred and wrinkled upland of the Central Negev on the east side of the watershed. A famous highway connecting the Arabah and Canaan ran through it. Had the Israelites been so minded, they could have followed almost a direct line from Kadesh-barnea in Sinai partly around and through it to Punon in the Arabah at the entrance to Edom.

The Inland Road

When Joshua and his fellow spies set out to reconnoiter the lay of the land and the disposition of the fortifications and armed forces in Canaan, they took the most direct inland road from Kadesh-barnea to the frowning wall of the mountains of Hebron. It was essentially the same route followed later on in the thirteenth century B.C. by the ill-fated expedition of the host of Israel from Kadesh to Hormah, where their hopes of gaining quick entrance into Canaan were shattered. The exact location of Hormah is unknown. It is undoubtedly east of Beersheba and west of the fortified center of Arad (Tell Arad), whose king and confederates stopped the invading Israelites in their tracks and forced them to retreat to Sinai.

Arbitrary identifications have been made of Hormah with Khirbet Mishash or Tell Milh, both located between Beersheba and Arad, and neither of which need be correct. It is possible that the Amalekites, under the leadership of the King of Arad, met the Israelites farther south at the strategic point of Bir Rekhmeh. It is more or less in the center of the highlands of the Northern Negev and was surrounded from earliest historical times on by agricultural settlements. Wherever Hormah was exactly, the Israelite line of march can be laid out along a whole series of springs and wells and water holes, which can be plotted in a generally straight direction from southwest to northeast. From Ain Qadeis and Ain el-Qudeirat (Kadesh-barnea) in Sinai, there is an irregular line of watering places which have been used from earliest antiquity on and are of much importance in modern times too. They include Bir Auja, Bir Birein, Bir Reseisiyah, Bir Hafir, Ain Mureifiq, Bir Rekhmeh, Bir Asluj, Bir el-Mishash, Biyar Ar'areh, Biyar el-Mishash, Bir Milh, and others.

The Way of the Wells, as it might be called, was the shortest, easiest, and most direct one between Sinai and Canaan. It was heavily traveled in the Middle Bronze I period of the Abrahamitic Age long before the Exodus, and earlier and later too. All along its length and around these sources of water, and on the slopes and in the beds of the wadis in which they occurred, were numerous Middle Bronze I sites and larger numbers of Judaean kingdom villages and fortresses, not to speak of the ubiquitous Nabataean to Byzan-

"THE WAY OF THE WILDERNESS" 89

tine settlements of later periods. There were other important travel routes in the Negev which could have been followed by the Israelites of the Exodus, but they would have been far more roundabout or difficult or both. Also there were considerable numbers of places of settlement in antiquity in other districts of the Negev. However, it is clear that the comparatively narrow, diagonal ribbon of land located mainly in upper reaches of the cross country watershed represented in its own right a "king's highway." It paralleled in economic, strategic and cultural importance the one which traversed the length of Transjordan.

Examine the map and you will see that to the east of this ancient travel route used by pilgrims, traders, armies and refugees, and still followed by modern Bedouins, the Negev is pitted with the forbidding and entirely barren depressions of the Wadi Hathirah (Machtesh Gadol) and the Wadi Hadhirah (Machtesh Qatan). Between them is a range of hills, which acts as a secondary northwest to southeast watershed leading down to the Wadi Arabah. A highway of great historic importance crosses it, descending from Kurnub (Mampsis) via the Naqb Sa'far and the Naqb Sufei and the Scorpion Pass (Ma'aleh Aqrabbim) to the strong spring of Ain Hosb in the Wadi Arabah. From there roads radiate to Sodom, Petra, Aqabah and Eilat. One can see why Ain Hosb was always one of the chief gateways from Edom and Arabia to Beersheba and Ascalon, which are reached by the westward continuation of the road from Kurnub. This was the pathway of the caravans as far back as the fourth millennium B.C., which transported raw copper ores from Punon on the east side of the Wadi Arabah to Tell Abu Matar, the Chalcolithic suburb of Beersheba.

It is obvious, however, that this Beersheba-Kurnub-Ain Hosb road would have been useless to the Israelites of the Exodus. They were interested in the most direct and practicable route from the southwest in Sinai to the northeast in Canaan. They wisely never attempted to reach the alluvial lands sloping to the Mediterranean, which at about the same time were being taken over by the Sea Peoples and were to become part of the Philistine kingdom. It would have led them from Kadesh-barnea to Bir Birein, Bir Auja, and then through the Wadi Khalasah, which is bounded by extensive stretches of sand dune areas, to the rich and thickly inhabited coastal plains of the northwesternmost Negev. That would have been a foolhardy undertaking, through a comparatively waterless region, to strongly held territory they had no hope of conquering. It was to take hundreds of years after the creation of the Kingdom of Israel before complete authority could be exercised there. The Israelites had only two choices in their attempt to gain entry into the Holy Land: the direct route explored by the scouts to southern Canaan and the other route through or east of Edom and Moab. They attempted both and it was only the latter, the longest and most arduous, which proved successful.

Soil and Water

More important than the hills in the Negev are the wadis which interlace them and make life possible in what appears during most of the year to be "a dry and weary land where no water is" (Psalm 63:1). They collect the soil washed down from the slopes by the brief and sometimes violent rains, and store large quantities of water in the sponge of the earth. Even in late summer, shrubs are sustained by the underground moisture. And not infrequently, in the midst of the blazing wilderness of presently unoccupied parts of the Negev, one comes across small oases, green with grapevines and with fruit trees bearing figs and pomegranates. There is no water in sight, but invariably across the wadi bed in front of the garden, the semi-Bedouin owners have flung a dam of dirt strong enough to check some of the flow of the winter and spring torrents and force it to sink into the soil. Enough of the transient flood is retained to keep the vines and trees alive and flourishing.

In addition, there is all summer long throughout almost all of the Negev, with the exception of the comparatively few *hamsin* days, an exceedingly heavy dew fall. In early morning, clouds of dew are often thick and extensive enough to obscure the face of the earth. Nor do they retreat precipitately before the burning rays of the rising sun, lingering on frequently for several hours. A wild melon growing in the Wadi Fiqreh near the Jebel el-Medhra on the way to the Wadi Arabah, a delicate crocus blooming in the Abdah plain or a fine, fall (S'tav) flower miraculously defying the meanness of its surroundings near the Sinai border, can be seen in late summer in the so-called desert of the Negev.

All this was known and appreciated by the ancients, who, undeterred by the unfriendly appearance of the land, terraced and dry-farmed the wadi beds and cultivable slopes above them and built thriving agricultural economies in much of its expanse. I have found wadis hidden in the heart of the Negev alive with waving stands of golden wheat, far from settlements of any kind or even of tent encampments. They had been lightly plowed and swiftly sown by Bedouin planters, who thereupon departed, meaning to return at the end of the season, *inshallah,* to harvest the grain. There is no question but that as early as the fourth millennium B.C. cultivation of the soil in the Negev was the mainstay of the Chalcolithic civilization there. We have seen that clear remains of that civilization have thus far been found as far south as the Rekhmeh Valley between Tell Rekhmeh and Kurnub.

As the centuries passed, the techniques and methods of collecting and storing and utilizing supplies of water improved radically. By the time of the gifted Nabataeans, in whose kingdom all of the Negev and Sinai were incorporated, the knowledge of how to obtain a sufficient amount of water in a marginal region where there was an average rainfall of about eight to four inches a year from the Northern to the Central Negev, and progressively less the farther south one goes, became a highly developed science. The Negev and Sinai were full particularly of Nabataean and Byzantine sites, which required comparatively large quantities of water for urban and agricultural and far-flung trade activities.

From the Wadi Arabah to the Wadi el-Arish and beyond to the borders of Egypt, there is abundant evidence of the genius displayed by the Nabataeans in securing sufficient water against seemingly hopeless odds to meet their needs. Dams, terraces, diversionary walls and channels, aqueducts, cisterns and reservoirs, the use of whole hillsides as catchment basins and the employment of extensive water-spreading devices, which included using as water channels long rows of low piles of stones on sterile soil, namely the so-called *"teleilat el-anab"*—all of these give evidence of the great skills employed by the Nabataeans and thereafter by the Romans and Byzantines to assure themselves of water supplies and to prevent soil erosion in the Negev and Sinai and elsewhere. This was the secret of their success.

Streams in the Negev

Terraces built across wadi beds to brake and exact tribute from the occasional winter and spring freshets, cisterns and reservoirs dug and plastered watertight to be filled from their meed against the certainty of many a rainless day, and all the other devices perfected or invented by the Nabataeans and utilized and even expanded in instances by their immediate successors, could never accomplish for the countryside at large the miracles of rebirth that a single rainfall over a wide area was able to perform. The grass and flowers fairly spring up after the first shower or storm, and the grim desert becomes a colorful garden overnight. It is as if a magic wand had been passed over the face of the earth. Flocks of birds suddenly make their appearance then, to sing and to swoop about in happy flight, and bands of gazelles and ibexes graze and cavort through the lush green. Camels and goats and sheep and their young wax fat. They drink their fill at pools of water collected in hollows, making it unnecessary for months on end to find other supplies for them. Springs flow more strongly, wells rise to their highest levels and the underground water is replenished in the wadi beds, there to remain long after the flowers have faded and the grass has withered and gone. Sturdy shrubs remain green all summer long because their roots tap the subsurface moisture. This is particularly true where the wadis are wide and shallow and terraced, with the result that the rain waters tend to sink into the ground. Otherwise, if unhindered, they race down narrow gullies and dry stream beds, stripping off the covering soil and gouging out for themselves ever deeper canyons.

The period of the rains is a glorious one and particularly so in the dry lands of the Negev. The gladness it brings is likened to the happiness that shall reign when "the ransomed of Jehovah shall return and come with singing unto Zion . . ." (Isaiah 35:10). For then "the wilderness and the dry land shall be glad; and the desert shall rejoice and blossom as the rose . . . Then shall the lame man leap as a hart and the tongue of the dumb shall sing; for in the wilderness shall waters break out and streams in the desert (Arabah). And the glowing sand shall become a pool, and the thirsty ground springs of water. In the habitation of jackals, where they lay, there shall be grass with reeds and rushes" (Isaiah 35:1.6-7).

The fullness of joy attendant upon the restoration from captivity is compared to the *Afiqim ba-Negev* (Psalm 126:4), that is, to the wadis in the Negev, whose soil has been saturated with life-sustaining waters of short-lived winter and spring freshets. In the lilt and beauty of his poetic imagery, the Psalmist sings:

> "Turn again, our captivity, O Jehovah,
> As the streams (Afiqim) in the Negev.
> They that sow in tears shall reap in joy.
> He that goeth forth and weepeth,
> Bearing seed for sowing,
> Shall doubtless come again with joy
> Bringing his sheaves with him" (Psalm 126:4-6).

The Invention of Cisterns

Many centuries passed before the art of building terraces and cisterns and perfecting water-spreading devices was fully developed. It did not reach its height until the advent of the Nabataeans. Even the science of digging cisterns and making them impermeable with many coats of cement or plaster seems, so far as our present knowledge goes, not to have been fully developed until about the thirteenth century B.C. There were cisterns before that, but they were hewn in solid rock, which itself was watertight. It is, nevertheless, possible that watertight cisterns will be discovered dating back to the fourth millennium B.C., knowing as we do that people already then had mastered the secret of burning limestone and making plaster. The fact that plastered cisterns have not yet been found, for instance, in any site of the Middle Bronze I Age of the period of Abraham is no absolute proof that they did not exist.

It is hard to realize what a revolutionary change was effected in the history of civilization when cisterns were invented—that is, when men learned to dig holes in any kind of ground and plaster them so that they could serve as storage places for water. Without cisterns, few of the Judaean fortresses and villages in the Negev could have been constructed. And without the still larger number of cisterns, dams and terraces in the Nabataean and Byzantine periods, the Negev could never have been made to sustain the tens of thousands of inhabitants who lived there then.

The great Nabataean to Byzantine cities in the Negev, some of which were built on hilltops, could never have come into existence without reservoirs and without at least one cistern in every house. Furthermore, to augment their supplies, artesian wells were sometimes sunk hundreds of feet deep. The Nabataeans dug one, for instance, some 65 yards below the base of the hill of Abdah until it reached the water table on a level with the strong spring of Ain Mureifiq (Ain Ovdat), situated at the bottom of the deep canyon of Wadi Murrah (Nahal Mor), several miles away. This was, however, not a new technique with them, although no one previously had ever attempted to tunnel so far into the bowels of the earth to find a subterranean water supply.

It was first in the Iron Age (thirteenth to sixth centuries B.C.), that brilliant engineers combined building techniques with knowledge of water resources to sink horizontal or, more often than not, vertical shafts straight through the center of hills crowned with fortresses to tap subterranean water sources, to which, even in time of beleaguerment, the inhabitants could have recourse in perfect safety. They have been found in Shobek and Kir-hareshet in Moab and at Lachish, Jerusalem, Gibeon, Gezer, Megiddo and Hazor in Judah and Israel.

These skills had, however, apparently not yet been achieved at the time of the Middle Bronze I period of the Abrahamitic Age, although tunnels of the subsequent Middle Bronze II period at Hazor indicate good engineering knowledge. It is obvious why all of the numerous Abrahamitic period sites we have found in the Negev are situated directly above or in the vicinity of springs and wells and on hilltops and slopes overlooking broad and shallow wadis which, all year long, retained underground moisture from the occasional rains. Dry farming could be and obviously was carried on in these wadis and along the slopes leading down to them.

If you compile the names of many of these fertile wadis or valleys, including among others the Wadis Qudeirat, Mitnan, Azeizi (Azuz), Hafir, Auja, La'anah, Reseisiyah, Abu Rutheh (Ruth), Raviv, Abyad (Lavan), Nafkh, Abdah, Haleiqim, Baqqar, Beqqarah, Rekhmeh, Jurf, Daiqa, Asluj, Khalasah, Ar'arah, Mishash-Sab'a-Ghazzeh, you will have a register of almost all of the best lands of the Central and Northern Negev. You will have more than that, because these names indicate areas in which agricultural civilizations were established with varying degrees of intensity and in widely separated periods from late Chalcolithic or from Middle Bronze I times on, that is from the late fourth or beginning second millennium B.C.

If you list the springs and wells and water holes which exist in them, such as Ain el-Qudeirat, Bir Mitnan, Bir el-Hafir, Harabat Atiqa (Borot Qedem), Bir Reseisiyah, Bir Birein, Bir Auja, Ain el-Mureifiq, Bir Asluj, Bir el-Mishash, Biyar Ar'areh, Biyar el-Mishash, Bir el-Milh, and the whole series of other wells in and around Beersheba, you will have a log of most of the sources of water around which centers of ancient civilizations clustered in the Negev between Kadesh-barnea and Beersheba and Tell Arad. If you trace the tracks that lead to them and through the arable lands around them, they will bring you to the realms of the Biblical past in the Negev and Sinai. If you examine the remains of ancient sites hard by them and in their vicinity that were scattered through the Negev in changing numbers during the course of millennia, you will know that it was never uninhabitable in historic times. Indeed, we have shown that it was occupied in early prehistoric times too.

From the vantage point of historical hindsight, made possible by archaeological exploration and excavation, one can see the tides of civilization advancing and retreating throughout the Negev and Sinai. From Chalcolithic invention and achievement to the height of Byzantine flowering, the whole story can be illustrated on a graph by a long, uneven, broken line, indicating the rise and fall of one civilization after another in discontinuous succession. Each was strong enough to thrive for a while in the austerity of the Negev, its fate bound up with that of its counterpart from Syria to Arabia. Each, however, was reduced in time to scrap heaps of artifacts, recalling on the one hand the thrill of peaceful accomplishment or even the excitement of martial achievement, and evoking on the other hand the terror of fading fortune or of violent end.

SITE 345

The border area of the high uplands, facing the approaches to Kadesh-barnea in Sinai, was one of the most intensively cultivated and settled of all the Negev in ancient times, due to fertile soil and a comparative abundance of water. The most thickly inhabited period there and elsewhere in the Negev was in Nabataean-Byzantine times, from the second century B.C. to the seventh century A.D. The next in density of population and number of sites was the Judaean Kingdom period of the tenth to sixth centuries B.C., when political and military conditions required the establishment of numerous fortresses on strategic hilltops. Open agricultural villages existed frequently below them, whose inhabitants practiced to a high degree the techniques of terracing which the Nabataeans and Byzantines perfected and most intensively and widely employed. Almost equally populous was the apparently peaceful Abrahamitic Age of the twenty-first to nineteenth centuries B.C.

There is a strikingly large number of antiquity sites in this district, extending for miles around the wells of Bir Birein. Little can be seen there now, especially since the wells have been enclosed in cement casings. But even in former days, their outward appearance did not correspond to their incalculable importance. These wells and others like them do not give much idea that they sustained large groups of settlements in their neighborhood.

A little less than two miles to the west-northwest of Bir Birein is the largest site of the Abrahamitic, Middle Bronze I period that we have discovered in our achaeological explorations of the Negev. It is a classic example of the fact that approximately four thousand years ago the Negev was not an empty wilderness, the haunt of rootless Bedouins and inhospitable to agricultural civilization. This site must have had a name, which, however, was not imbedded deeply enough in the minds of men or sufficiently associated with Biblical incidents and personalities to have escaped the erosion of the ages. There seems nowhere to be even a blur of memory of its former existence. Yet it must have played a significant role in the social and economic life of the entire Negev in the Age of Abraham, after which it ceased to exist and was never again reoccupied. We have no choice but merely to give it the number assigned to it on our map and call it Site 345.

Site 345 is situated on top of a long, low, somewhat flat rise, immediately above the west side of the Wadi Hafir (Nahal Nitsanah), whose comparatively broad, whitish bed weaves below it from southeast to northwest. It is a tremendous site for this early age of four millennia ago, however modest it may appear by modern standards. It was about a third of a mile long and over two hundred yards wide. There is no question in my mind but that it was the county seat or capital of the entire Bir Birein district in the time of Abraham. One wonders whether or not on his way across the Negev to Egypt, Abraham and his people may not have halted at this place, which was obviously large enough to offer abundant and lengthy hospitality. It is directly on the road to Kadesh-barnea in nearby Sinai, where he must have stopped for a considerable time. There was a powerful spring there, and on the slopes above it another settlement contemporary with Site 345, which would have been proud to welcome such an important guest.

In spite of its size, it is hard to find Site 345, whose maze of low piles of ruins is hardly visible except during the hours of the day when the slant of the sun and the ensuing shadows make objects stand out in plastic relief. When the sun is high in the Negev, its brilliance obliterates all distinctiveness of shape and substance, drowning almost everything in a sea of sameness. We had been scouring the countryside for days, discovering one ancient site after another and passing close to the low rise of Site 345 without seeing it. Then, early one morning, when the light conditions were good, we suddenly saw the low mass of ruins in the distance, which could no longer be mistaken for a natural part of the landscape.

Even from fairly nearby, they appear nondescript. It is only when one is in their midst that it becomes evident how extensive they are and what an important place this must have been. The view from the air is even more striking. The oval and circular foundations of houses with walled courtyards and the alleyways between them stand out clearly. An unusual sense of symmetry and order pervades the place, indicating that it was a better planned site than most of the other villages and towns of the Middle Bronze I period that we have come across in the Negev. Certain building-ruins were particularly outstanding, but it will take careful excavations to disentangle them from the debris of fallen stones obscuring the true lines of their walls. On a slight rise near the center of the site is a small, rectangular, platformlike structure. Was it a tomb, or the base of an altar?

There is no question, furthermore, about the dominant and practically exclusive period of occupation of this town, if one judges solely from the very large number of pottery fragments found among and around the ruins and on the gentle slopes below it. With the exception of a very small number of Roman to Byzantine sherds, they were solely Middle Bronze I in date, and could not be earlier than the twenty-first nor later than the nineteenth century B.C. Before then and after then, there was no settlement on the site.

Site 345 grew up and was cut down within the limits of the Abrahamitic Age. It was the permanent residence of several hundred souls, who derived their livelihood from their fields and flocks, and in all probability also from the traffic and trade on the highway to and from Kadesh-barnea in Sinai. As for their water supply, it must be remembered that they did not require very much according to the standards of their day and of many parts of the modern Near East, for that matter. Nor did they have far to go. They had to dig only a few feet or at the most a few yards into the wadi bed below them to find water, even during the height of the dry season. Then, too, the excellent wells of Bir Birein were only about two miles away. That was not a great distance in ancient days for the womenfolk and children to trudge or ride on their donkeys to fill their pottery jars with enough water to suffice for drinking and cooking purposes. Nor is it considered too great a distance for the inhabitants of many Arab villages to this very day.

It is possible, of course, that Site 345 was occupied only during the plowing, planting and harvesting seasons. It is well known that both in Biblical and modern times, many villages were lived in for only short periods of the year and then used as storage depots. During the remaining months, their inhabitants followed the crops and seasons in various parts of their domain, pitching tent encampments for as long as they cared to stay in any one place or district. This was the practice followed until recent years by the inhabitants of the Dura district in southwestern Palestine, where the average rainfall is higher than in any part of the Negev.

It is probable that this procedure was the rule in many of the Abrahamitic villages of the Negev, but there is no reason to believe that it prevailed in all of them. In places where there were wells such as those of Bir Birein or where a comparatively plentiful supply of underground water was known to exist, it probably did not apply. The scarcity and preciousness of water in the Negev limited the radius of wandering far away from it. The herds and flocks had to be watered every day. In view of its size and importance and the likelihood that it was an administrative center, and in view of the necessity of constantly utilizing and safeguarding the water supply, it would seem most likely that Site 345 was occupied all year round.

From all indications, or lack of them, this city, whose name and repute must have been widespread, was not concerned with security problems. There was no formidable outer wall encircling it to protect it from marauders or an invading army, and no complex, twisting gateway which could be nightly shut and barred. There seem to have been no guard towers of any kind or any means of defense. This was an open, easily accessible, completely unfortified town, which flourished in a prolonged period of peace.

With the exception of the walled hilltop site above Bir Rekhmeh, none of the numerous Middle Bronze I sites we have discovered in the Negev was fortified. They were utterly defenseless, unprotected by any kind of outer fortification walls. It would indeed have been extremely simple for beleaguering forces to conquer them simply by cutting off access to their water supplies, which in most instances were considerably beyond the perimeters of the settlements. To judge from the ease with which the Kings of the East, mentioned in Genesis 14, overran them, they were bound together, if at all, in only the loosest of political unions. As a result, they could be and were picked off one by one, like stragglers isolated from the main herd and torn to pieces by ravenous wolf packs.

The Journey of Sinuhe

Some day the original names of at least a part of the most important of these sites in the Negev, such as the very large one of 345, located on a major highway from Egypt to Canaan, or Retenu as it was called in the Egyptian tongue, may be recovered from the limbo of the past. That could happen as the result of literally patching up an ancient Egyptian malediction. The custom prevailed of writing out a curse against a person or place, out of favor and out of reach of the Egyptian court, on an earthen vase or statuette and then smashing it to pieces. It was thought or hoped that the recreant object of the royal wrath would in this fashion be properly punished, even though not near at hand. However psychologically soothing it may have been for the imperial feelings to be vented in this fashion, it enjoyed the additional, if unintentional, advantage of serving historical purposes.

These reconstructed twentieth and nineteenth century B.C. Execration Texts, written in extremely cursive, hieratic Egyptian, mention among other places the names of Jerusalem and Shechem, which Abraham visited. Indeed, under slightly different circumstances, it is not hard to imagine the Pharaoh of Egypt writing Abraham's name on such a jar and breaking it in order to punish him *in absentia* for telling him the partial truth that Sarah was Abraham's sister, whereas in reality she was both his half-sister and his wife (Genesis 20:12). Perhaps additional collections of purposely broken incantation cups or pottery sculptures will yet be found in Egypt, singling out by name this Negevite site 345. Being the most important place on the road leading northeastward from Kadesh-barnea through the Negev, it could well have offered haven to the noble Egyptian fugitive, Sinuhe, and thus have evoked against it fulsome and specific imprecations of evil. This would not be at all surprising in view of the fact that the strange word for "retainers" used in Genesis 14:14 in connection with Abraham's counterattack against Chedorlaomer is an Egyptian word, as William F. Albright points out, which occurs nowhere else in the Bible, but is employed in the Execration Texts to describe retainers of Palestinian chieftains.

The adventurous account of Sinuhe's escape from the jurisdiction of his king, Seostris (Sen-Usert) I, who ruled from about 1971 to 1928 B.C., to find refuge and riches in Canaan was read and narrated in wide circles in the Patriarchal Age and later. His sufferings in Sinai, his success in Retenu, his final return in honor to his homeland to prepare himself for life after death, were tales often told in lands of Egyptian control or influence. The Negev obviously figured in his odyssey. This site and others like them must have tempered the hardships of his pilgrimage. In similar fashion, we may assume that Abraham was received with the same warmth which he dispensed to others when they sought the threshold of his dwelling (Genesis 18:1-8). I, myself, have on repeated occasion enjoyed the same kind of welcome in Arab lands similar to the Negev, with my host being called Ibrahim instead of Abraham. The reception almost invariably accorded my companions and me, whenever we suddenly appeared at Arab encampments, can be described no better than with the paragraph in the Bible touching on Abraham's heart-warming reception of passing strangers:

". . . And when he saw them, he ran to meet them . . . and said . . . let now a little water be fetched and wash your feet and rest yourselves under the tree. And I will fetch a morsel of bread, and strengthen ye your heart; after that ye shall pass on . . . and Abraham hastened into the tent unto Sarah and said, Make ready quickly three measures of fine meal, knead it and make cakes. And Abraham ran unto the herd and fetched a calf tender and good and gave it unto the servant; and he hastened to dress it. And he took butter and milk and the calf which he had dressed and set it before them; and he stood by them under the tree and they did eat" (Genesis 18:1-8). This is the kind of hospitality that Abraham and Sinuhe before him must have received when they traveled through the Negev. Was it not occupied in their days by sedentary and semisedentary populations schooled in the Semitic culture of which Abraham was so strikingly representative?

Others too lived or sojourned in the Negev of this time: "Now Isaac had come from the direction of *Beer-lahai-ro'i* and had taken up residence in the land of the Negev" (Genesis 24:62).

A record of further travels through the Negev is contained in a mural painting in a tomb of about 1900 B.C. at Beni Hassan on the Nile. It is located between Memphis and Thebes, some 200 miles south of Cairo. The mural vividly portrays a group of well-clad and equipped Semites who had arrived in Egypt to exchange the popular black eye cosmetic of stibium for the staples they needed. They had to cross the Negev to get there. Their origin and background were obviously similar to those of Abraham, with their leader's name, Abisha(r), being somewhat related to his. Had the Bible given a popular etymology of the meaning of his name, it might have explained that it meant "the father of righteousness," even as it gave the explanation that Abraham meant "the father of a multitude of peoples" (Genesis 17:5), and might have added that Abram meant "exalted father." On his way to Egypt, Abishar and his companions must have walked familiar paths in the Negev and found lodging there with permanently settled communities, whose members were related to them even as they were to Abraham and his people in the brotherhood of a common language and culture and perhaps also of bloodstream.

The statement with which Sinuhe concluded the description of the arrangements for his prodigal return to his native land: "Then this servant headed for the South," may refer merely to the direction of his journeying. It need not necessarily mean the Negev, which, however, he had to cross again to get home, with stops at some of its towns and hamlets. Be that as it may, it is clear that the various trips of

Abraham and Sinuhe and Abishar and others like them are indicative of considerable travel and traffic through the Negev and Sinai during the Patriarchal Age, as in various periods before and after.

Ebbtide

The memory of Abraham's physical and spiritual adventures in the Negev and Sinai lingered on in the consciousness of his descendants. They alluded to these episodes in their Biblical account of the relationship of the God of Abraham, Isaac and Jacob to His chosen people. Abundant archaeological evidence bears out, as we have seen, the meager literary sources which mirror the catastrophic consequences of the invasion of the Kings of the East from Ashtaroth Karnaim to Kadesh-barnea and beyond and back again. Whether this destructive foray was a fairly isolated incident or whether, as seems more likely, it was an integral part of the happenings which brought about the collapse of the contemporary civilizations throughout all of Eastern and Western Palestine, remains for the present undecided.

Is it possible that the destruction and annihilation wrought by Chedorlaomer and his allies from Syria to Sinai through Transjordan and the Negev may be distant forerunners of the eruption of violent forces which resulted in the invasion and conquest of Egypt by the Semitic Hyksos? However, the fact remains that for about three hundred years between the twenty-first and nineteenth centuries B.C., tranquility prevailed in Transjordan, the Negev and Sinai. The town dwellers of this period may have purchased the peace they required through heavy tribute to the Bedouins, who pounced upon them savagely the moment their payments were not forthcoming. The brutal punishment inflicted by the tribal chieftain, Chedorlaomer, and his confederates upon the Dead Sea cities of Sodom, Gomorrah, Admah, Zeboyim and Zoar was occasioned by their refusal to be blackmailed any longer.

"Twelve years they served Chedorlaomer, and in the thirteenth year they rebelled" (Genesis 14:4). It was a foolhardy revolt, and was mercilessly crushed. The Negev cities of the Age of Abraham were, as we have seen, unfortified and hopelessly vulnerable. They were as defenseless against attack as the Aztec towns proved to be before the striking power of a small Spanish expedition equipped with weapons that the inhabitants of ancient Mexico, used to peace, were unable to cope with.

How different it was in the Negev in the next period of sedentary occupation marked by stone buildings and pottery and cisterns! This was not until about a thousand years later, beginning with the accession of the Judaean Kingdom to precarious power. During the more than three hundred years of its existence, almost all of its towns and villages were built with the expectation of attack and siege.

Very strong fortification walls, frequently with the addition of smoothed, sloping revetments tied into them to prevent their being undermined and tunneled through; regularly spaced guard towers; high embattlements from which the enemy could be speared or scalded; intricate gateways blocked sometimes by three sets of doors, all securely barred at dark against danger; long and deep tunnels vertically and sometimes horizontally piercing hill towns to underground springs to guarantee access to a secure water supply even under extended siege, as in Megiddo, Gibeon, Jerusalem and Shobek, among other places; the initial choice of strategically located and fortifiable hills—all these eloquently express the disturbed and dangerous state of affairs which the Judaean Kingdom had to contend with.

It was a time of turbulence and impending disaster throughout the Fertile Crescent. No kingdom could be sure of itself, no city remain dependent upon others to protect it. Even before the United Kingdom of Israel and Judah fell apart, and during the long and resolute and brilliantly successful reign of Solomon, every halfway important town was turned into a stoutly built fortress. Many of the inhabitants lived in houses or tents outside the confines of the city, taking refuge within its walls only during the threat of impending attack.

Hundreds of years earlier, however, as I have said, a "Pax Abrahamitica" prevailed in the Negev and in the countries with which it was geographically and economically integrated. It may be likened in effect, if not in form, to the continentally widespread Pax Romana of two millennia later. At that time, a strong, centralized government, by the wide delegation of much authority to capable governors, preserved peace throughout great stretches of the civilized world. During the beneficent centuries of Nabataean and Roman rule, multitudes of towns and villages escaped the hilltop restrictions of their walled straitjackets to be erected anew in the open plains of their inhabitants' employment. The Negev, too, flourished under the sun of this general well-being in a manner reminiscent of the more modest good fortune it had experienced ages previously when Abraham had sojourned in it.

The desolation, which had become the lot also of Canaan at the end of the Age of Abraham, was followed not too long after by a period of high prosperity. Numerous settlements took the place of those abandoned in Canaan as the result of economic decline, military defeat and political disintegration. This was not so in the Negev, where, generally speaking, civilization was unable to strike roots again until the tenth century B.C. Egypt too had been in a state of turmoil, and bereft of the strength which in other eras had enabled it to extend its sway from Sinai to Syria. The lure of its riches attracted the Hyksos hordes from Mesopotamia. There was no staying their sweep southward, using their startling innovation of horse-drawn chariotry to engulf everything in their path. They made their conquests secure with a new type of massive, rectangular fortifications of beaten earth (*terre pisée*). Examples have been found at Hazor, Shechem,

Lachish, Tell Beit Mirsim and Tell el-Ajjul, among other places, in Palestine. Egypt succumbed to their onrush about 1720 B.C. Setting up their own dynastic succession, they long maintained an uneasy hold over the lands of the Nile. Finally, some 150 years after their advent, they were unseated and expelled.

At the height of their power under Apophis and Khayana, their authority seems to have extended from the banks of the Euphrates in Mesopotamia to southern Nubia in Africa. Had they wanted to, therefore, they could easily have driven the Bedouins out of the Negev and built fortresses there, which would have protected the travel routes through it and enabled sedentary agricultural civilization to flourish there once again. They could also have restored the peace and prosperity which had existed in neighboring Transjordan in the Abrahamitic period. They did not choose to do so. The explanation lies, we believe, in the fact that they were really interested only in maintaining their line of communications between Egypt and Palestine via the famous Biblical Way of the Land of the Philistines, which went along the Mediterranean coast. It was the route invariably followed by Egyptian armies on their way to Palestine and Syria, and it was the route they themselves had taken with their horses and chariots.

It was all the more natural for the Hyksos to be concerned only with this coastal highway between Egypt and Canaan in view of the fact that they had built their own capital at Avaris in the northeastern corner of the Nile Delta. A direct and easy road suitable for heavy traffic led from it eastward and northward to Raphia and Gaza and Ascalon. When they were forced out of Egypt, the Hyksos followed this same route in their retreat, to make a vain, three-year stand at the great fortress of Sharuhen (Tell el-Far'ah), in the rich plains of the northwesternmost Negev. Thereafter, the forces of Egypt resumed their expansionist march northward. It was always along the "Philistine route" that, subsequently,

Thotmes I and Thotmes III led their victorious armies repeatedly through Palestine and Syria to the banks of the Euphrates.

Otherwise, during all this time, Sinai and the Negev as a whole were ignored and uninhabited by strong, civilized, permanently settled populations, possessed of fortified towns and deeply rooted in the land. Perhaps, if that had not been the case, the Exodus might not have taken place. There would have been no other area where the Israelites could have wandered about, halting at will at various places until sufficient strength had been gathered for advance and attack, or, in case of setbacks, for retreat and recuperation and renewal of effort. The centuries of alternate expansion of the Hyksos southward and of the Egyptians northward, and their respective withdrawals along the coastal road between the Nile Delta and the Gaza strip, created a power vacuum in Sinai and the Negev. It was accentuated during the period of decline and disintegration of the great powers of the Fertile Crescent, which took place between the thirteenth and twelfth centuries B.C.

From every direction, the old order gave way then to onslaught from abroad. Aramaean nomads erupted from the easternmost deserts and poured westward over Mesopotamia into Syria, where they established states of their own. Highly civilized peoples of the sea from Crete (Caphtor) (Amos 9:7) and related islands seized the opportunity to escape their confines and implant their standards firmly on the mainland of the eastern Mediterranean littoral. They invaded Asia Minor and overthrew the Hittite empire. Their attack on Egypt was beaten back by Rameses III, but they did succeed in establishing themselves on the southwestern coast of Canaan at the beginning of the twelfth century B.C. We know something about them from Biblical references and Egyptian records and from their pottery. The pottery is foreign to traditional Canaanite forms of the period, being patterned after wares from the Greek world whence they came. Nevertheless, their very language and script and culture still escape us. Appareled in armor when they went out to battle, and skilled in metallurgical crafts (I Samuel 13:19), this enigmatic people nearly succeeded in subjugating all of the land. The Canaanite cities of the time were both weak and impoverished on the whole and could offer little or no resistance. The Israelites were finally to win out in the long-drawn-out struggle for mastery that raged between them and the invaders from the setting of the sun. In the name of Palestine itself, however, which was derived from their presence and impact, the Philistines recorded for all posterity the nearness of the ultimate victory which eluded them.

CHAPTER V

"THIS IS THE BLESSING"

Spying Out the Land

IT WAS DURING THIS ERA of widespread turbulence and violent change that the Exodus from Egypt took place. Most of its history transpired in Sinai and the Negev. There was no governmental authority there to stay or aid its course. No civilized population existed there any longer, or had for centuries; in this it was unlike the coastal strip, which seems to have been continuously occupied. The villages that Abraham and his people had come across in their day had long ago disappeared, leaving ruins which were meaningless to the newcomers, if they recognized them at all. Cultivation of the soil had long since ceased. Any group of Bedouins or seminomads, which is what the Israelites were, large enough to protect itself against *ghazzus,* or raids, by others could pitch their tents and graze their flocks wherever it pleased them.

The Israelites were welcomed by the Kenites and related tribes that were friendly and kin to them through bonds of intermarriage. And so it was that the Israelites wandered at will throughout Sinai and the Negev, camping for long at such strong springs as those of En-mishpat (Ain el-Qudeirat), where Kadesh-barnea was located. But they were not content to remain homeless wanderers in the wilderness. Their hearts were set on penetrating as swiftly and directly as possible into the Promised Land, but their strength, at first, was not equal to the task. Ahead of them lay grievous years of difficult preparation and trial. In defeat and weariness, in hunger and despair, in testing and revelation their courage would be hardened and their faith matured.

A direct route I have already described, the one I called "The Way of the Wells," with water and grazing available, led between Kadesh-barnea and Canaan. It was, however, to prove a difficult road for the people of the Exodus, although in earlier times it had been traveled by Abraham and countless others. The spies sent out by Moses to reconnoiter southern Canaan had followed it along the watershed that snakes diagonally through the Negev, until they reached the difficult hill country beyond. Seeing the formidable defenses which commanded the approaches from the south to the Promised Land, they had returned with a dispiriting report to the Children of Israel awaiting them at Kadesh-barnea, between the Wilderness of Zin and the Wilderness of Paran. To demonstrate the fertility of interior Canaan, some of whose turreted cities they had observed with increasing apprehension, they brought back with them a great cluster of grapes and pomegranates and figs from the Valley of Eshkol near Hebron.

I can see them peering over the brows of hilltops and impassively taking mental photographs of everything within their range of vision, and follow them, as they slipped like shadows before daybreak into a garden to steal some of its fruits for their homeward journey. The instructions they had received were explicit enough: "And Moses sent them to spy out the land of Canaan, and said unto them, Get you

"THIS IS THE BLESSING" 113

up from here into the Negev and then into the hill-country. And see . . . the people that dwell therein, whether they are strong or weak, whether they are few or many . . . ; and what cities they are that they dwell in, whether in camps or in strongholds; and what the land is, whether it is fat or lean . . ." (Numbers 13:17-20).

They had completed their dangerous mission, retraced their way through the Negev and were back again among the congregation of their own people. In spite of the success of their venture, they had returned with some trepidation, for discord had broken out among their number. They said to Moses: "We came unto the land whither thou sentest us, and surely it floweth with milk and honey, and here is some of the fruit of it. Howbeit, the people that dwell in the land are strong, and the cities are fortified and very great, and moreover we saw the Children of the Giants there. And the Amalekites dwell in the land of the Negev" (Numbers 13:27-29).

The sound advice which all but two of them, namely Joshua the son of Nun and Caleb the son of Jephuneh, offered against attempting to invade the Promised Land from the south was ignored. They had said the right thing at the wrong time, and the result was that the people of Israel raised their voices against their leaders, while the ten who had demurred against the ill-considered adventure were grievously punished for their pains. ". . . The men whom Moses sent to spy out the land, who returned, and made all the congregation to murmur against him by bringing an evil report against the land, . . . died by the plague before Jehovah" (Numbers 14:36.37).

According to the point of view of later theologically oriented historians, the ten were judged not by the accuracy of their appraisal, which indeed merited gratitude, but by the unintentional incitement to rebellion against the leadership of Moses which it stirred up.

Ignoring the unpleasant intelligence, the exiles from Egypt

pressed swiftly northward from their temporary abode in Sinai, following, as I have said, much the same route between Kadesh-barnea and Beersheba that Abraham had traveled before them. Taking the shortest distance, they fought with all their might, but their strength was not enough. The reputation of their might was not yet great enough to strike paralyzing fear into the hearts of their opponents. Neither confederates from within nor earthquakes from without would help them breach the gates of the citadels that blocked them. Against this wall of Canaanite power, they battered in vain. Their onslaught was beaten off. Leaving their dead behind, together with some taken captive, they limped back to lick their wounds in Sinai, bruised, bewildered and bitter. A whole generation was to elapse, before they entered the Holy Land proper from a different direction and by a circuitous route. It had taken them only a few days to approach and be repelled from its southern flank. The miraculous experience at Jericho lay far ahead of them.

The Amalekites who claimed the Negev as their own and the Canaanites of the mountainous country made common cause against the incursion of the Israelites. "Then the Amalekites came down and the Canaanites who dwelt in the mountains, and smote them and beat them down even unto Hormah" (Numbers 14:45). It was the Negevite king of Arad who seems to have borne the burden of leadership against the attack by the Israelites, who had come via the caravan route (Numbers 21:1; 33:40).

It is likely that the "king" of Arad, who was in reality only a tribal chieftain, tented with his people on and around Tell Arad, but did not live in a fortified city there. It had been a center of civilization as early as the fourth millennium B.C., and again in the Abrahamitic period. It was not, however, to be the site of a city of houses of stone and brick enclosed within defensive walls until about the tenth century B.C., to judge from sherds found on its surfaces. (The same seems to be true of all the artificial city-hills in the Northern Negev, such as Tell Milh, Khirbet Ar'areh and Khirbet Mishash.)

In the Bible we are told that the "king" of Arad stopped the Israelites in their tracks "and took some of them captive" (Numbers 21:1). In the brief account in which this passage occurs, the Biblical editor immediately goes on to describe the defeat inflicted in turn by the Israelites upon the Canaanites at Hormah (Numbers 21:1-3). He does not explicitly point out, however, that several hundred years intervened between the two battles. Relishing the historical vindication of his people, he even puns on the word "Hormah." Its consonants (h-r-m) form the root of the word meaning "utterly to destroy." His story ends with the statement: "And Jehovah hearkened to the voice of Israel, and delivered up the Canaanites; and they inflicted upon them and their cities the absolute destruction of *herem;* and the name of that place was called *Hormah*" (Numbers 21:3).

Old Gods and New

The vehemence of the Biblical statements gives one pause. The battle between the people of Moses and the inhabitants of Canaan was a seesaw conflict. It raged for many centuries and in some ways was never resolved. The defeat inflicted by the king of Arad was merely the prelude to prolonged war. When the tables were turned, the triumph of the Israelites proved to be temporary. There was a regular merry-go-round of victors and vanquished. The question as to who conquered whom could not always easily be answered. New contestants for mastery kept appearing magically. Even after the adversaries had been annihilated or absorbed, their memory and influence remained amazingly alive. The iron armored Philistines were eradicated, but the impress of their power and culture was perpetuated in the name of Palestine.

Jebusites, Amorites, Canaanites, and Amalekites played out their roles and departed, but they left their gods behind them.

The prophets and priests of Israel had repeatedly to contend in this manner with the flare-up of pagan cult practices among their people. The long reign of Manasseh (circa 687-642 B.C.) was an extended instance of backsliding, made popular by royal example. "He did that which was evil in the sight of Jehovah, after the abominations of the nations whom Jehovah cast out before the children of Israel. For he built again the high places which Hezekiah his father had destroyed; and he reared up altars for Baal and made an Asherah . . . and worshipped all the Host of Heaven . . . And he made his son to pass through fire and practiced augury and used enchantments . . . And he set the graven image of Asherah . . . in the temple . . . Moreover, Manasseh shed very much innocent blood . . ." (II Kings 21:2-7.16).

It may seem strange, but our surface finds at Tell Arad illustrate some of the "abominations," as they are usually called in the Bible, which Israel adopted in its new surroundings. If you will join the circle of the expedition's staff for a moment, while I sort out the sherds we have picked up, I'll illustrate this. That cream-colored bowl rim with a band of reddish-brown paint belongs to the fourth millennium B.C., as does the fine flint scraper carefully tooled on three sides. This ribbed loop-handle and the sherd with horizontal lines of wheel burnishing over a reddish-brown slip stem from the ninth to the sixth centuries B.C.

But how about the fragment I put aside as being interesting, but not immediately clear? The ware obviously belongs to the period of the Judaean Kingdom, which the Babylonians destroyed in the sixth century B.C. Is it a cornet base? If so, it is new to me. When I tried turning the pointed end up, I understood it! It was not a cornet base at all, but a conical cap or crown set over a head, whose left side had been broken away. The nose is missing too, but the forehead and chin and the position of the eyes give a haunting character to the face, as if it were seen through a haze. The carefully braided hair reaching down behind the right cheek to the nape of the neck is completely intact. Seen in profile, the likeness of a goddess becomes apparent.

This was part of a pottery figurine of the goddess Astarte. Somewhat larger ones of the same period but of different type have been excavated at Beersheba, and at every contemporary site opened up north of it. Pressed into shape in previously carved stone molds and kiln-fired into lasting firmness, they formed a very common and indispensable part of the religious furniture of almost every household. The prototypes of their features were the women who fondled them, that they might readily conceive and bear numerous sons.

I have found these terra cotta statuettes or parts of them on tells also in Moab and Edom. They formed a bond of close community between the peoples on both sides of the Jordan. In Sabkhah, near southern Syria, I once purchased one of them of larger than usual size. She too wore a conical cap, but was somehow less elegant in style than the small one of Tell Arad. Her locks of hair were scraggly and her countenance was as coarse as her body was broad. Her breasts were scrawny. She was primarily a symbol of sturdy strength. In her, every woman of the land could find her counterpart, to whom she could familiarly turn for blessing of her womb and fields and cattle.

Even when they went on journeys, the first companions of the way were these sacred images. Rachel stole her father's teraphim before joining her husband, Jacob, in his flight from Padan Aram "to go to Isaac his father unto the land of Canaan." When Laban overtook them and frantically searched their encampment, her tent included, she concealed them, we are told, in her camel saddle, upon which she perched immovably. Claiming that "the manner of women is upon me," she guilefully explained away her lack of courtesy in failing to rise before her father. Nor was she moved by his bitter cry to Jacob: "And now, thou wouldest needs be gone because thou sore longedst after thy father's house, yet wherefore hast thou stolen my gods?" (Genesis 31:17-19.30).

Such gods were constantly denounced by the spiritually elect of Jehovah. Sometimes these "abominations" were publicly burned by a reform king like Josiah of Jerusalem. It was, however, to take an extremely long time before they were displanted from public acceptance and private attachment. This process neared final completion when synagogues replaced the temple and when the masses of people recognized the fact, however imperfectly, that the image of god must be found in their hearts. It was not till then that Canaan was truly conquered.

Retreat and Regeneration

The defeat of the Israelites of the Exodus at Hormah marked one of those decisive moments when history can take any one of countless turns. If they had won there against the armies led by the king of Arad and settled then in the highlands of southern Canaan, might they not completely have succumbed to the culture of those they had conquered? May not the toughening of their fiber and the resolution of their character by disappointment and disaster, coupled with increasing spiritual discipline and insight, be reckoned among the factors which prevented their disappearance into the void of an impenetrable past? If their way had been easy and their enemies impotent, would they have achieved the underlying singleness of force which gave them the uniqueness of identity and the fellowship of faith that have been their unfailing source of strength throughout history? They broke early with the barbaric practice of passing their sons through the fires of heathen sacrifice, but that was only a beginning. Would they, without intense suffering and seeking, have been able to produce out of their midst giants like Moses and Isaiah and Jeremiah and Job, and been molded in turn by them? The rush from Kadesh-barnea to Hormah was a race to near-catastrophe. The retreat from Hormah to Kadesh-barnea was the start of an extraordinary exercise in unparalleled regeneration.

Kadesh-barnea was a point of no return so far as Egypt was concerned for the Israelites of the Exodus. Yet the pull of that land would continue forever. Its fortunes inevitably affected the welfare of Israel and Judah, and apparently more frequently for ill than for good. It comes as no surprise, therefore, to find in Thebes, painted on the walls of the tomb of the soldier, Amen-em-heb, the statement: "I made captives in the country of the Negeb." Amen-em-heb had been a soldier in the army of Thutmose III, which in 1468 B.C. (?) had destroyed Megiddo in Canaan. Its fame as Armageddon, as it was later called, has endured. This performance was to be repeated a little over half a millennium later by another Pharaoh, Sheshonk I, known in the Bible as Shishak. During his campaign he also sacked the Solomonic temple in Jerusalem. An exaggerated list of his Asiatic conquests has been found at Karnak in Egypt. When, in due course, the flood of aggression from the south reached its crest and receded, the Assyrians and then the Babylonians invaded Egypt in turn. In battle and in bombast, they too were equally victorious.

Between the two poles of power in Africa and Asia there flowed a steady stream of traffic. Bedouins and planters, troops and traders, pilgrims and fugitives beat out a clear path, whose impress has always remained. From a distant perspective, they might have appeared like processions of ants surging in opposite directions to disappear into subterranean galleries, most of them never to reappear. The havens they sought were always illusory, buttressed as they were solely by the perilous fragility of power and possession. The riches they garnered ran out like grains of sand in an hourglass being perpetually upended. Unchanging were the drive to conquer and the pattern of change. Only the Law of the Lord, however dimly perceived by the many and dangerously taught by the few, was permanent and full of endless promise.

Turn the clock backward and take note of some of the milestones of history which can be traced in an undeviating line between the lands of the Nile and the Jordan. We find Isaiah urging that Judah make no political alliance and security treaty with Egypt: "Woe unto them that go down to Egypt for help and rely on horses, and trust in chariots because they are many, and in horsemen because they are very strong, but they look not unto the Holy One of Israel, neither seek Jehovah. . . . Now the Egyptians are men, and not God; and their horses flesh, and not spirit. And when Jehovah shall stretch out his hand, both he that helpeth shall stumble, and he that is helped shall fall, and they all shall be consumed together" (Isaiah 31:1.3). That was far different from the inception of the epic when Jehovah bade Moses say to Pharaoh: "Israel is my son, my firstborn. . . . Let my son go, that he may serve me . . ." (Exodus 4:22.23).

Then Israel, barred at Hormah from penetrating straight to the heart of their goal, had recrossed the Negev back to Sinai by the same path, the one already familiar to Abraham. Like refugees peering through unbreakable barriers to certain salvation immediately beyond, the wanderers had vainly glimpsed the Promised Land. They may have sensed that they themselves would never dwell in it. It was the more tantalizing, because their camping place in Sinai was located in the outskirts of the sanctuary they were seeking. On the way they had already crossed the River of Egypt, which is listed in the Bible as the southwesternmost boundary of Judah (Joshua 15:4.47; Numbers 34:4.5). Sinai to the east of it belongs physically to the Negev, and to the west of it to Egypt. These are the natural geographical divisions. Known today as the

Wadi el-Arish, its extensive system of generally dry stream beds drains the length of the Sinai peninsula into the Mediterranean. Its outlet is at the oasis of el-Arish, about fifty miles southwest of Gaza. The beginnings of some of its wadis reach well up the slopes of the watershed which Kadesh-barnea caps. This place became for Israel the crossroads of final decision. Their future depended on the outcome. Where should they go now?

The Israelites were compelled to turn eastward and southeastward through the Negev. The very slopes of much of the land and the direction of many of the usually empty watercourses which furrow its features are eastward too. Their descent culminated in the long, mineral-rich and history-laden depression of the Arabah, which has retained its name throughout the ages. The Dead Sea, known also as the Sea of Salt or the Sea of Lot, at its north end, and the Gulf of Aqabah, once known as the Yam Suph, at its south end were originally joined together over its length. The great geological fault to which they belong continues northward through the Jordan Valley, the Lake of Galilee, and indeed as far as and beyond the Beq'ah, the Valley of the Lebanon.

The importance of this immense fissure in the crust of the earth for the annals of Israel cannot be overemphasized. Eastern and Western Palestine were pendent upon it like wings to a body. It was vital in their defense, crucial in their economy and central in their orientation. The compulsions of geography, the imperatives of trade and the mandates of self-preservation have made and kept the Wadi Arabah, with its access to the Red Sea, the equivalent of a jugular vein in the body politic of the people and state of Israel. The path of the Exodus leads through it. The arrival at Punon, on its eastern side, signified a crucial stage in the wearisome journey. The direct distance between Kadesh-barnea and Punon, which are almost on a straight line from west to east, could easily have been traversed in four days. It took forty years.

"Thou Art the Man"

A roundabout journey brought the Israelites from Punon to Jericho, and in the course of time back to Ezion-geber:Elath again. Centuries elapsed in between, during which they established a firm base in the land of their inheritance. Happily, at the outset, they were unaware of the perils that loomed ahead of them. Awaiting them was hazardous conflict with numerous enemies. On one occasion, at Shiloh, they found themselves in such desperate straits that they gambled the Ark of the Covenant for victory and lost both the battle and their sacred heirloom to the Philistines. Not until the coming of David to power was the struggle with these adversaries from the Aegean Islands basically resolved in favor of his people.

His victories set the seal on their ultimate doom and disappearance, even as other brilliant martial and administrative feats enabled him to become the master of his own house. Without him, the new kingdom of Israel might well have foundered in its very beginnings, and the unfolding therefore of some aspects of divine purpose been left to others to execute. There is small wonder that messianic hopes were henceforth to be bound up with the house of David.

David had cleaved his way to the throne with a purposefulness as sharp as an unsheathed Damascus blade. Everything he did, or almost everything, contributed to the fulfillment of his schemes or to the consolidation of his power. It was a stroke of genius on his part to make Jerusalem his place of residence and to take steps to invest the sanctuary there with nationwide importance. Neither Hebron in the south nor Shechem in the north could be jealous because one was given preference over the other. David did not dream that the city of his choice was destined to become the capital of the conscience of mankind, even as the laws of nature had made it the center of the heartland of the earth.

David's successes at home were matched by his conquests

abroad. His smiting of the lands from Syria to Edom seems, however, to have been motivated by more than the desire to cut off at the source recurrent invasions into his own territory. He was the first of the heads of the new kingdom to realize, I believe, that its lifeline reached through the Negev and the Arabah to the Red Sea. This was fully understood and energetically acted upon by his son, Solomon, and by every strong occupant of the throne in Jerusalem after him.

The principle of keeping the way open to Ezion-geber: Elath and beyond, which became one of the cardinal and undeviating rules of all Israelitic and Judaean foreign policy, seems thus to have been established in essence in the time of David. It was basically over this issue that fierce war was waged frequently with Edom for several hundred years. Israel and later on Judah had no choice in this connection. They were forced by reason of the geographical position and the dominant topographical features of their land to face southward, with the same inevitableness that the sunflower is compelled constantly to turn its head toward the sun.

Early in his career, David came into familiar contact with the Negev. At one time, it almost proved to be his undoing. Fleeing from moody and suspicious Saul, whose tender love for him had turned to murderous hate, David found refuge in the remote village of Ziklag, located near the border between Judah and the Negev. We do not know exactly where, except that it was probably east of Gath and north of Beersheba. It had been offered to him by Achish, king of the Philistine city of Gath, who controlled it, and who acted apparently on the principle that "the enemies of my enemies are my friends." Otherwise, how could he possibly have offered hospitality and protection to one whose feats in battle against the Philistines inspired the chant: "Saul hath slain his thousands, and David his tens of thousands" (I Samuel 18:7)!

Ensconced at Ziklag, David accomplished the impossible. He succeeded in maintaining a delicate balance of loyalty to his own kinsmen, whom he would not hurt, and fealty to his Philistine patron, whom he was in duty bound to help.

While pretending to serve the Philistines with undivided loyalty, David would attack Negevite and Sinaitic tribes which looked to them for protection, but which David regarded as fair game for Israel. His Philistine overlord, Achish, assumed that these *ghazzus* were directed against his enemies. The question which the Bible reports his having put to David in this connection and the answer he received bear the ring of authenticity: "And Achish said, Against whom have ye made a raid today? And David replied, Against the Negev of Judah, and against the Negev of the Yerahmeelites, and against the Negev of the Kenites" (I Samuel 27:10).

David knew that it would please his host immensely to hear that he had attacked these areas, whose inhabitants were his own blood. "And Achish believed David, saying: He hath made his people Israel utterly to abhor him; therefore he shall be my servant forever" (I Samuel 27:12). But Achish could not possibly have been more deluded. He should have known that David would never attack his own people, and that his heart was too firmly set on becoming king of Israel in place of Saul to make himself hated in this fashion. The Calebite city of Hebron would never have rallied to his cause, as it did, to crown him there as the king of Judah, before he was also made king of Israel, had he ever harmed his own kind (II Samuel 2:4). The Negev of Caleb was also part of the larger region in which Judaeans and Yerahmeelites and Kenites tented (I Samuel 30:14).

On the very day that Achish had questioned him, David had carried out a brutal attack not only against the Amalekites, who were their mutual enemies, but also against the Geshurites and the Girzites (I Samuel 27:8), who may well have been related to the Philistines. They inhabited the coastal plains south of the Philistine territory as far as the Shihor, which is one of the eastern branches of the Nile (Joshua 13:2.3; I Chronicles 13:5). None of those he attacked could ever question his story, because "David saved neither man nor woman alive to bring them to Gath, saying, So did David, and so hath been his manner all the while he hath dwelt in the country of the Philistines" (I Samuel 27:11).

The day would come when David would no longer have to balance himself between keeping in the good graces of his Philistine master and at the same time protecting the Judaean and related tribes in the Negev. In the meantime, he could not afford to antagonize his Philistine patron by letting him know that he had plundered and slaughtered tribes such as the Geshurites and Girzites, who were probably as close to the Philistines as the Yerahmeelites and Kenites and Calebites were close to him. Following his theory that "dead men tell no tales," he blandly asserted the opposite of what he had actually done, and seemed to have been able successfully to carry off the deception.

A crisis arose, however, when Achish, who had absolute confidence in him, summoned him to join in the war against the forces of Saul. Unable to fight for Israel, David was certainly resolved not to fight against it. To have refused outright would have catastrophically imperiled his position. It was therefore a gravely perplexed man who, in obedience to the call, left Ziklag with his rough band of foreign legionnaires, composed of Cherethites, Pelethites, Philistines and Hittites, to journey to the Philistine camp. He did not know how he would manage, but he did know that somehow he would master the contingencies as they arose. David was a man of many parts, with great faults, but also with great virtues. Full of charm and courage, meek in the face of biting criticism by the prophet Nathan and as tender in his love for his wayward son, Absalom, as any father could possibly be, he was brilliant in his insights, merciless in his wrath, cunning and cold-blooded in his desires and mighty in his achievements. He was a natural-born leader. There was none to match him in all the land.

Fortunately for David, the other Philistine princes would

not accept him in any capacity whatsoever. They were rightly apprehensive about the honesty of his intentions and bluntly refused to take him along. Indeed, they "were wroth with . . . Achish, and . . . said unto him, make the man return to his place . . . where thou hast appointed him, and let him not go down with us to battle, lest in the battle he become an adversary to us" (I Samuel 29:4). The fact that they were unable to persuade Achish of his protegé's unreliability is indicative of David's remarkable charm and of the deep affection he often evoked. Had not Jonathan, Saul's heir-apparent, been ready to forfeit his own rights to the crown for the sake of David's preferment? It was, therefore, truly with great reluctance that "Achish called David and said unto him: . . . the lords favor thee not. Wherefore return now, and go in peace . . ." (I Samuel 29:6-7).

David's heart must have leaped with joy when he heard this! He feared no longer being ground to pieces in a dilemma in relationships which seemed to be insoluble. Nevertheless, he made vehement and convincing protestation to Achish, saying: "But what have I done, . . . that I may not go and fight against the enemies of the lord my king?" Only after Achish had strongly reassured him with the words: "I know that thou art good in my sight as an angel of God" (I Samuel 29:8-9), did David subside and visibly manage to overcome his feigned disappointment. They parted company then. Achish went with the Philistine armies to Jezreel and Gilboa, where the deaths of Saul and his three sons opened the way to David's taking the throne, while David with his men turned back to Ziklag, full of happiness and self-satisfaction (I Samuel 29:11). These stuck in his throat when he saw what had happened there in his absence, the effect of which was to govern his future policy toward the Negev, when he ruled over Israel as king.

David and his troops had been away only two days from Ziklag, but it was two days too long. Left behind were the women and children and old men. The countryside had been pacified. David himself had seen to that. No immediate danger threatened, or so it seemed. His departure, however, was immediately noted by Bedouins hovering in the distance and made known to the ever-hungry Amalekites tenting in the vastness of the Negev and Sinai. With amazing speed they flocked together from far and wide and pounced upon the defenseless community. There was no one to hinder them in their frenzy of looting and burning. Soon they were done and had disappeared beyond the horizon, with their bellies and saddlebags stuffed full and driving their captives, numb with terror and shock, before them. Behind them they left precious little except smoldering ashes.

This was the scene that confronted the travelers upon their return. "And it came to pass, when David and his men were come to Ziklag on the third day, that the Amalekites had made a raid upon the Negev and upon Ziklag, and had smitten Ziklag and burned it with fire. And had taken captive the women and all that were therein, both small and great. They slew not any, but carried them off and went their way. . . . And their wives and sons and daughters were taken captive. Then David and the people that were with him lifted up their voices and wept until they had no more power to weep. And David's two wives were taken captive, Ahinoam the Jezreelitess and Abigail the widow of Nabal the Carmelite" (I Samuel 30:1-5). Wild with grief and rage, David's men turned upon him, ready to stone him for having taken them away and having left no rearguard in their absence. There is no question but that they would have killed him had not he, too, suffered the loss of his wives and goods.

David had indeed committed a shocking error. Experienced as he was in the ways of the desert, he should have envisaged the possibility of a lightning attack by nomads, who can materialize like magic or disappear as suddenly. He might have expected that sooner or later the Amalekites would attempt to repay him in his own coin for the frightfully cruel raid he had previously carried out against them.

Had he been less concerned with creating a stir in his patron's camp by taking along with him as large a contingent of soldiery as possible, and had he been less lost in thought as to how he might avoid joining the Philistines in battle against his own brethren, he could have taken steps to prevent this calamity. Still, it might yet not be too late to pursue the hated Amalekites southward, as far as Sinai, if necessary, in order to take vengeance against the despoilers of Ziklag and above all to rescue the captives.

At this point, David was unaware of the identity of the attackers, knowing at first little more than the direction in which they had fled. Discarded pieces of booty marked their trail, although the footprints of men and beasts were clear enough for experienced eyes to discern even after the lapse of several days. Of particular significance was the fact of the pursuit iteslf. The return of the Israelites to the Negev, toward which they were attracted as by an irresistible magnet, was approaching full circle. The Amalekites, who once at Hormah had been able to frustrate the attempt of the Israelites to enter Canaan directly from Kadesh-barnea (Numbers 14:45), could no longer prevent their coming or going or staying. The best they could do now was to hit and run. Even this became nearly impossible or extremely perilous when Solomon and his successors built fortresses throughout the Negev which dominated its lands and roads and water holes. Until then it had been impossible for agricultural civilization to be reestablished there following the destruction of that of the Abrahamitic communities in the nineteenth century B.C.

It was natural for the Amalekites, "that dwelleth in the land of the Negev" (Numbers 13:29), fiercely to resent and violently to oppose the intrusion of the Israelites into their territory. The scanty water and limited grazing in the lands which were traditionally theirs "as thou goest to Shur, even unto the land of Egypt" (I Samuel 27:8), spelled the difference between life and death for them. The intimation of trouble was already made clear in the unvarnished report of the spies to Moses about the Promised Land, which stated flatly that "Amalek dwelleth in the Negev" (Numbers 13:29). Conflict over its possession was inevitable. The Biblical account of the fierce battle which had already taken place during the course of the Exodus at Rephidim in Sinai concludes with the statement written from the hindsight of bitter experience: "And (Moses) said: . . . Jehovah will have war with Amalek from generation to generation" (Exodus 17:16). And, indeed, so it was to be. We find Saul smiting the Amalekites "from Havilah as thou goest to Shur that is before Egypt" (I Samuel 15:5-7). And David was to go on where Saul had left off in the running fight over the resources of the Southland and Sinai.

When he had discovered the tragic situation at Ziklag, David and his men set out in pursuit of the raiders. The pace he set was so strenuous that by the time his party got to the Nahal Besor, two hundred of the original six hundred men had to be left behind. Which particular dry stream bed is meant by the Wadi Besor is impossible to determine. It may be one of the branches of the Wadi Khalasah, such as the Wadi Asluj or the Wadi Themeleh, or one of their offshoots, whose final junction is with the Wadi Sab'a-Ghazzeh.

On the way, they came upon an ill and famished Egyptian who had been abandoned by his Amalekite owner as an unnecessary encumbrance after the sack of Ziklag. "We made a raid," he said, "upon the Negev of the Cherethites and upon that (Negev) which belongeth to Judah and upon the Negev of Caleb; and we burned Ziklag with fire" (I Samuel 30:14). Promised his life and liberty, the grateful Egyptian led David and his warriors to the camp of the Amalekites. Thinking themselves safe, after having traveled a considerable distance from Ziklag, they had halted to examine and divide their loot.

So secure did they feel that no guards were posted. When David came upon them, "they were spread abroad over all the ground, eating and drinking and dancing, because of all the great spoil that they had taken out of the land of the Philistines and out of the land of Judah" (I Samuel 30:16). David's men, appearing out of nowhere, descended like a raging torrent upon the Amalekite raiders, smiting them mercilessly. Abandoning everything, many of the Amalekites flung themselves upon their camels and escaped. They would raid again some other day, boasting in the meantime of the damage they had inflicted, and minimizing the defeat they had suffered.

David now proceeded to make capital out of the Ziklag affair. He had wrested victory out of defeat. His repute as the doughty champion who could be relied upon to protect the Negev and Judah against the gadfly attacks of the Amalekites and others was now further heightened. He worked hard and steadily to enlarge his popularity among the masses of his people and to magnify the character of his leadership and generosity, which already enjoyed wide acclaim. Included in the spoil he had recovered from the Amalekites was their booty from the Negev of the Cherethites. This, of course, he did not return. Instead, he very judiciously distributed it to important sheikhs in various places in the Negev and southern Judah, where he was storing up for himself a treasury of good will.

A politician never waged a cleverer campaign among his constituency for election to office. His ambition was the kingship of Israel. His tremendous ability and very great natural charm, his unswerving doggedness and his tendency to allow nothing to stand in his way, his bold planning, inspired improvisation and the compelling needs of his day were to bring him finally to his goal. And so "when David came to Ziklag, he sent the spoil unto the elders of Judah, even unto his friends, saying, Behold a present for you of the spoil of the enemies of Jehovah" (I Samuel 30:26). Among other places he sent gifts to key people in Ramoth of the Negev (Joshua 19:8) and to Aroer, "and to them that were in the cities of the Yerahmeelites, and to them that were in the cities of the Kenites and to them that were in Hormah . . . and to all the places where David himself and his men were wont to haunt" (I Samuel 30:27-31).

The reference to the "cities" of the Yerahmeelites and of the Kenites must not be taken too seriously. They were cities to be sure, but not in the sense in which that word is employed today. If there was one thing which the Yerahmeelites and the Kenites did not have in the Negev, it was cities of stone houses with all the paraphernalia of permanent, sedentary civilization. Their cities were tent encampments. These were moved from place to place within certain districts, which became distinctively their own and became known in time, as we have seen, as the Negev of the Yerahmeelites or the Negev of the Kenites. Nor are the exact locations of Ramoth of the Negev or of Hormah known, although the latter has arbitrarily been identified with Tell Milh or Khirbet Mishash in the Northern Negev.

Of all the places in the Negev to which David so carefully distributed his largesses, the location of only one is definitely known, and that is Aroer, undoubtedly to be identified with Khirbet Ar'areh. Soil, water, means of communication, general location and sameness of name, plus the presence of numerous, datable fragments of pottery, make that identification almost absolutely certain. The large, squat, partly artificial mound is located in the Northern Negev, dominating a fertile plain which extends northward to merge with the plains in which Khirbet Mishash and Tell Milh are located. Close to the mound are the perennial wells of Biyar Ar'areh, extensively used by the Bedouins of the district to this very day. A direct track leads from Beersheba to Khirbet Mishash and then forks south-southeastward to Khirbet Ar'areh and past Harabet Umm Dimneh to Kurnub and thence down to the Wadi Arabah. We recall in passing that Harabet Umm Dimneh may well reflect the name of Madmannah, which is included in the Biblical list of "the uttermost cities of the tribe of Judah toward the border of Edom in the Negev . . ." (Joshua 15:21.31; I Chronicles 2:49).

Very few artificial city-hills exist in the Negev in general. With the exception of Tell el-Kheleifeh at the head of the Gulf of Aqabah, every one of them is to be found in its northernmost district. There the same mantle of security could be placed over them which enabled the cities of Judah to rise and remain in being after the conquest of Canaan. They were usually built over the ruins of the previous Canaanite cities. In the Negev, however, there were no Canaanite cities that had been constructed in the long interval of absence of law and order following the end of the Abrahamitic Age in the nineteenth century B.C. Such villages as did spring up and fortresses as were built there can almost all be dated to the times of Solomon and of some of his successors, whose strength sufficed to checkmate the Bedouins and keep open the lines of communication. The pottery remains on the surfaces even of such striking tells in the Northern Negev as Khirbet Mishash, Tell Milh, Tell Arad and Khirbet Ar'areh, indicate that their main period of occupation in the Iron Age commenced with the tenth century B.C. and lasted till the Babylonian conquest of Judah in the sixth century B.C.

The Kenites of the Negev

The Kenites of the Negev, whom David favored with gifts, were associated with the history of Israel from the times of Moses on. He married into their tribe (Judges 1:16; Exodus 2:15-22), and the closest connections seem to have been maintained between them and Israel thereafter. They were native to the Negev and seem to have mingled freely with the Amalekites. Before engaging these implacable enemies of Israel in battle, which Saul hoped, in vain, would result in their annihilation, he "said to the Kenites, . . . get ye down from among the Amalekites, lest I destroy you together with them; ye showed kindness to all the children of Israel when they came up out of Egypt. So the Kenites departed from among the Amalekites. And Saul smote the Amalekites from Havilah as thou goest to Shur that is before Egypt" (I Samuel 15:5-7).

The Kenites were at home in all of the Negev and of the Wadi Arabah, but the region south and east of Tell Arad in the Northern Negev seems particularly to have been their own (I Samuel 27:10). There is an interesting if somewhat confused or perhaps overedited passage which deals with the settlement of the Kenites in the Negev south of the great tell of Arad. It reads: "And the children of the Kenite, the father-in-law of Moses, went up out of the city of palm-trees with the children of Judah into the wilderness of Judah, which is in the Negev of Arad; and they went and dwelt with the people" (Judges 1:16).

The passage in its present form does not make much sense. We are confident that some ancient commentator made a marginal note about the children of Judah and the Wilderness of Judah, which some well-intentioned scribe of more assiduity than sense later on inserted into the Biblical text proper. It is obvious that the Wilderness of Judah cannot be south of Arad or in the Negev of Arad, and it is unkind treatment of whatever the original text may have been to locate it there. This is borne out by Judges 1:9, which tells us that "the children of Judah went down to fight the Canaanites that dwelt in the hill-country, and in the Negev, and in the lowland."

It is hardly likely that the "city of palm-trees," which is mentioned in Judges 1:16, should be identified with Jericho, which is correctly described as being just that in Deuteronomy 34:3. A more likely place would be Ain Ghadyan in the Wadi Arabah, where there is much water, large numbers of palm trees and a fortress of the Judaean Kingdom dating from the tenth to the sixth centuries B.C. In addition, it was one of the centers of copper and iron mining operations, which were carried on then extensively in the Wadi Arabah. This was also familiar territory to the Kenites and Kenizzites, who, as their name indicates, were metalsmiths by profession. Indeed, the Wadi Arabah may well be identified with the Biblical Valley of Smiths (I Chronicles 4:12-14). There is little doubt but that the Kenites were the ones that introduced the Israelites to the art of metallurgy and taught Moses how to make a copper serpent (Numbers 21:9). Furthermore, a Kenite is recognized in the Bible as having been the first creator of copper and iron instruments (Genesis 4:22). His name was Tubal-Cain, that is, Tubal the Kenite, or Tubal the smith.

The Kenites were a wandering lot, which conforms with the fact that many of them were itinerant metalsmiths. As indicated by Balaam's punning proverb with regard to them: "Everlasting is thy habitation and set in the Rock (Sela) is thy nest (Ken)" (Numbers 24:21), their headquarters were regarded as being at the great Edomite-Nabataean center of Sela-Petra in the hills above the east side of the Wadi Arabah. There was, for instance, Jael, the wife of Heber the Kenite, who had traveled as far north as the Jezreel Valley. She achieved dubious fame by striking a tent pin through the temples of the defeated Canaanite general, Sisera, who lay in deep sleep, spent and feeling secure in her tent, where he had sought refuge. Her husband "had separated himself from the Kenites, even from the children of Hobab, the father-in-law of Moses, and had pitched his tent as far as the oak in Zaanannim, which is by Kedesh" (Judges 4:11-23).

Districts of the Negev

In addition to the Negev of the Kenites, mention is made in the Bible of four other sections of the Northern Negev, namely, the Negev of Caleb, the Negev of the Yerahmeelites, the Negev of Judah and the Negev of the Cherethites (I Samuel 27:10; 30:14). These divisions comprised most of the agricultural and grazing lands in the Beersheba Basin extending north-south from Beersheba to Bir Rekhmeh and west-east from the Mediterranean to the top of the slopes leading down to the Dead Sea fault. This does not mean that there weren't others, any more than the very limited number of villages and towns mentioned in the Bible represents by any means an inclusive list. There were hundreds of them that were passed over in silence, because for one reason or another the tales connected with them were not woven into the tapestry of the theologically colored text of Sacred Writ. Not only were whole districts and important places thus completely ignored in the Scriptural accounts, but important persons were either dismissed with a dry sentence or two or not even named.

There is, for instance, Omri, one of the most capable rulers ever to sit on the throne of Israel, yet his career and works are dismissed with a curt paragraph, because "he did that which was evil in the sight of Jehovah, and dealt wickedly above all that were before him." Fleeting recognition of Omri's achievements is, however, contained in the statement: "Now the rest of the acts of Omri which he did, and his might that he showed, are they not written in the book of the chronicles of the kings of Israel?" (I Kings 16:25-27). In other words, the editor of the Book of Kings was saying in effect: "Omri does not concern us, because the pattern of his life was contrary to the precepts of Jehovah. If you want to learn more about him, go to the library and look up the records yourself."

The editors of the Bible were interested in mentioning the Negev in whole or in part only insofar as it figured in the lives of the elect of the Lord from the time of Abraham on. Their concern with individuals was whether or not they were profoundly subservient to the will of God, however errant on occasion they might prove to be. David is quoted as saying: "Wherefore, thou art great, O Jehovah God, for there is none like Thee, neither is there any God besides Thee . . ." (II Samuel 7:22). As the gifted leader of his people, the progenitor of its noblest strain, who had been brought low through suffering and was penitent of his misdeeds, he was one of the great heroes of their story. And there is every reason to believe that their delineation caught the elusive compound of strength, wisdom, fierceness and sensitivity that made up the personality of David.

No detail was too small to be included in his spiritual biography, whether it portrayed him in a good or unfavorable light. He and his household were become Jehovah's chosen instrument. "When thy days are fulfilled," said Nathan the prophet speaking to him in the name of the Lord, "and thou shalt sleep with thy fathers, I will set up thy seed after thee, that shall proceed out of thy bowels, and I will establish his kingdom. He shall build a house for my name, and I will establish the throne of his kingdom forever. I will be his father, and he shall be my son: if he commit iniquity, I will chasten him with the rod of men . . . but my loving kindness shall not depart from him . . ." (II Samuel 7:12-15).

Editorial Favorites

To the west of the Kenite part of the Negev were the tent encampments of their closely related clans, each with a farming and grazing district of its own. These included the Kenizzites, Calebites, Rechabites and Yerahmeelites. Their names may sound strange to unaccustomed ears, but their mention struck chords of grateful and glorified memory among the defenders and expounders of the Mosaic faith. Their role in David's life and Israelitic history was underscored in Sacred Writ, because it was felt that God's purposes were advanced through them. Darlings of the Biblical exposition were the Calebites. Some of them lived in the Negev of Caleb (I Samuel 30:14), but the main body of them was ensconced immediately to the north of it in the hill country of Hebron.

Much is left unsaid in the Biblical account dealing with their settlement there, but the implications are very clear. Was it not indeed an act of poetic justice, divinely ordained, that the descendants of Caleb should call Hebron and its surroundings their very own? Had he not been one of the twelve who had penetrated the outskirts of this fortified town and returned to Moses and Israel in Sinai with grapes plucked from one of its gardens? It mattered not that the minority report he and Joshua bin Nun had rendered resulted in Israel's attempting to break into Canaan from the Negev and being disastrously defeated and turned back at Hormah. It mattered only in Scriptural retrospect that Caleb and Joshua had been supremely confident of the fulfillment of God's word.

Israel achieved its goal from a different direction, returning to occupy as of right the lands its scouts had viewed by stealth. The original merit of Caleb was richly rewarded. Hebron "became the inheritance of Caleb, the son of Jephuneh the Kenizzite . . . because he wholly followed Jehovah, the God of Israel" (Joshua 14:14). What Caleb had once espied, his descendants took possession of. The city sanctified by the sepulchre of Abraham, Isaac and Jacob in the Cave of Machpelah (Genesis 49:31; 50:13), became the center and chief stronghold of their particular domain. It is noteworthy that Caleb's Kenizzite ancestry is remarked upon. This is not mere happenstance. The Kennizzites were related to the charmed circle of the Kenites, into whose tribe Moses had married, and who thereafter were forever treated with favor by the people of Israel both in historical fact and in historical writing.

We cannot help having a special liking for the author of the text dealing with Caleb and Hebron. He had very definite antiquarian interests, which are invaluable to the archaeological explorer of Bible lands. In a valuable historical aside in the next passage, he mentions the fact that Hebron in former times was called the City of Arba (Kiriath-arba), "who was the greatest of the Giants (Anakim)" (Joshua 14:15). A similar type of person comes to mind in this connection, whose name was Adino the Eznite. He belonged to the immediate entourage of hardy warriors that David had originally assembled about himself at the Calebite city of Ziklag, and he was reputed, together with another like him, to have accounted for "eight hundred slain at one time" (II Samuel 23:8). Frontier life everywhere seems to breed heroic figures and tall stories.

To judge from his name, Adino the Eznite may well have hailed from one of the places or districts in the Negev, conquered and meticulously listed by the Egyptian king Shishak (Sheshonk I), when he invaded the Negev and Palestine five years after the death of Solomon. The equivalent of the Negev of the Shuhatites is mentioned by him, which corresponds with the name of the family of Shuhah in I Chronicles 4:11. Although most of the Negevite names in Shishak's catalogue of conquests cannot positively be identified, their importance lies in the evidence thus furnished of areas inhabited and fortresses occupied there at the end of the tenth century B.C.

This is in full accord with what we have established to be archaeological fact. Solomon and the strongest of his successors, as I will show later, erected strategically placed fortresses and police posts in the Negev to keep the lanes of travel and the lines of communication open between Jerusalem and Kadesh-barnea in Sinai and Ezion-geber on the eastern arm of the Red Sea. Among them was the Calebite Madmannah (I Chronicles 2:49), whose name may be reflected in the modern Arabic site of Harabat Umm Dimneh, located a little more than four miles north-northwest of Kurnub (Mampsis). The Wadi Kurnub may have marked the southern limit of the Negev of Caleb. The northern part of the Calebite territory seems to have extended west of the lands of Tell Arad and east of the Wadi Khalil, which, descending from the Hebron hills, joins the Wadi Sab'a near Beersheba.

The relative abundance of rain and the scores of springs in the highlands of Hebron and Judah immeasurably outweigh the miserly showers and mean handful of springs in the

Negev. Were it not for population pressures forcing people in more fertile and less parched lands to spill over into marginal areas, the Negev would never have been occupied as extensively as it was at various times by agricultural civilizations (cf. Obadiah 1:19.20; Ezekiel 20:46.47). Some groups, like the tribe of Judah and the subtribe of Caleb were spread over both types of territory. The striking difference between the Calebite hill country of Hebron and the Negev of Caleb below it is emphasized in the request addressed by Achsah to her father Caleb with regard to her wedding gift.

He had promised her hand to whoever conquered the Canaanite city of Kiriath-sefer, or Debir, as it was later called. His own nephew was the lucky man: "And Othniel, the son of Kenaz, the brother of Caleb, took it; and he gave him Achsah his daughter as wife" (Joshua 15:17). She was not content, however, to embark upon her married career with the land assigned her in the nearly arid Negev. As a chieftain's daughter of rare spirit, she felt she was entitled to more, and more she would demand in spite of obvious reluctance of her gallant but apparently bashful groom to approach Caleb for further aid. We are told "that she urged him to ask of her father a field," but apparently did not get very far with him. Undaunted, she journeyed forth to make the request herself: "And she alighted from her donkey, and Caleb said, What wouldest thou? And she said, Give me a blessing; for thou has set me in the land of the Negev. Give me also springs of water. And he gave her the upper and lower springs" (Joshua 15:18-19; Judges 1:14-16). What she got were the springs above and below the Canaanite city that her husband had subdued.

I have often stood by these very springs, located above and below the artificial city-hill called Tell Beit Mirsim, which is the modern Arabic name of Biblical Kiriath-sefer or Debir. For a number of years I was a member of the staff of the great William F. Albright, under whose brilliant and exacting direction the mound was excavated. Beginning from the top down, the ruins of one city after another were exposed and removed till bedrock was reached, making possible the reconstruction of the development of civilization on that site from about 2200 to 586 B.C. Among the layers of the remains of houses and fortifications, with their pottery, tools and fertility figurines, there was uncovered the stratum of the simple Canaanite town of stone construction that Othniel had laid low, winning a wife in the bargain.

Frequently in the course of the dig it became difficult to remember that there was a curtain of millennia between our own world and the one we were unearthing. Some of the ancient houses we exposed to the light of day for the first time in thousands of years were not much different from those of the neighboring village, whence we drew our workmen. Listening to the high-pitched chatter of their womenfolk drawing water at one or the other of the nearby springs, I often thought that Achsah could hardly have been distinguished from among their number. I wondered how long it had taken before child bearing, goat tending, wool carding and spinning and weaving, and the endless burdens of other household duties had drained her youth and withered her body long before her time.

It would have been nice, I daydreamed on occasion, to have been able to roll back the centuries, as well as to recover their artifacts. There would have been innumerable questions to address to the daughter and son-in-law of Caleb about people and places in the Negev, and about the interrelationships between the Kenizzites, to whom they belonged (Judges 3:9; I Chronicles 4:15), and the Kenites, Rechabites, Israelites and others too (I Chronicles 2:55). Most specifically, I would have inquired about their connection with the Yerahmeelites, knowing that Yerahmeel is listed in the Bible as a brother of Caleb (I Chronicles 2:42). In the name and district of Bir Rekhmeh (Be'er Yeruham), at the southern end of the Beersheba Basin, we believe it possible, with

FIG. 20. The author reading to members of his expedition passages from the Bible telling about the arrival of the Israelites at Elath on the Red Sea, visible at upper right (see page 160).

FIG. 21. Ancient cistern in the Negev, lined with roughly hewn stone blocks; in the background are terraced fields

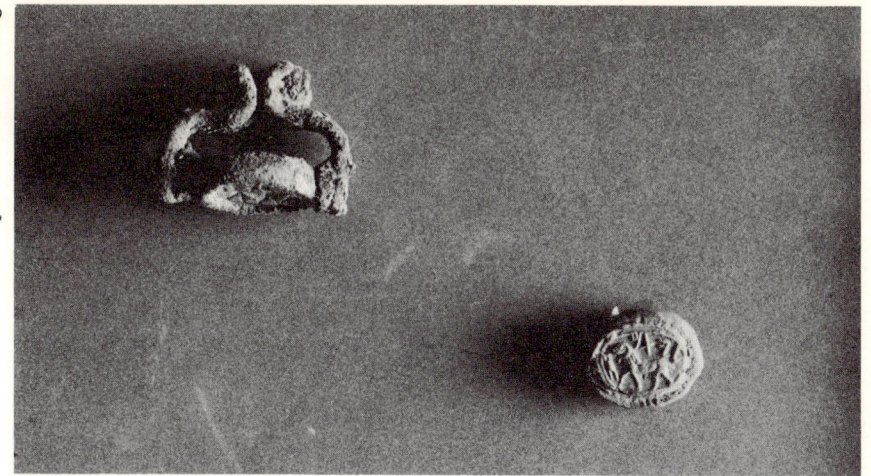

photo: S. J. Schweig

FIG. 22. The only seal signet ring of a Judaean king ever found was discovered in the excavations of Ezion-geber: Elath. The impression shows, from left to right: a figure of a man, a horned ram, and above it ancient Hebrew letters reading LYTM, meaning "belonging to Jotham" (see page 167).

photo: Royal Air Force, Levant

FIG. 23. Airview of excavations of Ezion-geber: Elath. The large building at upper left is King Solomon's smelter; at lower right are visible rows of bricks, with which original city was constructed (see page 165).

FIG. 24. Cornerstones of a fortress of the Judaean kingdom, showing typical header and stretcher bonding (see page 106).

Fig. 25. Remains of outer fortification wall, with sloping revetment built against it, at Judaean fortress of Khirbet Gharrah (see pages 106, 174-178).

FIG. 26. A Bedouin chieftain of the Negev (see pages 183-184).

FIG. 27. Bedouins at the well by Khirbet Mishash, where Judaean and both earlier and later settlements once existed (see page 183).

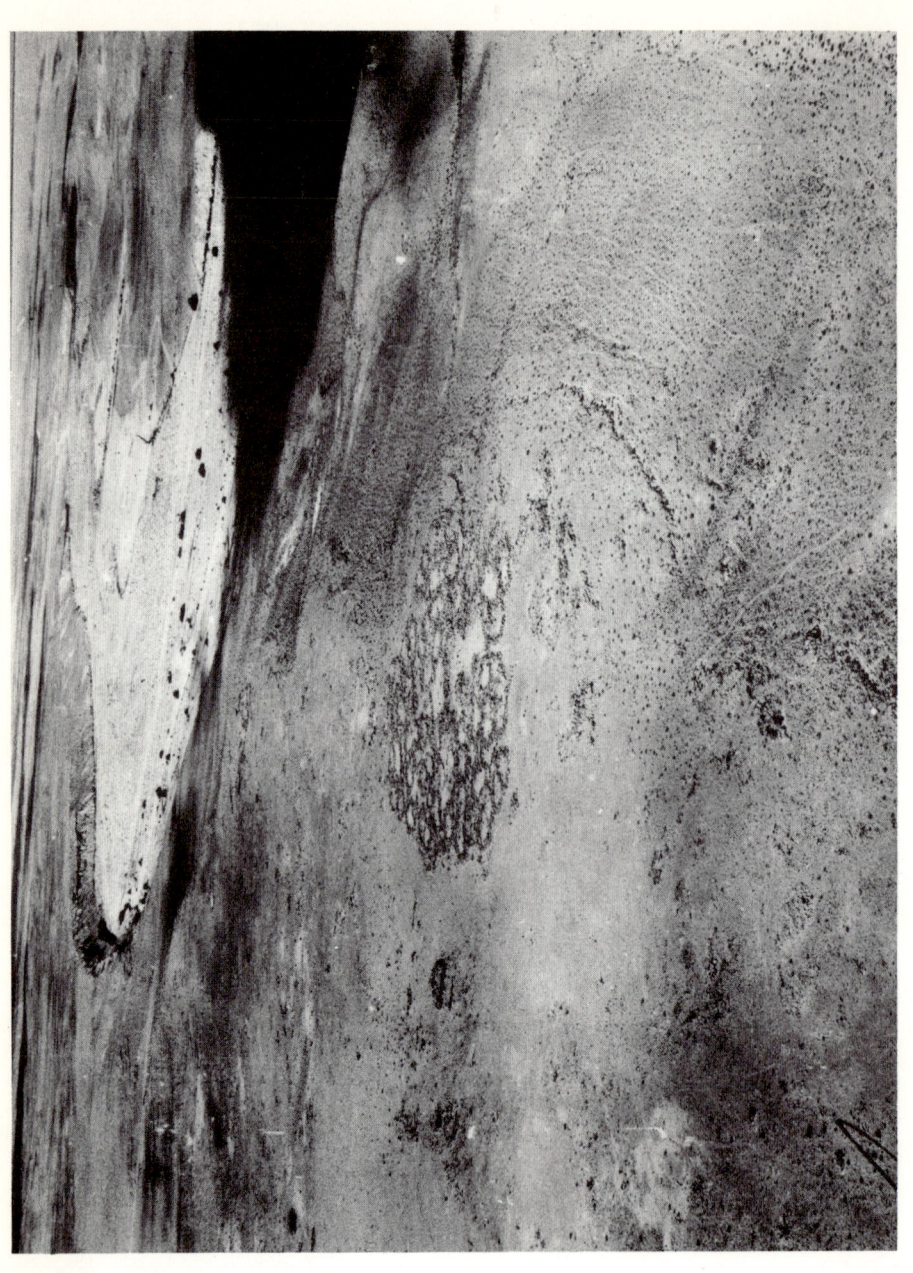

FIG. 28. A Middle Bronze I village of the Abrahamitic period, Site 345 (see pages 97-101).

Palmer, to find a reflection of the original name and location of the Negev of the Yerahmeelites (I Samuel 27:10).

It was natural also for part of the Negev to be assigned to the tribe of Judah and in time for its authority to prevail over all the Negev from Beersheba to Elath. The central part of the Northern Negev became known thus as the Negev of Judah (I Samuel 27:10; 30:14), with its seat of authority at Beersheba. In addition, to the west of it, reaching to the Mediterranean, was the Negev of the Cherethites (I Samuel 30:14). It was from among them and the Pelethites (II Samuel 8:18) that David recruited a large part of the mercenaries who formed his bodyguard when he became king. That made him independent of both Israelite and Judaean forces and safe from both. The Cherethites and Pelethites were undoubtedly part of the Sea Peoples, to whom the Philistines belonged. This relationship and the location of the Cherethites on the coastal plain is apparent from the Biblical passage: ". . . behold, I will stretch out my hand upon the Philistines, and I will cut off the Cherethites, and destroy the remnant of the seacoast" (Ezekiel 25:16; cf. Zephaniah 2:4-5).

Desert Ways

Common to the Kenites, Kenizzites, Calebites, Yerahmeelites and Rechabites in the Negev was a way of living which became idealized in the religious philosophy of Israel. The simplicity, austerity and selflessness imposed by desert conditions corresponded to the prophetic ideals of society. The leanness, clarity and uncompromising qualities of Sinai and the Southland were favorably contrasted with the abominable fertility practices and idolatry of the Canaanite civilization, which so many of Israel so fervidly aped. The fellowship of faith, the unity of brotherhood and the awareness of the existence of one universal God, which underlay Israel's evolution as a "kingdom of priests and a holy nation" (Exodus

19:6) were correctly associated with its wilderness experience. Even as the position and resources of the Negev, extending from the River of Egypt to the Vale of Arabah, made it the *sine qua non* of a viable state, so did its very ground become and remain the touchstone enabling the people of the Exodus and their descendants to find and ever renew their spiritual values. As though drawn to a magnet, it was natural for Elijah to flee southward to the Negev and Sinai from Jezebel of Samaria and find refuge and restoration of strength with Jehovah of Mount Horeb (I Kings 19:8-15; Exodus 3:1).

Little wonder that the Biblical writers drew attention to the Negevite clans, among whom the Rechabites were perhaps the most highly esteemed. Connected with the Kenites (I Chronicles 2:55), they were regarded as an outstanding example of spiritual rectitude. Practicing what the Prophets preached, they incorporated into their daily lives the commandments of the Moral Law, and neither knew nor tolerated any deviation from it. Their like was known in later Nabataean times and was reflected in the Wahabi movement of Saudi Arabia in our own. Untouched by the comparative lushness of Canaan, uncontaminated by its wanton cults, unimpressed by private wealth and great possessions, unswerving from their fierce adherence to the concept of the brotherhood of man and the fatherhood of God, they sought to perpetuate the conditions they had met and surmounted in the Negev and Sinai. Agricultural civilization, with its evil by-products of abuse of power, oppression of the poor and reversion to heathendom was abhorrent to them. Abstemiousness became a part of their creed, and refraining from plowing and planting, drinking wine and building stone houses a puritan demonstration of an inviolable faith.

The Tent of Meeting of the Lord was undoubtedly more preferable to them than the Temple of Solomon. Had it not been for fear of the Babylonians who had invaded the land (Jeremiah 35:11), the Rechabites would never have left the encampments of their preference in the Negev for the security of the walls of Jerusalem. There they dwelt in a compound of their own, withdrawn from the rest of the community (Jeremiah 35:2). When an attempt was made to have them drink wine, they pronounced their classic creed: "Jonadab ben-Rechab, our father, commanded us, saying, Ye shall drink no wine, neither ye, nor your sons, forever. Neither shall ye build houses, nor sow seed, nor plant vineyards, nor have any; but all your days ye shall dwell in tents; that ye may live many days in the land wherein ye sojourn" (Jeremiah 35:6-7). For failing to follow the praiseworthy example of the Rechabites of obeying their father's commandment, Jeremiah pronounced God's judgment of doom upon the people of Judah and Jerusalem (Jeremiah 35:16-17).

A direct line of connection can be traced from Moses in Sinai to the Calebites and Kenites and Rechabites in the Northern Negev. It continues to the House of Rechab in Jerusalem and is tied up with the settlement of the Essenes and related communities at Jericho in the Jordan Valley and at the monastic settlement of Qumran, overlooking the northwest shore of the Dead Sea. Such a scroll as the *Manual of Discipline,* found in one of the Qumran caves, bears the imprint of the Rechabite spirit and reflects strongly the influence of the religious atmosphere and instruction of Sinai and the Negev. Containing the detailed code of rules and principles of faith of the religious sect of this Dead Sea retreat, it insists that each man submit "his soul to all the ordinances of God" and warns that "unclean, unclean will he be as long as he despises the commandments of God."

There is a striking resemblance to the following Biblical passages: "Then came the word of Jehovah to Jeremiah, saying: Go, and say to the men of Judah and the inhabitants of Jerusalem, Will ye not receive instruction to hearken to my words? . . . Forasmuch as the sons of Jonadab ben-Rechab have performed the commandment of their father, but this people hath not hearkened unto me, . . . behold, I will bring . . . all the evil I have pronounced against them. Because I have spoken to them, but they have not heard; and I have called unto them, but they have not answered" (Jeremiah 35:12.13.16.17).

Throughout the entire history of Israel, the physical and spiritual influence of Sinai and the Negev remained paramount. The understanding of God's will achieved there has been transmitted over the centuries through such elect of the Lord as Elijah and Jeremiah and Hillel and Jesus. Like the Rechabites, their emphasis has always been upon the simple and essential in seeking out the ways of God. With the kind of clarity and puritanism that are characteristic of the desert atmosphere, they have insisted upon the rockbound realities of innermost attitudes and upon concrete actions of love and mercy and justice as demonstrations of religious faith.

Thus it is that a single entity embraces the tablets of law of Mount Sinai, Israel's painful growing to maturity during the sojourn in the wilderness, the creed of the Rechabites of the Negev and the scrolls of the ascetic community at Qumran. They are all bound together in one indivisible whole. From the time of Moses on, prophets and priests and rabbis impressed upon the hearts of their people and into the conscience of mankind that fealty to the kingdom of God took precedence over obedience to the government of man, that the needs of no state could supersede the ethical criteria of universal brotherhood, that the elemental freedoms of the desert dwellers were the inalienable rights of all human beings.

As seminomads, Israel had swept into Canaan at a time of cultural decay and physical decline there. Compared to Sinai, it was "a land of wheat and barley, and vines and fig-trees and pomegranates, a land of olive trees and honey . . . (Deuteronomy 8:8). Soon they absorbed the agricultural civilization of those they had conquered, and fell prey to all its attendant evils. Against this backsliding the prophets of Israel inveighed with all their might, emphasizing unceasingly the supreme value of God's moral imperatives as the guides and goals of human conduct. They enlarged constantly upon the disastrous end awaiting those who ignored His directives. No wonder they idealized the unspoiled simplicity and the uncompromising social consciousness of Israel's early days in the desert. It was with a distinct spiritual nostalgia that they commended to their people the precepts of Jonadab ben-Rechab and always found space in their crowded narrative for mention of the Calebites and Kenites and others like them, who lived in the Negev and the Arabah and preserved in their tent-cities many of the habits and practices of desert life.

CHAPTER VI

FACING SOUTH

The First Line of Defense

THE IMPORTANCE attached to the Negev by the Judaean religious leaders and Biblical writers was paralleled from an altogether different point of view by those responsible for the defense and economic well-being of the new state. The roads to Egypt, Arabia and Edom led through the Negev. They gave access to the Wadi Arabah, with its great stores of copper and iron and its strategic importance as a natural highway, and to the commerce of the Red Sea. We can understand why Judah warred so fiercely with Edom for centuries over control of the mines in the Arabah and the lands between Beersheba and Ezion-geber. The country that dominated them stood astride the center of the heartland of the ancient Near East.

The nearly harborless coast on the Mediterranean offered less permanent attraction to Israel and especially to Judah than the land and sea gateways to the south and southeast, which opened to the riches of the Orient. David and Solomon were the first to be fully aware of the implications of their country's geographical position, which oriented it perforce more from the north to the south rather than from the east to the west. With David's enthronement over Israel and Judah, the conquest of the Negev was begun in earnest. It was evident to this far-visioned ruler, who had schemed his way to control over an inchoate kingdom, that undisputed possession of the Negev was vital to its very existence.

When David obtained the crown that Saul was the first to wear, he avenged the defeat that the Philistines had so grievously inflicted upon his predecessor. Schooled in their ways and fully conversant with their tactics, he engaged them in decisive battle and broke their offensive power once and for all time (I Chronicles 14:16; II Samuel 5:20-25; Isaiah 28:21). There would be more battles with the Philistines later on, but they would take place in Philistine and not in Judaean territory. The ebbtide of their fortunes had set in. David's victory marked the beginning of the end for them.

But the Philistines were far from being the only enemy of Israel, although the one that had been most threateningly dangerous. As the united kingdom waxed in strength and wealth under David's rule, so did the list of encircling states opposed to it grow larger. It was perhaps natural for them to think that the development and expansion of the new kingdom could take place only at their expense. They fought therefore to forfend in good time the danger they thought threatened them. It would have been better had they accepted the newcomer in the arena of the ancient Near East and worked with it for their common welfare. They chose war instead. And so David was forced to fight on all sides to save the skeletal structure of the state he had inherited.

Syria and Ammon made common cause against Israel and were jointly subdued, with the result that "the Syrians feared to help the children of Ammon any more" (II Samuel 10:19). Rabbah, or Rabbath-Ammon, as it is sometimes called, the capital of the kingdom of Ammon on the east side of the

Jordan, was beseiged and captured and its inhabitants savagely dealt with. Next in line were the kingdoms of Moab and Edom, which, several centuries earlier, had denied Israel transit permission through their territory. "And he (David) smote Moab" and "put garrisons . . . throughout all Edom" (II Samuel 8:2.14; I Kings 11:15.16).

Though none of these conquests was to prove permanent, they had at least for a long time rid Israel of peril from without. The Amalekites and their confederates had been driven into northwesternmost Sinai and the Philistines contained within their seacoast perimeter. The young state had not been killed aborning. Forces of separatism from within, which David had not been able to fuse into lasting cohesion, were later on to shatter what he had so heroically joined together. As a result of irreconcilable conflict, Israel and Judah fell apart later on, so weakening the strength that had carried them victoriously from Syria to Sinai, that each one succumbed separately to overwhelming forces. In the meantime, however, David's reign marked the beginning of a period of unforgettable glory in the history of Israel and Judah.

As a result of David's direction, a nation had been hammered out on the anvil of war, its enemies pushed back or crushed, its territory enlarged, its wealth and power increased, its dream of becoming its own master in the Promised Land fulfilled. The forms of this reality would be altered in time, but the phenomenon of Israel's being rooted in the Holy Land would remain unchangeable. Israelites might henceforth be dispersed and the kingdoms of Israel and Judah disappear, but Israel itself would remain. A new entity had been fashioned, whose faith in God made it resistant to the attrition of time. The fortunes of the house of David would be forever entwined with its future.

What David had so brilliantly achieved, his son, Solomon, magnificently exploited. During his long rein of almost forty years, from approximately 960-922 B.C., fortune smiled on Israel as never before or after. "And Judah and Israel dwelt safely, every man under his vine and fig tree, from Dan even unto Beersheba, all the days of Solomon" (I Kings 4:25). It was a reign without parallel and he was a ruler without compare. Actually, his territory extended "from the entrance to Hamath to the Brook of Egypt" (I Kings 8:65), that is, as I have shown, from southern Syria to the Wadi el-Arish in Sinai. His influence and sway reached from Mesopotamia to Egypt: "And Solomon ruled over all the kingdoms from the River (the Euphrates) unto the land of the Philistines and unto the Brook of Egypt. They brought tribute and served Solomon all the days of his life . . . and he had peace on all sides round about him" (I Kings 4:21.24).

The seeming contradiction between the Biblical statements that in Solomon's days Judah and Israel dwelt from Dan to Beersheba and that his territory extended from the entrance to Hamath as far as the Brook of Egypt is more apparent than real. The one refers to the most thickly inhabited part of his kingdom, the other to its farthest reaches, which he controlled and utilized for military and economic purposes. This applies particularly to the Negev south of Beersheba. Strongly held and strictly administered by Solomon, this strategic Southland with its highways leading to Egypt and the Red Sea and with its mineral-rich Wadi Arabah may be described as having been forcefully occupied and then intensively settled and cultivated by the people of Israel. Their domination of it was characterized mainly by fortresses and farming communities. The latter, as already noted, existed there in large numbers in the much earlier Abrahamitic Age and in still larger numbers in the later Nabataean and Byzantine periods.

It was first under Solomon's regime that the Negev assumed its proper place in the make-up of the burgeoning state. David's victories had made this possible. It had become evident that the kingdom of Israel could not long endure, let alone thrive, without the Negev. It was vital to its defense and indispensable to its economy. It was the key to Egypt and Arabia. It barred or opened the way to India and Africa. It is obvious, therefore, why the worldly wise and infinitely gifted monarch, Solomon, who was the epitome of an enormously able Oriental potentate, placed the safeguarding of its travel routes, the exploitation of its resources and the enlarging of its commerce in the forefront of his developmental program. It was inevitable that Solomon should have built the famous seaport and great copper smelter and industrial center at Ezion-geber on the north shore of the eastern arm of the Red Sea. It was natural that his ships should have carried its finished products to distant Ophir and brought back in exchange the frankincense and spices and gold and other precious goods of Arabia and India and Africa.

Solomon completed what David had commenced. David had hewed out the clearing in the wilderness, conquering the enemies of Israel, consolidating its territory and preparing the way for internal growth and external expansion. It remained for Solomon to build on the foundations David had laid, to organize and strengthen the affairs of the state both at home and abroad, which he did with brilliant aplomb. He accomplished this by thorough-going military preparedness, broad gauged industrial and commercial undertakings and highly successful diplomatic and marital alliances. He was wise and winning, and made full use of his enormous, natural talents. His personal qualities won him legendary repute. Almost everything he touched seemed to turn into the gold of glittering accomplishment.

Israel shone in Solomon's glory, at the expense of having foisted upon it a despotic Oriental monarchy. The evil he did lived after him. Much of the good perished with his passing. During his reign, however, Israel was raised by his genius to a position of importance and power without equal in its earlier or later history. Most appropriately was he called "Jedidiah," that is, "beloved of Jehovah" by Nathan the prophet (II Samuel 12:24). He erected in Jerusalem the temple that David had contemplated constructing there.

Through this sanctuary, he put the seal of his personality upon the physical and spiritual centrality of this city, which it has retained ever since.

Solomon could not possibly have chosen a more propitious period to make his entry and prolong his stay upon the stage of history. To the northeast, the once mighty Assyria had fallen on evil days under its weak king, Tiglath-pileser II. Several centuries later, restored to great power and impelled as always to advance southward towards the Mediterranean and Egypt, it overwhelmed the northern kingdom of Israel, which had parted company with Judah, scattering its inhabitants to irretrievable exile. The southern kingdom of Judah alone survived for less than a hundred and fifty years more. That was long enough, however, to continue the story and perpetuate the traditions of Israel and the testament of Jehovah.

From the far north, Solomon had nothing to fear. The power vacuum created by the fall of the Hittite kingdom had not adequately been filled, and no danger threatened from that source. Phoenicia immediately to the north of Israel on the Mediterranean coast provided no threat. Its mounting prosperity paralleled that of Israel, but there was no competition nor conflict between the two. On the contrary, the economies and interests of both, bound together by commercial and marital bonds, were mutually complementary. The friendly relationship between the two countries, and particularly between their kings (II Chronicles 2:11.12), both of whom, incidentally, were extraordinarily successful business men, is reflected in the help given by Hiram to Solomon in constructing and furnishing the Phoenician type temple in Jerusalem.

It was manifested also in their use of the same kind of Tarshish ships, which were built and manned by Phoenician craftsmen and sailors (I Kings 9:26-28; 10:22). This type of sea-craft, based on the home port of Tyre, the island capital of Phoenicia, sailed the Mediterranean, carrying on a brisk trade with cargoes of silver, iron, tin, lead and dye-stuffs (Jeremiah 10:9; Ezekiel 27:12.25). A main port of call was Tarshish (Tartessus) in southern Spain, near Gibraltar. The same type of ships, based on their home port of Ezion-geber, plied the lanes of the Red Sea, making round trips once every three years to fabled Ophir (I Kings 9:26-28; 10:11.22; 22:48; II Chronicles 20:36.37). It was as natural for Phoenicia to seek its fortune westward through the Mediterranean, as it was for Israel to pursue its destiny southward through the Red Sea. It was only from the Hellenistic period onward, when artificial harbors were constructed along the practically unbroken curve of the Palestinian coast, that any appreciable amount of commerce developed between Judah and the west. There ensued then the corresponding exchange of cultural forces that always flow along the channels of trade.

With Egypt, too, Solomon was at ease. The compulsion to advance northeast through Sinai, the Negev and Palestine towards Syria and Mesopotamia, which has always been an ineradicable feature of Egypt's foreign policy, was dormant at the time. The fires of its expansionist fury were merely banked, however, and were soon to erupt again. Hardly had Solomon died and his kingdom been split lastingly asunder, than Shishak (Sheshonk I), the founder of the 22nd dynasty of Pharaohs, invaded the Negev and Palestine, as I have shown, devastating the country and despoiling the temple. With an eye to the immortality that every Egyptian king started working for as soon as he was crowned, it was Shishak who inscribed his victories on a pylon at Thebes, preserving thus names of districts and places in the Negev, however obscure their locations still remain, which might otherwise have completely been lost.

Under Solomon, however, Israel maintained the friendliest relationship with Egypt. He cemented it by adding an Egyptian princess to his *harim* (I Kings 3:1; 9:24). There was, furthermore, a flourishing trade between the two countries, undoubtedly heightened by the amity which prevailed between them. To judge both from Biblical records and archaeological finds, Solomon was, in addition to everything else, an excellent horse trader. He shipped horses from the Asia Minor gateway of Hittite Cilicia to Egypt in return for chariots and other goods manufactured or obtainable there, which he then disposed of in the markets of Syria (I Kings 10:28.29). It was of supreme importance to Solomon to keep open the lanes of traffic which led through the Negev to Sinai and Egypt to the southwest, and to his copper and iron mines in the Arabah and to his industrial and shipping center of Ezion-geber on the Red Sea to the southeast.

King Solomon's Copper Mines

The rise of Israel cut across the vital interests of Edom in the Arabah, the Negev and Sinai. After Edom's complete defeat by David, faithful servants of its royal house spirited the young Edomite crown-prince, Hadad, away to Egypt. Otherwise, he would have been slain by Joab, the captain of David's host. Maturing and marrying in Egypt, he returned to Edom after David's death, to become a constant thorn in Solomon's side (I Kings 11:14-22). The Pharaohs hedged their interests in mutually antagonistic Edom and Israel with Egyptian princesses. One was married off to Hadad, while he was in exile in Egypt, and another, with fine impartiality, to Solomon.

It is significant that when some of the Edomites, carrying the child Hadad with them, escaped Joab's dragnet to flee to Egypt, they paused long enough on the way through Sinai to pick up some cohorts there out of (the Wilderness of) Paran. David himself had wandered in this Wilderness of Paran south of Kadesh-barnea as a refugee from Saul (I Samuel 25:1). And Ishmael, the son of Hagar, had tented there long before him (Genesis 21:21).

There is confusion in the Bible with regard to the relationship of Seir and Edom. They are equated with each other, and are located variously both on the east and west sides of the Wadi Arabah. The solution, I believe, lies in remembering that when Edom was conquered by the Babylonians in the sixth century B.C., large numbers of the Edomites were pushed out of their country by the Nabataeans. They crossed the Wadi Arabah and settled in southernmost Palestine, where they were Judaized and became known as Idumaeans. The names of Seir and Edom also traveled for a while westward and became associated with Paran in Sinai (Deuteronomy 1:2.44; 33:1; Joshua 11:17; 12:7; I Chronicles 4:42-43; Judges 5:4-5; Habakkuk 3:3). It is only in the light of this background that it becomes possible to understand the Biblical injunction: "Thou shalt not abominate (treat as outside the pale of brotherhood) an Edomite (Idumaean), because he is thy brother" (Deuteronomy 23:7). Otherwise, generally speaking, Edom is mentioned in the Bible with anger and bitterness (I Kings 11:14-22; Isaiah 34; Jeremiah 49:17-22; Ezekiel 25:12-14; Amos 1:11), and is considered as being on the east side of the Wadi Arabah.

The early Edomites were no less at home in the Wadi Arabah than the Judaeans, and no less concerned with it. They fought with them fiercely for its possession and exploitation. The secret of its riches was familiar to them too, gained perhaps from the Kenizzites (Genesis 36:9.11), who, as I have said, were also related to the Calebites. Like the Kenites, they were masters of the art of metallurgy, which was practiced there of old. The struggle between Judah and Edom lasted for centuries, with fickle victory alternating between them. Finally, mutually exhausted, they were both overcome by Babylonia. Indeed, their enmity was of ancient vintage, hailing back to the early antagonism between the two brothers Esau (Edom) and Jacob (Israel) (Genesis 36:1; 32:28).

It was only after I had finished exploring the Wadi Arabah and had discovered Solomon's copper mines in it, that it was possible to understand fully why this great fissure, extending between the southern end of the Dead Sea and the northern end of the Gulf of Aqabah, must have served as the chief bone of contention between Judah and Edom. Its importance as a natural highway was long known. The Israelites of the Exodus had trekked through it as far north as Punon on its east side. To retrace the ancient pilgrimage and trade-route through it was one of the main purposes of our expedition. Riding camel-back, we spent weeks crisscrossing its width many times, as we moved steadily southward, halting at every spring and water-hole, and examining every "khirbeh" or ancient ruin, no matter how poor its remains or insignificant its appearance.

Our guide and chief assistant was Sheikh Audeh ibn Jad of the Injadat Arabs. In name, which reflects that of the tribe of Gad, and in appearance, he could have been one of the Israelite chieftains who had journeyed with Moses and the children of Israel during that part of the Exodus which led through the Wadi Arabah, before they turned eastward to circumvent Edom and Moab to reach the Promised Land. As we advanced slowly towards the Red Sea, eating the unleavened bread he baked for us each night and sleeping on the ground wrapped in our *abayehs* wherever darkness overtook us, it was sometimes hard for me to remember that he was really not a member of the ancient tribe of Gad and that he himself had not been a companion of the Biblical pilgrims, showing them, as did the Kenites, the best trails and camping places in the Negev and the Arabah.

And then, one day, we came across a great copper mining and smelting site, called Khirbet Nahas (the Copper Ruin), which we could date by pottery fragments on the surface of the ground to the time of Solomon and of the kings who followed him down to the sixth century B.C. It possessed the features which we found to be characteristic of all the other mining sites discovered subsequently on both sides of the Arabah as far south as the hills overlooking the present shoreline of the Gulf of Aqabah. The raw ores dug in open mines in the vicinity were given a preliminary "roasting" in numerous small, stone-block furnaces. The waste slag was thrown aside, forming the large, black piles that had first attracted our attention as we neared the site. Both the furnaces and the slag piles were contained within a strongly walled enclosure, which could have served no other purpose than to prevent the slave labor employed in the mines and at the furnaces from escaping. It was killing work for expendable human beings, who must have suffered greatly under the fierce heat and miserable living conditions.

The fate of captives taken by the Judaeans and Edomites in the relentless war they waged against each other was literally to be consigned to the mines. It is in this light, perhaps, that we can understand more fully than hitherto the prophet's excoriation of Edom, which was the prelude to his condemnation of Judah and Israel: "Thus saith Jehovah, For three transgressions of Edom, yea, for four, I will not turn away the punishment thereof; because he did pursue his brother with the sword, and did cast off all pity, . . . and he kept his wrath forever" (Amos 1:11). We learn from the fourth century A.D. writings of Eusebius, bishop of Caesaria in Palestine, that early Christians and criminals were herded together in slave camps in the Wadi Arabah, for the purpose of mining and smelting its ores.

We believe that the Arabic name of the first great copper and iron mining and smelting site we discovered in the Wadi Arabah, namely Khirbet Nahas (the Copper Ruin), may well be the same as the *'Ir Nahash* (the City of Copper) mentioned in the Bible, and that the *Ge-harashim* (the Valley of the Smiths), referred to in connection with it, was used interchangeably in Biblical times for the Arabah itself (I Chronicles 4:12.14). Above all, however, the demonstration of the existence of these ores in large quantities in the Wadi Arabah, underscores once again the amazing accuracy of the historical memory of the Bible. Every syllable of the hitherto enigmatic description in the Bible of the Promised Land as being, among other things, a land "whose stones are iron and out of whose hills thou canst dig copper" (Deuteronomy 8:9), has now been proven to be literally correct.

These mines also furnish the explanation of one of the chief sources of Solomon's fabulous wealth. The mineral deposits of the Wadi Arabah had also been worked in previous ages, in fact as early as the time of Abraham and before that in the Chalcolithic period, too. Never, however, were they worked as intensively and in as coordinated a fashion as from Solomon's time on. It is revealed now that not only was he a great ruler of legendary wisdom, and a highly successful merchant prince and shipping magnate, but that he was also a copper king of first rank, who transformed Israel into an industrial power. The elaborate copper smelter and manufacturing center constructed by him at Ezion-geber is the largest that has thus far been discovered.

It is impossible to figure out why the Biblical writers omitted this latter phase of Solomon's career from their record of history. Nor will it ever be known why, beyond the vague hint that there was copper and iron in the Promised Land, they failed to mention specifically the natural, mineral riches of the Valley of the Smiths, as the Arabah may have been called on occasion. And, lastly, by the same token, it is idle to speculate why they refrained from mentioning that Ezion-geber:Elath was not only Israel's only seaport, but also, for its day and age, one of the largest, if not the largest of metallurgical centers in existence.

Ships to Ophir

The progress of the bitter and protracted struggle between Israel or Judah and Edom can be correlated with the development, destruction, abandonment, reoccupation and final disappearance from history of the port city and industrial center of Ezion-geber:Elath. Serving a multiplicity of interests, it was strategically located at the south end of the Wadi Arabah, on the north shore of the eastern arm of the Red Sea, known as the Gulf of Aqabah today. Hemmed in by Sinai on the west and Arabia on the east, this long and narrow body of water is further restricted by several islands at its south end. The question of control over these straits, which have been the cause of much concern in modern times, projects on an international scale the geopolitical compulsions which animated the Edomites and the Judaeans in their interminable combat with each other. Domination of the Wadi Arabah and of Ezion-geber and thus of the land and sea-routes which led to the spices and gold and precious products of Arabia and Africa and India was of life and death importance to them. Free access to the Gulf of Aqabah and the undisturbed right of innocent passage through it, are of no less importance to the modern states bordering it.

When the Israelites of the Exodus first reached the north shore of the gulf, an Ezion-geber was already in existence. It was probably a straggling village, with a few mud-brick houses and a small palm grove, located near the east side of this shoreline, where there is sweet water in abundance and shelter under the lee of the hills from the fierce winds which blow down the center of the funnel-like rift of the Wadi Arabah. All traces of this earliest site have disappeared. In its place, and on a site better suited to his purposes, which is situated about half way between the hills on either side of the Wadi Arabah, Solomon built a new city of the same name. Furthermore, he "made a navy of ships in Ezion-geber, which is beside Eloth, on the shore of the Red Sea, in the land of Edom. . . . And they came to Ophir, and fetched from thence gold, four hundred and twenty talents and brought it to king Solomon" (I Kings 9:26.28). Not a word is written about the smelter and workshops he erected in Ezion-geber nor about the copper ingots and tools that he exported in exchange for the gold and exotic goods obtainable in Ophir!

One of his successors, Jehoshaphat, was not so successful with his shipping undertakings. He, too, "made ships of Tarshish to go to Ophir for gold; but they went not, for the ships were broken at Ezion-geber" (I Kings 22:48). Nearly a century had passed since Solomon's banners fluttered on the high seas. The disaster to Jehoshaphat's ships, dashed ashore and probably wrecked in a storm, may have contributed materially to the decline in Judah's fortunes. Its full impact was felt in the reign of his son, Joram, when Edom regained its complete independence from Judah and utterly destroyed Ezion-geber. The next city, built years later on its ruins, became known as Elath. That name remained current, until the entire site was finally abandoned late in the fifth century B.C. Becoming buried under a cover of drift sand, it took on the typical form of a small, artificial mound, which became known in modern times as Tell el-Kheleifeh. No one associated that tell with the ancient site, whose location had been erased from the memory of man. For about twenty-five hundred years, its whereabouts remained unknown. It fell to our lot to examine and excavate and identify it beyond all question of doubt.

Even before coming across Tell el-Kheleifeh and commencing excavations there, we were certain that the site of ancient Ezion-geber:Elath would have to be looked for along the present shoreline. Because of the notion, widely prevalent among previous explorers, that the Wadi Arabah had advanced seaward many miles during the last two and a half millennia, the ancient site was always looked for far inland where it never was or could have been. Our previous discovery of Solomonic mining sites close to and immediately overlooking the north tip of the Gulf of Aqabah, had convinced us that Solomon's city must be relatively near, if not exactly on the existing shore. Coupled with that was our belief in the complete reliability of the Biblical statement that Ezion-geber "is beside Eloth, on the shore of the Red Sea, in the land of Edom" (I Kings 9:26). Furthermore, in years gone by, in the course of a complete archaeological survey of all of Transjordan, we had examined Nabataean to Byzantine Aila. It is situated but a short distance to the west of modern Aqabah, which overlooks the northeast end of the Gulf of Aqabah. Nabataean Aila was founded about two thousand years ago. It probably reflects the Biblical name of Elath, which may well have existed in the beginning of its history on the site of the modern village and have belonged to the kingdom of Edom. In other words, from the points of view of history, archaeology, geography, Biblical credibility and common sense, it stood to reason that the site of Ezion-geber, built anew by Solomon and renamed Elath later on, had to exist somewhere in the vicinity of Aila.

I shall never forget the day we came to the crest of the inconspicuous watershed near the southern end of the Wadi Arabah, and saw the deep blue tongue of the Gulf of Aqabah ahead of us. It extended southward as far as one could see between haze-shrouded hills of forbidding mien, forming a jagged barrier on either side. Our camels, sniffing the moisture in the air and anticipating the sweet water they must have sensed awaited them, quickened their pace and soon broke into a steady run. Our weariness suddenly vanished. At this junction of the continents of Asia and Africa, the boundaries of Arabia, Transjordan, Palestine and Sinai touch the northern end of the gulf, with parts of all of them becoming visible to us. This was the scene that had presented itself to the people of the Exodus. We were racing forward into the past. And soon we reached the water's edge, near which Ezion-geber had once stood.

It was not long before we came across the inconspicuous mound of Tell el-Kheleifeh, located about five hundred yards from the actual shoreline and situated about half way between the east and west sides of the Arabah rift. On its surfaces were the same kinds of pottery fragments as we had discovered at all the Solomonic copper mining and smelting sites in the Arabah north of it. They informed us, without any digging whatsoever, that its first city was erected in the tenth century B.C. and the last one in the fifth-fourth century B.C. There was no other site within the purview of possibility which could fit the requirements as well as this one. Tell el-Kheleifeh had to be Ezion-geber:Elath!

At the time of our first visit to Tell el-Kheleifeh, we were unaware of the fact that shortly before our arrival there, Fritz Frank had come across it, and had correctly suggested that it might conceal the ruins of Solomon's Ezion-geber. This was all the more prescient, because he did not know how to date the fragments of pottery strewn on the surfaces of the mound. They served as conclusive evidence to us. To him, therefore, belongs the accolade of priority of discovery. And so, the search was over, and the secret that had puzzled generations of scholars was solved! What had been lost, was restored; what had been forgotton, was remembered. We could hardly wait to unearth the ruins of the Judaean and Edomite cities buried there. If Solomon had used Ezion-geber as a point of departure to win for himself the gold and other precious products of the Orient, we would use it as a book of history, beginning, however, at the end and reading backwards from the fourth to the tenth centuries B.C.

One can easily visualize the conditions existing about three millennia ago, when the idea of building Ezion-geber was first conceived and then translated into reality. Hundreds of laborers had to be assembled, housed, fed and guarded at the chosen building site. Perhaps they came over each morning from the more salubrious location of the equivalent of modern Aqabah, about four miles to the east, with its good water and kindly breezes and palm tree groves. Skilled technicians of all kinds had to be recruited. And then, when construction was completed, an effective business organization had to be called into existence to regulate the profitable flow of raw materials and finished or semi-finished products.

There was, so far as we know, only one person in Israel who possessed the wealth and wisdom capable of initiating and carrying out such a highly complex and specialized undertaking. He was King Solomon. He alone in his day had the ability, vision and power to establish an important industrial center and seaport such a long distance from the capital city of Jerusalem. His far-flung net of activities extended from Egypt and Arabia to Syria and Phoenicia and Asia Minor.

Evidence of the international role that Ezion-geber played in the economy of the ancient Near East was furnished, among other things, by an inscription on fragments of a large storage jar we discovered there. It consisted of the first South Arabic letters ever discovered in a controlled excavation. They belonged to the Minaean script. The Minaeans are reputed by Pliny to be the oldest known commercial people in South Arabia, controlling the famous Incense Route and monopolizing the trade in myrrh and frankincense. We were able to restore most of the shape of this jar, which may have been a container of precious products brought by caravan from as far as South Arabia, and whose ultimate destination may have been Damascus or Tyre. It was in this fashion that the caravan of the Queen of Sheba may have come heavily laden with the much-sought goods of her kingdom, when she made her famous visit to Solomon in Jerusalem. In addition to huge jars filled with the extremely valuable spices and incense, she apparently brought with her "very much gold and precious stones" (I Kings 10:2).

The incurable romantic who penned the account of their highly publicized meeting, portrayed her as having been so overwhelmed by his wisdom and prosperity, that "she gave the king a hundred and twenty talents of gold, and of spices very great store, and precious stones. There came no more such abundance of spices as these which the queen of Sheba gave to the king Solomon" (I Kings 10:10). He passes over in silence the products that Solomon undoubtedly gave her in exchange, beyond saying that "king Solomon gave to the queen of Sheba all her desire, whatsoever she asked"

(II Chronicles 9:12). It may be taken for granted that there was some hard and shrewd bargaining between the two, and that they arrived at a mutually satisfactory trade treaty before she took her departure. Otherwise, she had hardly been worth her salt, or in this instance, her spices. Among the goods that Solomon must have given her in exchange, there were most probably some of the copper and iron products of the Arabah and Ezion-geber.

The Unexpected

We are of course speaking from hindsight about the copper and iron products of the Arabah and Ezion-geber. To our immense surprise, the excavations demonstrated that while Ezion-geber was undoubtedly a seaport, it was no less important as an industrial center. There were nails and timbers and resin and ropes, which had undoubtedly been used to build and repair ships. There were fishhooks and net-weights and piles of sea shells related to the extensive fishing that had obviously been carried on in the rich waters of the eastern arm of the Red Sea, which is a fisherman's paradise even today. There were, to be sure, no traces of docks, but perhaps we should not have expected any. It is highly possible that the Tarshish ships were little more than small *dhows*, which were anchored offshore. And when, at times, a sudden storm blew up, and their mooring lines did not hold, they could be dashed to shore and broken to pieces on the rocks in the shallows. That is exactly what happened, as we have seen, to Jehoshaphat's fleet, about the middle of the ninth century B.C.

What puzzled us greatly when we first commenced operations at Tell el-Kheleifeh was what seemed to us to be the particularly unfortunate location of the site. Situated in the center of the Arabah rift, which is banked on either side by high hills leading, respectively, into Arabia and Sinai, it is open to the full fury of the almost constant winds that blow fiercely down the Wadi Arabah, as if forced through a wind tunnel. The result is an endless series of sandstorms, frequently so severe as to obscure vision. The architects of Ezion-geber could not possibly have chosen a more inclement site along the entire shoreline. It was understandable why they had not built farther to the west where the soil was poor and the water was worse, being completely undrinkable by either man or beast. But why, we asked ourselves at first, in irritation at having to work, eat and sleep in frequent sandstorms, had they not chosen a site farther to the east at Nabataean Aila or Arabic Aqabah, where the water is excellent, the soil is fertile and the winds are tempered by the hills? We began digging at the northwest end of Tell el-Kheleifeh, in order at least to have our backs and not our faces turned to the biting winds and blinding sandstorms. In the meantime, we fumed and fussed at what seemed to be the folly of Solomon's town planners. Their seeming madness, however, was soon explained.

The very first building brought to light at the northwest corner of the mound turned out to be the largest and most elaborate smelter ever discovered in antiquity. Each of the walls of its rooms was pierced by two rows of carefully constructed apertures, which could only be flues. The upper rows opened into a system of transverse air-channels, utilizing the winds blowing almost constantly from the north and northwest to fan the flames in the furnace rooms. The lower rows were intended to permit the gases formed in one chamber to penetrate into the second and so on and preheat its contents. It was easy to reconstruct the smelting process. The ores were given a preliminary "roasting" at the individual mining sites in the Wadi Arabah, and then brought for further smelting and refining to Ezion-geber. Layers of ore were placed between layers of lime in large, thick-walled, pottery crucibles.

Piles of charcoal from the wooded hills of Edom were packed all around them in the open furnace rooms of the smelter, with the fires being ignited in successive order at proper intervals of time. No hand-bellows system was necessary, because with brilliant calculation, Solomon's engineers had harnessed the winds to furnish a natural draft. The Bessemer principle of forced-air draft, discovered less than a century ago, was, in essence, already familiar some three millennia back. So well had the smelter been constructed, that when it had been completely exposed, we could place our hands on the flue holes in the wall at the south end of the structure and feel the air emerging, which had entered through the flue holes on the north side, a number of rooms away.

It became more apparent than ever, as a result of our excavations, why Edom and Judah had fought so long and so bitterly with each other over the Arabah and Ezion-geber, although the Bible, however, as I have already pointed out, passes over in complete silence one of the main reasons for the prolonged warfare between them. The copper and iron mines of the Arabah and the control of access to the Red Sea were as much a cause of inextinguishable rivalry between them as oil in Arabia and along the Persian Gulf is a source of competition and conflict among many nations today. Both for Edom and Judah, the command of the resources of the Arabah and of the highway which led through it and the control of Ezion-geber:Elath, with its industries and access to the Red Sea, were indispensable to their safety, economic well being and potentialities of growth.

The turnabout ownership of Ezion-geber:Elath is illustrated by two names, one Edomite and the other Hebrew, which we came across in the excavations of the city of Elath. Built by the Judaeans on the ruins of Ezion-geber, it had been captured from them by the Edomites (II Kings 16:6), with whom it exited from history. The Edomite name occurred in seal impressions on the handles of a whole store-room full of fine pottery jars. On the handle of every one of them was stamped the following inscription: "Belonging to Qausanal, the Servant of the King." We know that Qausanal is a typical Edomite name, the first part of which, Qaus, is the designation of a familiar Edomite, Nabataean and Arabian deity. It seems likely that this Qausanal, who was undoubtedly an Edomite, was the governor of the district of Elath when it was under Edomite dominion. He acted as the personal representative, that is, the "servant" of the Edomite king of the time.

The other inscription was found in an earlier level of Elath, when it was still in Judaean hands. It was part of what turned out to be the only seal signet-ring of a Judaean king ever discovered thus far. And thereby hangs a tale. At the last minute of the last day of the last of the three seasons of our excavations, I decided to make a final farewell tour of the site. Our Arabic foreman, Abbas, made the rounds with me. Yielding to a sudden impulse, I asked him to tear down with his pickaxe a bit of mud-brick wall that we had left standing until it was measured and photographed. As he pushed it over, he saw a tiny object that had lain underneath it, and quickly picked it up. "What have you there, Abbas," I asked him. Instead of replying, he asked me if the system of paying *baksheesh* for every object found still held good, even though the expedition were formally over.

I must explain here that we paid our workmen a special reward for every object found, related to its market value, whether it was a broken bead or an ivory fragment or a piece of gold. This was necessary to ensure that every object found got into our hands rather than into those of dealers, whose rates, incidentally, we were always prepared to match. Instead of keeping accounts, we would pay each workman immediately for the things he had found and had turned over to the staff member supervising the section he worked in as a pick-man, shovel-man or basket boy. By the time everyone concerned had looked carefully through the earth being dug up and removed, there was very little of value that escaped attention. In addition, we sometimes put the debris of entire rooms through sieves to make this assurance doubly sure.

I told Abbas that I would be delighted to pay him *baksheesh*, even at this stage of the game. He persisted and asked if I were willing to pay as much as a shilling or two for what he held in his closed fist. "Hand it over, Abbas," I said to him. He gave it to me. I took a hurried look, stuck it into an inner pocket, and told him to hold out his hands in cupped form. With that, I emptied into them all the silver and paper money in my pockets. It may have been the equivalent of fifty dollars. It was a lot of money for that part of the world. I could easily have engineered a minor revolution with it. He looked at the heap of shillings and pounds, which was indeed a veritable fortune to him, and, after a moment, said to me: "Ya Mudir (O Master), but I can't possibly take all that money from you." I assured him that I thought what he had found was worth a good reward, and that anyway I had intended giving him a parting gift. He had been most faithful and helpful during the years we had worked together, and we had become good friends. We embraced and took leave of each other, he back to Aqabah and the rest of us to our cars on the way to Amman and Jerusalem.

As soon as possible, I examined the find. It had been apparent immediately that it was some sort of a seal-signet ring, with an intact copper casing around a dirt encrusted stone. It was the kind that was hung by a cord on the belt of a prominent person and served in effect as a badge of office (I Kings 21:8; Haggai 2:23). Cleaning it somewhat, I was able to make out what was engraved on the stone seal, which was stained green from the copper band around it. A horned ram, with a little man standing in front of it, was carved on it; and incised above it, in retrograde, in the clearest possible ancient Hebrew characters, was the inscription *LYTM*. The letter *"L"* means "to" or "belonging to." And, making allowance for the omission of vowels or vowel letters, which is characteristic of ancient Canaanite writing, the three remaining consonants *"Y T M"* could signify nothing else than *"YOTAM,"* which is the proper name of "Jotham." The translation of the entire inscription, therefore, is "Belonging to Jotham." This had to be a seal-signet ring of Jotham, King of Judah!

We know that a Jotham ruled Judah as regent during the last years of the reign of his father, Uzziah, who had been afflicted with leprosy, and that he succeeded him as king after his death. It was Uzziah who had built the new city of Elath on the sand-covered mound of the previously ruined and abandoned Ezion-geber, and it was during the reign of his grandson, Ahaz, the son of Jotham, that the Edomites drove out the Judaeans and established themselves firmly in Elath. It was, therefore, quite appropriate that the Qausanal impression should have been found in the Edomite stratum of Elath and the Jotham ring in the preceding Judaean one. There is little question but that this unique seal-signet ring lent royal authority to the governor, ruling the southernmost city of the kingdom of Judah in the name of its king, Jotham.

Reoccupation of the Negev

The Negev lay empty of permanent settlements for a long time after the end of the Age of Abraham. It was not until the reign of David that Israel became strong enough to make use of it, after placing the Bedouins, who had roamed there unchallenged for centuries, under the leash of its authority. This had come about through David's breaking the ring of enemies that encircled Israel and threatened to choke off its life. Although Israel had built or rebuilt cities and villages and fortresses in the parts of Canaan it had conquered in the centuries after its advent there, it had not been able to establish itself firmly in the Negev, south of Beersheba. To be sure, most of the Northern Negev was occupied by semi-nomadic tribes which were closely related to Judah, such as the Kenites and Calebites and others. As we have seen, however, they lived in tents and not in walled towns of stone houses and made little or no use of the pottery current in Judah from the late thirteenth to the beginning of the tenth centuries B.C.

The Amalekites, who in earlier days had halted Israel's initial attempt to penetrate into the Holy Land directly from Kadesh-barnea, were disastrously defeated by David and forced to flee into the recesses of Sinai. Other Bedouin groups, too, that for centuries had roamed about the Negev like untamed beasts of the field, were undoubtedly also brought to book by him. With the Negev subjected to the discipline of governmental control for the first time since the formation of the new kingdom, it became possible for Israel to move to the fulfillment of its destiny, conditioned by ineluctable geopolitical factors, of expanding southward towards the Red Sea. The yawning gap in the record of permanent, sedentary civilization based on agriculture and trade, which had characterized the story of the Negev from the nineteenth century B.C. on was now closed. The Negev again resumed its rightful place in the annals of history.

Only half of the necessary task had been completed by David when he drove the Bedouins of the Negev back to the perimeters of the desert whence they came. Strong measures were required to hold them in check and prevent them from flooding back and inundating the accomplishments of civilization. The Bedouins are always prepared to break into the rich or comparatively fertile lands at the first appearance of weakness there, and they can always retreat into the wilderness whither few can follow. Perpetually homeless and hungry, they have everything to gain and nothing to lose by swooping down upon planted fields and settled communities in order to reap what they have not sown and to break and loot what they have not built or nurtured. It is only when they themselves become rooted in the soil, that they are subject to the forces of growth and decay, from which they are secure in their native estate. In turn, then, they must remain ever on guard against incursions of other raiders lurking on the rims of the waste lands. The lean who are left behind can afford to bide their time. They can live on next to nothing and have the patience of the ages. The struggle, over a sufficient length of time, is inevitably weighted in their favor. It may be said of them that it is the weak who shall inherit the fruits of the earth.

It remained for Solomon to establish firmly throughout the entire Southland the kind of iron-fisted security which had to prevail there if his vision of empire and economic aggrandizement were to be fulfilled. The routes of travel and the channels of trade between Jerusalem and its distant seaport of Ezion-geber had to be kept open at all costs, if either city were to flourish. Judah had to have access on its east side to the Arabah with its mineral riches and strategic position, even as it did to the Brook of Egypt to the west, because, other considerations aside, they formed the natural, geographical boundaries of the Negev. The Negev has ever been the chief frontier land of Israel, with the peaks of its prosperity always dependent upon undisturbed possession of it.

There was only one way for Solomon to exorcise the chaos that had existed in the Negev and in Sinai since the end of the Age of Abraham, and that was to introduce strong military rule there. To achieve this, he called into being a whole system of fortresses throughout the entire southern extension of his realm. In the maintenance and renewal from time to time of these strongholds, he was copied perforce by all his successors who were powerful enough to hold what they had inherited or recapture what their predecessors had lost. There is, to be sure, no specific mention of Solomon's activities in the Negev, the Arabah and Sinai, other than may be deduced from references to "all the store cities that Solomon had, and the cities for his chariots and the cities for his horsemen" (I Kings 9:19). It is, however, impossible to believe that this great statesman and organizer, whose industrial and commercial centers and depots reached all the way from Ezion-geber on the Red Sea to Tadmor (Palmyra) in the desert of Syria (II Chronicles 8:4; I Kings 10:22), would have failed to safeguard his lines of communication with fortresses and guard-towers and settlements of former soldiers who tilled the soil wherever possible. Similarly, the "fenced cities" (II Chronicles 14:6.7; 17:2) erected by Asa and Jehoshaphat of Judah must have included some in the Negev and the Arabah. It has been clearly demonstrated by our archaeological explorations in the Negev, that Judaean strongholds existed there between the tenth and sixth centuries B.C.

More or less inaccessible and easily defendable hilltops rather than fertile slopes or valleys were preferred for their locations. The primary factor animating the choice was public security rather than availability for agricultural pursuits. Although there were many open villages in the Negev in the time of the Judaean kingdom, most of the sites were protected by walled fortresses, which dominated roads, water and tillable fields and acted as a deterrent to Bedouin attacks. The lack of concern about impending danger which apparently characterized the numerous settlements of the much earlier Patriarchal or Abrahamitic period in the Negev, did not return even during the reign of Solomon. As a result of all his security measures, which included the construction of forts, assembling a foreign legion, instituting a military draft among his own people (I Kings 9:20-22), and concluding trade and friendship treaties with his neighbors, Solomon "had peace on all sides round about him" in all of his dominion, which extended, as we have seen, from the Euphrates to the Brook of Egypt (I Kings 4:24).

When, many years and half a dozen kings later, Uzziah mounted the throne in Jerusalem and restored to Judah much of the glory it had enjoyed under Solomon, he found it necessary to replace many of the bastions originally constructed by his famed predecessor. The star of Judah rose high again with his ascent into the firmament of power. The flaming and smoking furnaces and bustling harbor of (Eziongeber:)Elath, which he rebuilt from the ground up, testified that the reins of government were once again in firm and creative hands. Pushing back the restive Philistines and checking the encroachments of the constantly probing Ammonites and Arabians, his repute grew "till his name spread even to the entrance of Egypt, for he waxed exceeding strong" (II Chronicles 26:6-8). To achieve this and maintain his gains, Uzziah re-enforced the defenses of Jerusalem and "built towers in the Wilderness (the Negev), and hewed out many cisterns . . ." (II Chronicles 26:10). He was fully aware of the importance of the Southland, which tied continents and cultures together.

The centrality of the Negev as a keystone in the bridgehead of Canaan between seas and land masses and civilizations was illustrated, for instance, by some of our finds in the excavations of the topmost and last city of Elath, which belonged to the fifth-fourth centuries B.C. Among them were black glazed sherds and ink-written ostraca, which in their origin were literally worlds apart. The sherds were parts of ointment vessels imported from the Aegean area of the Mediterranean. The ostraca were business receipts written in Aramaic, which at that time was beginning to be the *lingua franca* of much of the ancient Near East. Several centuries later, the Nabataeans from Arabia, who spoke and wrote Aramaic and learned to worship gods sculptured with the features of Greek deities, incorporated the Negev into their kingdom, and lifted it to a height of importance even greater than it had enjoyed in the times of Solomon and Uzziah. It remained in the limelight of history till the end of the Byzantine period, after which it fell into an obscurity, created by political ineptitude, economic dislocation and international conflict, from which it is only now again emerging.

photo: S. J. Schweig

FIG. 29. This Hellenistic-Semitic statue from Khirbet Tannur shows the Nabataean Zeus-Hadad seated on a throne, flanked by two bulls, with the thunderbolt symbol over his left arm and a double lion-headed torque around his shoulders (see page 196).

FIGS. 30 (a) and (b). Front and side panels of Nabataean altar from Khirbet Tannur, with Greek-Semitic dedicatory name (ALEXA)NDROS AMROU (see page 194).

photos: *Royal Air Force, Levant*

FIG. 32. Terraces in the beds and along the banks of dry watercourses (*wadis*) were designed by the Judaeans and especially by the Nabataeans and Byzantines to retain moisture in the soil from occasional flash floods and to prevent erosion (see page 202).

On opposite page: FIGS. 31 (a) and (b). Walled fields of et-Telah, once irrigated and cultivated by the Nabataeans (see pages 201-202).

FIG. 33. Subsurface moisture in the dry stream bed of the Wadi Luzan nourishes numerous pistachio trees. In the upper center, right, can be seen rows of terraces (see page 202).

Fig. 34. Closeup of a Nabataean terrace (see page 202).

FIG. 35. Jebel Medhra, equated by some with the Biblical Mount Hor, where Aaron died (see pages 205-206).

FIG. 36. These rows of *teleilat el-anab* on hillsides at Mishrefeh, near the Nabataean-Byzantine city of Isbeita, were used to channel rain water to terraced fields in the dry stream-beds below (see pages 218-220).

Fig. 37. Mouth of a Nabataean-Byzantine cistern, showing rope marks (see pages 22, 94, 223).

"Walls, Towers, Gates and Bars"

The phenomenal progress of Israel under Solomon would not have been possible had not some unsung genius several centuries before him, as I have described earlier, found out how to collect and store rain water in impermeable, underground reservoirs. It is not surprising, therefore, that, until the problem of water supplies was more or less solved, the development of the Negev lagged behind that of the rest of the country. It had to wait, also, until a strong government such as that of Solomon could enforce its authority and preserve peace throughout its reaches.

The chief type of construction in the Negev between the tenth and sixth centuries B.C. consisted of strategically placed strongholds and well-built open villages below them. A sufficient amount of water to supply the modest needs of garrisons and settlers could be caught in the impermeable cisterns from the rare rains. The art of soil and water conservation was already well advanced. In the preceding period of civilized occupation of the Negev, which occurred between the twenty-first and nineteenth centuries B.C., almost all centers of habitation, both of semi-nomadic and completely permanent nature, were located by springs or wells or easily tappable supplies of underground water. The ability to bring water to the settlements, instead of the compulsion of bringing the settlements to the water, spelled the beginning of a long era of renewal and expansion of civilization in the Southland. It reached its zenith, as I have mentioned, in the age of the amazing Nabataeans. It came to an end when the Byzantine empire fell apart.

To judge from Biblical records, Uzziah of Judah understood thoroughly that the availability of dependable water supplies and the widespread prevalence of law and order were prerequisites for rebuilding the seaport and industrial center of Elath, reestablishing firm trade connections with Egypt and Arabia, and radically improving the economy and security of his entire country. The importance attached by him to digging cisterns and building or rebuilding fortresses in the wilderness and throughout the entire land indicate his deep appreciation of the measures that had to be undertaken to advance the welfare of his kingdom. We are told that "he had husbandmen and vine-dressers in the mountains and in the fruitful fields" and that "he loved the land" (II Chronicles 26:10). His love of the soil, as well as his numerous public works, won him enduring renown. And, above all, together with David and particularly Solomon, he was cognizant of the fact that the political economy of all of Judah rose or fell in accordance with the improvement or deterioration of conditions in the Negev. The cisterns dug there at his command were as essential to his expansionist plans as the seaport he rebuilt at its southern tip. Little wonder that Judah prospered under his regime, as it had not since Solomon's time, and that the remains of many of the fortresses and villages which we found in the Negev may be attributed to him, as well as to Solomon.

KHIRBET GHARRAH

It is not hard, after wandering about in the Negev for months and years, to project one's self back into its past and feel less like an observer of ancient events and objects than like a participant in contemporary happenings. This sense of witnessing works in progress rather than of observing their latter day wrecks overcame us when we were examining the impressive remains of a very strong fortress that had in all probability been erected under Uzziah's orders. Let me relate my impressions as I imagined them at the time in connection with the visit to this particular stronghold. I gave myself the role of a member of the chief architect's entourage, awaiting the visit of a royal commission to examine and take over the fortress he had designed and the construction of which he had supervised.

He was distinctly nervous, as he awaited the arrival of the king's messengers. If anything were wrong, he would be blamed. He had chosen the site, laid out the plans, fixed the lines of the massive outer walls, determined their thickness and height, figured out the angle of the cyclopaean revetments built against them in lean-to fashion to prevent their being undermined or breached, plotted out the locations and nature of the barracks and commanding officer's residence and decided where the huge cisterns should be dug. It was he who had directed and coordinated the entire program of construction. And now the work was done! Would it be received with the loud silence of disapproval or with the accolades of enthusiastic praise?

There were no outward insignia to set the architect apart from the throng of overseers, workmen, officials of various kinds and visitors from neighboring sites, who were standing about in expectation of the arrival of the deputation from Jerusalem. He clutched no sheaves of architectural drawings in his hands, because he carried all the plans in his head. When something had to be illustrated, he drew an exact sketch on the ground or scratched it on a piece of pottery or on a mud-brick of the type used in building walls the thickness of two and one-half bricks. He seemed to know without consulting exact specifications and detailed layouts exactly where every stone should be placed and how high a wall should go and exactly how best to make use of the contours of the land. Indeed, I have often seen unlettered Arabs, who could not have read architects' plans if they had had them, build elaborate, vaulted stone structures with a skill that would have done credit to highly schooled engineers, who had previously solved on reams of foolscap the mathematics of the structural problems involved.

A sudden shout alerted everybody that the expected visitors had been sighted. In the distance, a troop of riders could be made out, raising a small cloud of dust as they traveled along the road which led eastward from Beersheba to the edge of the plateau overlooking the south end of the Dead Sea. Banners were broken out, buglers stationed on the parapet above the twisting gateway, with its three pairs of doors and two opposite sets of guard-rooms between them. A delegation, including the architect, advanced half way down the hill to greet and welcome the oncoming guests. There was a flourish of the trumpets to receive them as the gates were ceremoniously opened! Normally, they would be swung back early in the morning and shut only at nightfall. And then, after several hours' delay, which, in addition to the usual welcoming amenities, included food and rest, the inspection tour commenced.

The head of the delegation that had come for the purpose was a man of great experience and quick perception. Already from afar, he and his companions had noticed that the building site had been selected with a keen awareness of both military and economic considerations. Planted on top of the southernmost hill of an outrunner range of the Mountains of Judah, the fortress commanded an excellent view of much of the Northern Negev. Many of the most important sites there between Beersheba and Arad could be seen from it. It was obvious that if this hilltop were strongly fortified, it would serve as a kingpin in the protective framework set up by Uzziah to safeguard the Negev. As the inspector-general of the king's forces strode alongside the walls of this newly completed bastion, he made no effort to conceal his growing satisfaction with what he saw. No activity could take place for many miles round about in the plain about a hundred yards below without the let or stay of its garrison.

With expert eyes, he took in the details of construction. There were the corners of the walls bonded together in an interlocking pattern of headers and stretchers, so that they could not pull apart; the plastered cisterns, already filled with an adequate supply of rain water, caught in the great area of the wall-enclosed hilltop, which measured some 330 by 90 yards in extent; the massive revetment or glaçis sloping sharply inward against the outer wall, in order to compound its defensive strength; the small, subsidiary fort on a promontory on the far side of an intervening canyon, which guarded against any surprise attack from the hill-country to the north. All these and many other features made a clearly favorable impression upon him. His praise was lavish. The architect was now smiling. The work had been well done, and the king would be highly pleased. If the rest of the Negev were equally well protected, Uzziah's people could occupy it and his caravans traverse it without fear of disturbance. . . .

The examination of the site in the hot sun had been tiring. I sat down to rest in the shade of a wall and was soon lost in thought about all I had seen. It had been an exciting occasion. After a while, my eyes focussed on an isolated pile of building stones lying about on the ground in careless disarray. I wondered vaguely about that, until, with a sudden start, I realized that they had not been left there by the builders, but had fallen and remained there after the destruction and abandonment of the stronghold. The tour of the completed fortification in the company of the architect and the envoy of the king had indeed been the result of a flight of imagination. But the picture I had conjured up had not been made out of whole cloth. I had, as a matter of fact, walked along the outer walls, noting carefully the height and angle of the supporting glaçis or revetment. To be sure, neither wall nor glaçis were any longer intact, but still sufficiently so to enable them to be reconstructed easily in one's mind's eye.

Given the funds, workmen and materials, it would not have been too difficult a task to restore this site to its former appearance. It seemed completely natural to drift through the gate of its present into the crowded chambers and thronged corridors of the past, with its familiar sights and sounds and smells. On the way eastward from Beersheba, we had passed some Bedouin women separating chaff from wheat by means of vigorously shaken sieves. In appearance and form of daily activities and the use of closely related language, they were hardly distinguishable from their Biblical sisters. Their pronunciation of the Hebrew words of a seal impression found on the surface of this site by its discoverer, Johanon Aharoni, which read: "belonging to the king," would probably not have been much different from what it was in the time of the Judaean kingdom.

One thing, however, escaped us completely, and that was the original name of this prominent fortress. Extraordinarily well built, strategically located and of unusually large size, it is known today as Khirbet Gharrah. It must necessarily have played a considerable role in the affairs of the country more than two and a half millennia ago. It controlled a commanding position between the Mountains and the Negev of Judah. Nevertheless, the name by which it must have been widely known has been completely forgotten. It may be one of the "twenty-nine cities with their villages," listed among "the uttermost cities of the tribe of Judah toward the border of Edom in the Negev" (Joshua 15:21-32), only a very few of which can be identified positively. To judge from the pottery finds among the ruins of Khirbet Gharrah, it was not occupied before the tenth century B.C. Solomon was the one who probably erected the first fortress there, which was then radically rebuilt and enlarged by Uzziah. There is no question but that it exercised decisive military and civil jurisdiction over a large part of the Northern Negev between Beersheba and Arad. No armies could move or caravans pass or Bedouins dare raid in this area, without taking into account the position and power of Khirbet Gharrah.

From the airplane view alone, we would have been willing to assign Khirbet Gharrah to Iron Age II, that is, to the period extending between the tenth and sixth centuries B.C. This judgment presupposed the possibility of its having been refashioned in part and utilized later on, as indeed it was, from the Hellenistic through the Byzantine periods. Flying over it, we could clearly see how the entire hilltop of some twelve acres was enclosed by the remains of a great, fortification wall, against the inner side of which a whole series of rooms had been built. The site, from on high, has the appearance of an immense harpsichord, with the keyboard on the west side and the inward curve on the north side. The narrower, east end is covered with foundation ruins of numerous stone structures, most of which in their present form were built or rebuilt in the Byzantine period. Several large cisterns were visible, too, with others undoubtedly being hidden under the ruins.

KHIRBET GHAZZA

There are few sites in all the land which convey more sharply than does Khirbet Gharrah a sense of the power of the Judaean kingdom in its heyday. Very much like it in function and force was the contemporary site of Khirbet Ghazza, located near the easternmost edge of the broken plateau of the Northern Negev. It was a multi-towered fortress and caravanserai with massive walls and large courtyards, perched on a ledge immediately above the beginning of the abrupt and jagged descent to the Dead Sea and the Wadi Arabah. Planned and built as a pivotal stronghold, it possessed no history of occupation before the tenth century B.C. and little after the sixth century B.C. In the plain paralleling the curve of the wadi bed below it are numerous remains of ancient stone houses. The families of the members of the garrison were undoubtedly the ones who lived in them and tilled the available soil. They sought the fortress only in times of danger. Together with its smaller outpost fortress, called Khirbet Umm Radin, situated less than two miles to the south-southeast of it, this fortress guarded the approaches to and from the Arabah and the land of Edom.

These particular fortresses and many others like them were built by fiat and assured the tranquility necessary for trade and settlement in the raw lands of the Negev. The time span of most of them is contained largely within the five centuries of the kingdom of Judah. Other sites, such as the tremendous tell of Arad, about five and a half miles to the northwest of Khirbet Ghazza, merely included this period among numerous others which it had experienced. It was like adding another service stripe to the cluster of ribbons of history it already wore. Situated in the midst of fertile fields on top of the gradual watershed which separates the direction of the watercourses between the comparatively near Dead Sea to the east and the more remote Mediterranean to the west, it was the seat of many successive cities. They flourished, as we have already seen, during every cycle of history that left its mark on the Negev. Tell Arad figured in the story of the Exodus, and has throughout all the millennia of civilization remained faithful to its name.

Between it and Beersheba there were other places of lesser size but of equal significance for the story of settlement in the Negev. Invariably located near sources of water and surrounded by good farming lands, they were inhabited from earliest historical times on. Among them in the Northern Negev may be listed such names as Tell Milh, Khirbet Mishash, Khirbet Medhbeh, Khirbet Ar'areh, and others of no names at all, to which I have had to give numbers for purposes of identification. Some of them, like Tell Arad and Khirbet Ar'areh, clearly reflect their original Biblical names of Arad and Aroer. Others have been identified arbitrarily and by no means certainly with Biblical sites. Tell Milh, for example, has been equated with Hormah. All of them came into being not because of royal edicts and *a priori* military considerations, but in natural response to the needs of local inhabitants. It cannot, however, be repeated too often that their rise and fall and rebirth were not predicated upon radical climatic changes in historical times. Whenever there was firm-handed governmental rule, they sprang up like grass in the desert after a sprinkle of rain, and withered and disappeared whenever it was absent.

The Structure of Security

TELL MILH

Dead and deserted for many centuries, Tell Milh is today again coming to life as a result of the reestablishment of state authority in the Negev. The forces which of old made for the development of this artificial city hill are again coming into play. Its location on the major highway between Beersheba and Arad and at a junction of numerous trails, the centrality of its position among the fertile lands which surround it and the existence of a good well have repeatedly in historical times attracted people and dwellings and activities to it. It is plainly visible from the eagle-nest position of Khirbet Gharrah, about two and a half miles to the west-northwest of it.

A new town is being built at the foot of the mound of Tell Milh. It already has a noisy little grain-mill, a police post, a small general store and several permanent, stone houses which belong to the local sheikh. The colorful animal market held there every Wednesday is as indicative as anything could possibly be of the changes presently taking place in the Negev. The concourse of *fellahin* and shepherds and tradesmen, the shrill babel of hawking and bartering, the incessant chatter attending the constant drawing of water at the well, the sputtering and coughing of the anemic, one-lunged, diesel engine of the grain-mill, the dust and flies and cheerful confusion of hobbled camels, straying goats and sheep and braying donkeys are all part of the robust character and color of the region.

We flew over Tell Milh one morning in the early autumn, having frequently visited it on foot. The bare ground below was black with people congregated for the weekly market. We knew from experience that some of them had brought camel loads of sacks of grain grown in the lands round about to be milled at Tell Milh. Only enough was ground each time to last for several weeks, since it was easier to store the grain than the flour. As we circled the site, we could see tracks and travelers converging upon it from all directions. Groups of tent-encampments stood out within a large radius of Tell Milh, with the most distant of them appearing from our vantage point like collections of dots and dashes. Looking down upon Tell Milh itself, we could make out the lines of the outer walls of the rectangular Judaean fortification, showing through the thin skin of soil that covered them.

If it were possible to excavate this tell, the foundation remains of a whole series of cities superimposed upon each other would appear in the order of their construction. It would be necessary, after thoroughly examining the topmost level, to slice it off, in order to expose the one underneath, and to keep on repeating this process until the first village ever constructed on this site had been uncovered. To judge from the fragments of pottery we found on the top and slopes of Tell Milh, the story of civilization there, reading perforce backwards, extends from the Byzantine period, which ended in the seventh century A.D., to the Chalcolithic period, which came to a close in the thirty-second century B.C. There were, to be sure, occasional blank chapters in between, when only nomads roamed about, leaving no traces of their former presence behind them.

KHIRBET MISHASH

Not far away, about three and a half miles to the west-southwest of Tell Milh, is the smaller site of Khirbet Mishash, with much the same history. It, too, was within the range of vision of the impressive hilltop fortress of Khirbet Gharrah. Cultivable soil, a steady supply of water in the shallow wells of the nearby Biyar Mishash and good road connections have always made Khirbet Mishash a natural center of settlement.

Unmarked by any surface ruins and hardly different in size and shape from other low hilllocks in the vicinity, there is little to draw the attention. It, too, is cloaked in anonymity. If the casual passers-by only knew that its shabby appearance undoubtedly conceals numerous articles not only of cultural but of intrinsic value, there would be a mad scramble to open up and loot this abandoned treasure chest of ancient history. Since the discovery of the Dead Sea Scrolls, every Bedouin in the Negev has become an incipient archaeologist of sorts. They well understand that a piece of parchment or leather with some writing on it is worth many hundreds of sheep to the lucky finder.

As we drove up to one of the water holes in front of Khirbet Mishash, a black-garbed Bedouin woman and her young son were loading a tethered donkey with metal water-containers they had just filled. Their deeply branded camel, which had been drinking from a pan on the ground, raised its head to give us a supercilious look, while a baby donkey stood momentarily in its shadow. If you substitute beautiful pottery jars for the ugly receptacles abandoned by or appropriated from modern armies, this scene could have been much the same in Biblical times. Not far away we could see the black tents of the sub-tribe these two belonged to, which derived its living from animals and from the wheat raised in season on the lands surrounding Khirbet Mishash. On the slopes were innumerable fragments of the distinctive, wheel-turned, kiln-baked pottery vessels, which belonged to the times of the Judaean kingdom, and to a lesser degree to both earlier and later periods, too.

While we were standing about, the chieftain of the nearby encampment approached us to offer us coffee in his tent. He was politely curious about the potsherds we were picking up and putting into carefully labeled sacks. As we talked, discussing their significance and many other things, I found myself wondering about his background. There was a keenness and sharpness in his appearance, which reminded me of an unhooded falcon I had seen, ready to take off from the gloved hand of an Arab falconer. The chief was a man of warrior breed. I was tempted to ask him against whom he had fought and when and where, and whether he recalled or had been told about the incursion of the Israelites into the Negev. But then I suppressed the questions, remembering that all the Bedouins of the Negev had infiltrated there in comparatively recent times from Arabia and that their tribal lore could not assist my quest into antiquity.

KHIRBET AR'AREH

Although the original identity of Khirbet Mishash seems to have been erased completely from the minds of men, there is one site, about four and one half miles to the south-southeast of it, whose name has remained faithful throughout the ages. It is called Khirbet Ar'areh. Both by spelling and archaeological criteria, it is undoubtedly to be identified with the Aroer of the Negev, which is mentioned in the biography of David (I Samuel 30:28). "Shamah and Je'iel, the sons of Hotham the Aroerite" are listed as being among those "that came to David to Ziklag, while he yet kept himself close because of Saul the son of Kish" (I Chronicles 11:44; 12:1). How helpful it would have been if the Bible had been more explicit and told us exactly where David's Ziklag, near the north border of the Negev, was located!

Khirbet Ar'areh is a sturdy, fat mound, which has developed throughout the ages on top of a natural knoll. Standing in the midst of cultivable fields in the center of the Northern Negev, with wells both above and below it, it was bound to attract settlements to it. There seem to be the remains of a dry moat around it, particularly on its western side. A tremendous pit, which may be a natural depression, is located at its northern end. Excavations, however, might reveal that this pit served a particular purpose, such as that of a small amphitheatre in Roman times. We found great numbers of unusually large fragments of Judaean pottery of the tenth to sixth centuries B.C. at Khirbet Ar'areh, in addition to very large numbers of Hellenistic to medieval Arabic sherds.

There are, however, very few places in the Negev like Khirbet Ar'areh or the other mounds located there, that embraced many periods of history and developed only in the northern part of the Beersheba Basin. The only other manmade hill that can be compared to them is that of Tell el-Kheleifeh, at the southernmost tip of the Negev, which can be identified, as I have pointed out, with Ezion-geber:Elath. There were Judaean kingdom sites south of Khirbet Ar'areh, but none of them formed or became parts of tells. They were, first of all, the fortresses on the high hills, which were built to guard the cultivators of the limited fields around them and naturally to protect the roads leading to them and throughout the country. Their main purpose was to serve as strongholds and defend the centers of settlement. They were watch towers against Amalekite and Edomite and Bedouin encroachment in a border land of high strategic importance. Their existence enhanced the defensive position and striking power of Judah and opened up sources of wealth which could not otherwise have been tapped.

SITE 306

Characteristic of these Judaean strongholds, which, from Solomon's time on, occupied commanding positions in the Negev and Sinai, is Site 306, located a little over ten miles south-southeast of Khirbet Ar'areh. It stands on a completely isolated, steep-sided, flat-topped hill, with an unimpeded view over the fairly fertile countryside around it. A massive fortification wall enclosed the entire summit of the hill, with a row of rooms built against its inner face. At one end stood a blockhouse with a cistern on the slope below it. We located the site from far off through our field glasses. The occupants of this nameless site could have observed everything that went on in the surrounding district.

Although everything was in ruins when we got there, the outer fortification wall was still sufficiently intact to give a good idea of its original appearance. It was constructed of large, crude, limestone blocks, with the corners well bonded together in classic header and stretcher fashion. As we ascended the hill, following a distinctly banked roadway, we came across the clear remains of the gateway of the fortress. Aside from the general architecture, numerous fragments of pottery scattered about testified unmistakably that this had been a Judaean kingdom outpost. It had been abandoned in the sixth century B.C. and had never again been reoccupied except by passing shepherds. It was typical of many other places like it in the Negev, which bolstered the authority of the kings of Judah there.

A certain amount of dry farming is still carried on in the fields below Site 306. It consists, however, of little more than scratching the ground and sowing the seeds haphazardly and then hoping for the best. In the past the protection furnished by the fortress made it possible to raise crops on a regular basis, which involved leaving probably as much as half or even more of the fields fallow every other year. It served also as a link in the elaborate chain of military posts that guarded the highways in the Negev. They inhibited nomadic forays or made them exceedingly unhealthy. They also enabled the king's agents to travel between Jerusalem and Ezion-geber: Elath or between Jerusalem and Kadesh-barnea in complete safety. It was possible for a Queen of Sheba to traverse the Negev on her way to meet Solomon with no danger threatening her rich caravan.

The Permanence of Change

The structure of security in the Negev, based on hilltop

fortifications erected by the kings of Judah, lasted a fairly long time. It served its purpose for nearly four hundred years, collapsing finally like a sand castle before the blows of the Babylonians early in the sixth century B.C. (Jeremiah 13:19; 33:13). Orderly government in the Negev dwindled and disappeared altogether during the next century and a half. A power vacuum developed there, which was not filled by the return of the exiles to Jerusalem under the leadership of Ezra and Nehemiah. As a result, during this long interval, the Bedouins again swept in, planting their flimsy tents on the ruins of Judaean fortresses that had for so long held them stoutly in check. Such caravans as passed through the Southland must have paid heavy tolls to many tribal leaders. All agricultural civilization there came to an end. It made no sense for farmers to toil under conditions which at the best were difficult enough, only to be robbed in the end of the gains of their labor. And soon the Negev, which in many places had been coaxed and badgered into reluctant productivity, again took on the appearance of a "howling wilderness." It remained a "desert land" for centuries, with not a village nor fortress being constructed to relieve the monotony of its emptiness.

Although, in the course of events, a kingdom of Judaea was reestablished, it was never able to repossess the totality of its former estate and reach out again as far as the Red Sea. That was accomplished only by the creation of the modern State of Israel. But even though the Negev remained outside the limits of Judaean control, it could not forever lie unclaimed and unutilized, any more than Palestine as a whole could escape the rivalry of world powers about it. The names and languages, cultures and capitals of these countries might change, but the unvarying compulsions of their geographical positions and economic needs and military requirements, convinced them, sooner or later, of the importance of the Holy Land as an indispensable part of their *Lebensraum*. The moment that occurred, their armies would be on the march, driving southward or northward as the case might be, in the endless and ultimately always idle attempt to achieve security through conquest.

Change followed change in Palestine, with the Persians replacing the Babylonians as the overlords of the land, and yielding in turn to the Greeks as the masters of its destiny. When the empire of Alexander the Great, the warrior high-priest of Hellenism, was split asunder after his death in 323 B.C., Ptolemaic Egypt and Seleucid Syria replaced it in part. Each of them sought to extend its rule over Palestine. Serving, however, as a common bond of union between all of them, was the irresistible influence of Greek culture, which overleaped borders and embraced bitter rivals. Even the bungling attempt of the Seleucid king, Antiochus IV, known also as Antiochus Epiphanes, to introduce the worship of Olympian Zeus into the Temple at Jerusalem and force the Jews, under penalty of death if they resisted, to accept pagan practices, failed to blight the attractiveness of Greek dress, sports, philosophy and arts for thousands of them. All Antiochus IV succeeded in doing was to ignite the Maccabean rebellion in 168 B.C.

In spite of the tenuous freedom achieved for little over a century under the Hasmonean dynasty, the appeal of the civilization of the Hellenes remained strong in Judah. No one could have been a greater admirer of it than Herod the Great, however staunch he was in his loyalty to Rome and however dauntless he proved to be, in spite of all his horrible shortcomings, in his championship of his people. His brilliant and brutal reign over them extended from 37 to 4 B.C., during which time he did extraordinarily much to give a Greek appearance to the face of the land. Even though Latin was current then and the use of Aramaic was widespread indeed, the Greek tongue remained in general use. Indeed, it persisted in coarsened form down to the end of the Byzantine period in the seventh century A.D.

It is all the more amazing, therefore, that with the glitter and pomp of the Graeco-Roman world about them, the humble, common people of the land continued to adhere with amazing tenacity to the severely simple faith of their forefathers. Inwardly untouched by the resplendent structures of such places as Caesaria Maratima on the Mediterranean coast of Palestine, which Herod the Great constructed, or Caesaria Philippi, which his son, Herod Antipas, built at one of the main sources of the Jordan, or other cities like them in Eastern and Western Palestine, the people moved about serenely in an unostentatious world of their own, a world made glorious by their unswerving belief in the majesty and power and loving kindness of the one, invisible and universal God of Israel and of all mankind.

Following the downfall of Judah as a result of the Babylonian conquest, the tides of empire bypassed the Negev. The contending armies of antipodal forces used "the Way of the Land of the Philistines" along the western coast. Palestine was important as a passageway, but the harsh interior of the Negev and Sinai was of little moment to them. When the Maccabees finally snatched their independence from the Seleucids and rose to fugitive power, they still failed to exercise control over the Southland. Either they were unaware of its possibilities or indifferent to them, or, what is more probable, were unable to take advantage of them.

For some years, during the reign of the redoubtable Maccabean cleric-king, Alexander Jannaeus, 103-76 B.C., the territory of Judaean Idumaea included the well known caravanserai of Mampsis (Kurnub). It is twenty-two miles southeast of Beersheba, and marked the high point of the penetration of the Maccabees southward. Otherwise, both before and after his time, their authority stopped short at the natural, northern boundary of the Negev, below the foothills of the Mountains of Hebron. Not even under Herod the Great, whose achievements were Solomonic in character, and whose domain to the north more or less paralleled that of his famous predecessor, was this condition changed. Long before his time, however, a new order, originating from the east, had been established in the empty spaces of the Negev. The newcomers, who filled the void which had then existed there for centuries, were known as the Nabataeans.

CHAPTER VII

THE NABATAEANS

Out of the East

WHEN WE THINK OF Palestine about two thousand years ago, we often overlook the fact that the Nabataeans were very much a part of its general cultural world. The Judaeans and the Nabataeans knew each other well. There must have been much intermarriage between them. The Judaean king, Herod the Great, for instance, had Nabataean blood. While his father, Antipater, was of Idumaean ancestry, his mother was of Nabataean origin. When the ablest of his sons, Herod Antipas, married the daughter of the powerful Nabataean king, Aretas IV, who ruled from 9 B.C. to A.D. 40, the relationship between the two peoples improved, only to deteriorate when he divorced her in order to marry his niece and sister-in-law, Herodias, the wife of his half-brother, whom she abandoned. Under the circumstances, the fact that his province of Peraea abutted Nabataean territory on the east side of the Dead Sea, proved to be a curse rather than a blessing. He had inherited Peraea, together with Galilee, as his testamentary share of his father's kingdom.

John the Baptist was to pay with his head for having condemned the marriage of the doubly divorced and doubly related Herod Antipas and Herodias. The execution was at the instigation of Herodias, who never forgave the rabbi for his fearless rebuke, based on the law forbidding a man to marry his brother's wife during his brother's lifetime (Leviticus 18:16). This tragedy took place at the mountain fortress of Machaerus, located above the northeast end of the Dead Sea. It was there, some time earlier, that Herod Antipas's Nabataean queen found refuge in good time, after she had learned of his plan to rid himself of her in favor of Herodias. She found it easy then to escape to her Nabataean kinsmen across the border to the south. Herod Antipas was to rue the day. Her father, Aretas IV, dispatched a punitive expedition, which soundly thrashed the army of his former son-in-law. He was not the first Nabataean king to engage and defeat Judaean forces. Shortly after the beginning of the first century B.C., a decisive victory was gained by the Nabataean king, Obodas I, over the aggressive Maccabean, Alexander Jannaeus. This greatly facilitated the Nabataean occupation of the Hauran and Jebel Druze in southern Syria.

The Nabataean kingdom had by then become a formidable power in the affairs of the ancient Near East. Paul of Tarsus discovered that fact to his sorrow when he arrived in Damascus, after a long stay in the desert spent in lonely contemplation. We are indebted to him for a graphic description of his experience at the hands of the Nabataean governor, who ruled there in the name of the great Nabataean king, Aretas IV: "In Damascus, the governor under Aretas the king guarded the city of the Damascenes in order to seize me; but through a window in the wall, I was let down in a basket and escaped" (II Corinthians 11:32-33).

They Came from Arabia

The story of the Exodus of the Israelites and the rise and fall of their kingdom is paralleled in many respects by that of the Nabataeans. They took advantage of a vacuum of power to press into lands more fertile than their own and to prosper there astonishingly. Their rule prevailed for several centuries from Arabia to Syria and across the Negev to Sinai. They may be accounted one of the most remarkable peoples of history. Sprung swiftly out of the desert of Arabia to a position of great power and affluence, they were thrust back by the Romans even more swiftly into the limbo whence they came. While their turn lasted, the Nabataeans wrought greatly, developing almost overnight into builders of magnificent cities, which are unique in the history of the handiwork of man. They became tradesmen, farmers, engineers, architects and artists of outstanding excellence. The phenomenon of their appearance and disappearance between the first centuries B.C. and A.D. may be likened to the brilliance of a meteor flashing briefly across the skies to blazing extinction.

The discovery of great numbers of their villages in southern Transjordan and now in the Negev, in addition to those previously known, has made it possible to piece together an imperfect but revealing mosaic of their amazing civilization. They were a story-book people with almost magical accomplishments, which included exquisite pottery, exciting architecture and imaginative agriculture. The towers and temples they erected or at times hewed out of the solid rock, as well as their innumerable cisterns and reservoirs and terraces testify to their extraordinary abilities. Almost everything they put their hands to took on the patina of their genius, like their fantastically beautiful capital city of Petra.

Petra had been the site of Biblical Sela (the Rock). Even in its present condition of dilapidated elegance, with crumbling and pock-marked façades and broken pillars and ruined staircases left hanging in mid-air, it continues to be an unforgettable monument of the high estate they had so quickly achieved. Wherever they turned, their creative abilities came into play. No terrain was too difficult, no soil too poor, no area too arid to resist their efforts to transform wastelands into gardens and to establish the activities of an advanced civilization, where none had existed before. We filled our maps with dots and numbers marking the remains of their towns and villages and caravanserais and fortresses. We came across some of their temples and open sanctuaries, too. They knew how to exploit fertile lands, but they also knew how to wrest a hard livelihood from an inhospitable environment. Yet their heyday lasted for less than three centuries.

Moving in from the spawning grounds of Arabia, the Nabataeans seized Edom and Moab, the Negev and Sinai, as well as other lands, which had been shorn of their defenses in the vain effort to stem the Babylonian juggernaut. Speaking and writing a dialect of the widespread Aramaic tongue, they developed a distinctive script of their own. Furthermore, in the course of the Hellenization of the ancient Near East, many of them became well versed in Greek and to a lesser degree in Latin. When we excavated the Nabataean hilltop temple of Khirbet Tannur in central Transjordan, we found inscriptions in Nabataean, Aramaic and in Greek. One of them, in particular, incised on a small, free-standing incense altar, emphasized the eclectic nature of the fully developed Nabataean civilization. Composed of four superimposed lines, the first of which is missing, and occupying a narrowing, triangular space, it read: "[ALEXA] NDROS AMRO U." The latter part of the name is typically Nabataean or Semitic, while the former is typically Greek.

When we brought this altar to Jerusalem, a Christian Arab friend of ours marveled at the name of Alexandros Amrou, until we reminded him that his own name, Demetrius Salameh, was likewise composed of Greek and Semitic elements.

The sculptures on the front panel and on the two side panels of the altar were also indicative of the cross-fertilization of Semitic and Hellenistic cultural forces which met and merged in the extraordinary art and architecture of the Nabataeans. The central figure combined features of the Greek god, Zeus, and of the Semitic god, Hadad. On his left arm was Hadad's symbol of the thunderbolt. The two figures on the side panels were representations of Nike, the Greek goddess of victory. All three of the figures were placed between representations of attached columns capped with Corinthianized, horned capitals, which are uniquely Nabataean.

Another dedicatory inscription from Khirbet Tannur in Nabataean Aramaic, recorded that a monument had been erected by a person named Natayr'el, "for the life of Haretat (Aretas), king of the Nabataeans, who loves his people, and for the life of Huldu, his wife, in the year II." That dates it to the second year of the reign of the great Nabataean monarch, Aretas IV, who, as I have already said, ruled from 9 B.C. to A.D. 40. He was an ardent exponent of Hellenism, in this respect being much like his former son-in-law, Herod Antipas, and particularly like Herod the Great. Aretas, too, did much to impress the Greek spirit upon the character of his country. In such places as Khirbet Tannur, one phase of which was built during his reign, and in the Nabataean capital of Petra, which he must have helped fashion, are revealed both the variety of cultural influences and the vigor of ethnic attachments, which animated him and his people.

Foundations of Empire

The spectacular rise and development of the Nabataean kingdom to great wealth and power between the first centuries B.C. and A.D. may be attributed in part to the fact that it was situated on important trade routes between Arabia and Syria. Along them were carried not only the spices and incense of southern Arabia, but also goods which had been transported from Africa, India and very possibly even from China. Heavily laden caravans converged on the great trade emporium of Petra, with some of them coming from the related centers of Meda'in Saleh and Teima in Arabia. Other caravans came from as far away as Gerrha on the Persian Gulf. Both in Petra and Meda'in Saleh, bold architects carved buildings out of the solid rock, as if they were slicing through the most insubstantial material.

From Petra, goods were reexpedited northward to Syria, southwestward across the Negev and Sinai to Egypt, and westward across the Northern Negev to Gaza and to Ascalon on the Mediterranean. From Ascalon, the precious freight was transshipped to Alexandria in Egypt and as far away as Puteoli in Italy, with the ships hired by the Nabataeans touching Rhodes and Greece on the way. Their boats also traveled the length of the Red Sea. Along with their merchandise, the Nabataean traders carried their gods, so that by worshipping familiar deities in foreign ports they would always feel at home and secure. Long before their time, Rachel, the wife of Jacob, acted in much the same way. Departing from Padan Aram, on the trip that was to take her far from her ancestral hearth, she clandestinely appropriated her father's idols, so that they might protect her and hers in the strange, new world of Canaan she was headed for (Genesis 31:19.34-35).

In Ascalon, at the end of their trade route across the Northern Negev, the Nabataeans built themselves a temple of their own. There they worshipped Atargatis, the goddess of fertility, in the form of a mermaid. At Khirbet Tannur, too, the emphasis on fecundity and fortune was expressed through the symbolism of two dolphins over the bust of Atargatis. On another Atargatis sculpture there, the theme of the yield of the soil was underlined by representations of sheaves of wheat placed next to her head. And when at journey's end at distant Puteoli, a few miles north of Naples, the venturesome Nabataeans unloaded their valuable cargoes and disposed of them, they could visit there also a temple of their own, and give thanks for a safe voyage and pray for favorable winds homeward. We are confident that a Nabataean temple must have existed also at Rhodes, where a Graeco-Nabataean inscription has already been found. Among the gods they worshipped at Puteoli was the likeness of Zeus-Hadad, whose face and body were veiled by large leaves. The countenance of a great bust of Atargatis at Khirbet Tannur was similarly guarded from direct mortal gaze. It will be recalled that Moses could not look at the face of Jehovah in Sinai and live (Exodus 33:22-23). The Bible relates, also, that after speaking with God, Moses' face shone so that "he put a veil on his face" (Exodus 34:30).

The extensive trading activities of the Nabataeans and the heavy taxes imposed by them on goods in transit through their territory were far from being the only sources of their riches and of the livelihood of the masses of the people. They reopened and worked the copper and iron mines in the Wadi Arabah and Sinai, the ones which had once been exploited by Solomon and others before him. Above all, however, in order to meet the food requirements of their population, which increased tremendously in numbers as their kingdom grew in extent, wealth and power, they pursued agriculture intensively. They engaged in it not only in the fertile lands of Edom and Moab, but in every available nook and cranny elsewhere, which they could call or make their own. Their capital of Petra was much more than a "caravan city," as it has so frequently been called. It was also the center of a great farming area. The advanced nature of the agricultural civilization of the Nabataeans at the zenith of their development between the first century B.C. and the second century A.D. can best be illustrated through their fertility deities and the temples dedicated to them, such as Khirbet Tannur.

Intense population pressures forced the Nabataeans to make use of all the marginal lands of their kingdom and taught them to sustain themselves in inhospitable environments. They created places of permanent settlement, even in the desolate rift of the Wadi Arabah. Spreading westward, they seized the lands of the Negev, transforming thousands of waste acres into cultivable fields, from which they extracted a rewarding yield. As we wandered in their footsteps, it became evident why the Hasmoneans and the Herodians could not extend their power southward into the Negev proper. The Nabataeans had entrenched themselves there firmly and had made it an integral part of their kingdom. One of their greatest rulers, Obodas, was buried there, as if to emphasize its importance to them. His memory is perpetuated in the massive ruins of the Nabataean-Byzantine hill-city of Abdah, which was named after him. However, it serves as a monument for all the Nabataean kings with the name Obodas, because we do not yet know exactly which one of them found his final resting place there. It is clear, however, that the western boundary of the Nabataean kingdom is not demarcated by the Wadi Arabah, as we once thought, but rather by the River Egypt (Wadi el-Arish) in Sinai.

Metamorphosis of Nomads

The metamorphosis of the Nabataeans from nomads to prosperous traders and agriculturists parallels in many ways the experiences of the Israelites. We learn from the ancient historian, Diodorus, as I have mentioned earlier in this book, that the Nabataeans knew nothing about agriculture in the fourth century B.C., although they already then trafficked in the products of Arabia. Indeed, in the early part of their history, they had acted as if they were descendants of the Rechabites. Like them, they seemed, at least at first, to make a virtue of abhorring agriculture, banning the use of wine, and preferring to live in tents rather than in stone houses.

There is also a striking closeness of their creed then to that of the later Essenes and of the related inhabitants of

Qumran, where the Dead Sea Scrolls originated. The discovery of some Nabataean papyri in caves of the Wadi Murabba'at in the vicinity of Qumran is of considerable interest in this connection. Particularly striking is the fact that although these papyri deal with commercial transactions between Jews, they were penned in a beautiful, cursive Nabataean script by a professional Nabataean scribe. They may possibly indicate that some of the Nabataean clans persisted in their early asceticism and joined with others of similar tendencies. On the other hand, being ordinary business documents, they may merely signify the existence of commercial connections between the two groups.

Soon, however, the Nabataeans lifted the ban on strong drink. The use of wine was given a prominent place in their religious ritual. The grape and vine motif became one of the most commonly employed in their decorative arts. By the turn of the era, at the transition between the first centuries B.C. and A.D., the Nabataeans are described by Strabo as living in stone houses, being devoted to trade, and tilling the soil with might and main. We have been able to confirm this through archaeological fact. The change in their form of living was accompanied also by a radical change in the kind of gods they worshipped.

In the beginning, the main Nabataean deity partook of some of the characteristics of the God of Sinai, who could not be seen face to face, let alone be represented in human form. In Petra and in many other places, the god most commonly known to the Nabataeans took on the physical shape of an unhewn, four-cornered stone. He was known as Dhu-Shara (Dushara, Dusares, and subsequently identified with Dionysus). Reminiscent of this depiction of the deity is the black, igneous stone, which is revered to this day by the Moslems in the central sanctuary at Mecca. With the passage of the centuries, however, and the transformation of the Nabataeans from nomads into extraordinarily skillful tillers of the soil, they adopted the Semitic fertility deities and practices of their surroundings. As they became increasingly Hellenized, their deities were sculptured in the likenesses of Greek gods. They adopted and improved upon the agricultural civilization of the Edomites and Moabites. In many ways, they far surpassed them and others in greater ability to subdue wildernesses and harness the evanescent rivers of the desert. No one before them had been quite as successful as they were in storing up for many months each year the waters of the flash floods that roar down the dry wadi beds on infrequent and brief occasions.

The keys opening the portals of the vanished Nabataean kingdom were the innumerable pieces of deceptively fragile, but exceedingly durable Nabataean pottery left behind on the surface of the ground. George and Agnes Horsfield were the first to recognize and describe the striking characteristics of Nabataean pottery. Once seen, it can never be forgotten. Nomads could never have produced this extraordinarily fine and sophisticatedly ornamented ware. Only a few completely intact specimens have ever been recovered, but we were able to recognize the locations of dozens of Nabataean villages in the Negev by means of these distinctive, Nabataean sherds, and found about five hundred Nabataean farming communities in Transjordan by the same method.

Most of the fragments of Nabataean pottery which we found belonged to unbelievably thin, beautifully shaped plates, bowls, cups and jugs of various kinds. Many of them were ornamented with painted designs. They consisted usually of stylized floral or leaf patterns in a solid, reddish-brown color, superimposed over very delicate parallel or crisscross lines. Sometimes, leaf and floral designs were most faithfully depicted, and at other times represented in highly stylized form. One of the partly reconstructed Nabataean bowls from Khirbet Tannur was decorated with pomegranate, palm leaf and date or grape designs in reddish-brown paint on a buff background. Other forms of decoration included bands of rouletting, with the sharp little indentations fitting into each other like rows of diminutive cogwheels. There were, of course, also coarser types of Nabataean pottery. It has always amazed me, however, to find the presence of Nabataean pottery of exquisite workmanship and ornamentation at even the most isolated Nabataean caravanserais, such as Bayir Wells in the easternmost desert of Transjordan.

Garden Cities in the Desert

The resourcefulness and energy of the Nabataeans, which enabled them to prosper greatly in fertile lands, accomplished also miracles of achievement in more forbidding regions. While exploring the Wadi Arabah on camel back, we came across the remains of a garden city on the east side of its dreary wastes. It is called et-Telah (Toloha) and turned out to be a Nabataean caravanserai on the trade route leading from Edom to the Mediterranean. Almost a mile before we got there, we could see, even from our high seats on the camels, that the ground was strewn with masses of sherds. It was easy to identify them as Nabataean when we dismounted several times to examine them. The puzzle of their origin was solved when we arrived at et-Telah. A small spring there nourishes a patch of green which stands out prominently in the midst of its gray surroundings. Another spring rises a short distance above it in the wadi leading down from the hills of Edom.

Large quantities of Nabataean sherds and sigillata ware and glass were found there. Particularly impressive was a large *birkeh* or reservoir, to which the waters of the springs had been led. Even more striking were the several square miles of carefully walled fields, which were irrigated from the supplies thus stored. The laboriously erected stone walls, which fenced in every square plot of earth, are still largely intact. Only those sections have been swept away during the centuries which were in the paths of the occasional floods caused by runoff rain waters from the Edomite hills. The terraces which once restrained and channeled them have fallen into disrepair. When, later, we flew over et-Telah, it appeared even more impressive than when we had examined it on foot. From the air, the elaborately walled fields resembled a gigantic checker board. Many of them are as ready for cultivation today as they were approximately two thousand years ago.

Elsewhere, too, in the wastelands of the Arabah, we came across similar Nabataean garden villages. One of them, on its east side, is named Qasr Feifeh. Its wide stretches of terraced fields would respond again quickly to the husbandman's care. The walls about them have withstood the erosion of nature and time. They testify as eloquently in their way to the creative genius of the Nabataeans as do their temples, paintings and pottery. They were indeed a wonderful people, whose abilities were directed to the arts of peace rather than to the science of war, to the fructification of deserts rather than to the sowing of their neighbors' fields with salt, to the conservation of the soil and the skillful gathering and utilization of water rather than to the squandering of natural resources and to the scorching of the good earth to prevent others from enjoying its blessings.

To achieve their goal of making as much as possible even out of marginal and dry lands, they built hundreds of miles of terraces and dug thousands of cisterns and used entire watersheds to garner every possible drop of the rare rainwater. They found their reward in the survival values they created for themselves and their children and their children's children, planning and undertaking soil and water conservation schemes which sometimes must have taken generations to complete. It was in this way that they reconquered the wilderness of the Negev, planting more agricultural colonies there than it had ever known before. At the same time, they were extremely mindful of the gains of commerce and the profits of trade, which they continued to pursue energetically throughout their entire realm. Their garden places in the Wadi Arabah served also as way stations for their brisk caravan trade between the east and the west.

It took a day's time for the Nabataean caravans to cross the width of the Wadi Arabah from et-Telah or Qasr Feifeh to the fine spring and caravanserai of Ain Hosb (Eiseiba) on its extreme west side. At least it took that long for our small train of a dozen camels and as many men to negotiate the same distance. During the hours of the midday heat, intense even in March, we halted in a shady fissure of the Wadi Jeib, which broadly grooves the length of much of the Arabah rift. The Bedouin track we followed lay between two gray areas covered with stones and boulders. They bordered a central, golden, sandy stretch, tinged green during the furtive springtime of our journey with a sparse growth of grass and shrubs and tiny wild flowers. We passed several herds of camels and goats there, watched over by Howeitat shepherds. Our own camels foraged on the way. Occasionally, the cameleers, without disturbing the rhythm of our advance, would slide off their beasts to pluck some succulent grasses for them and then remount with the agility of monkeys. Having started early in the morning, we reached Ain Hosb in the late afternoon. The prominent landmark of its huge, old *sidr* tree had been visible to us from afar. The ride would have been much harder had we been traveling at any other time of the year except spring, and had not the expectancy of finding plentiful water at Ain Hosb made the weariness of the way easily bearable.

That supply of water attracted settlements in ancient times, with the Nabataeans leaving behind the most distinctive remains of their former existence. We found thousands of fragments of the almost egg-shell thin, hard-baked, wheel-turned, plain and painted and rouletted Nabataean pottery, including many pieces of their own type of terra sigillata ware. Bits of the delicate glassware they produced were also found, as well as some coins of Nabataean mint. These were too corroded to be cleansed, but were very much like some we had found at et-Telah. On one of them were the busts of a king and queen, jugate, on the obverse side. On the reverse side, between and below two crossed cornucopiae, were Nabataean letters spelling Shaqilath, the name of the royal consort. Other Nabataean queens bore the same name. The size of this coin, however, suggested that she was the queen of the Nabataean king, Malichus II, A.D. 40-71. The potsherds and bits of glass and coins at Ain Hosb were found particularly among the foundation remains of a large Nabataean caravanserai, that had continued to exist until as late as the first part of the twentieth century A.D. It was torn down then to provide an easy source of ready-cut building stones for the police post erected there after the end of World War I.

Ain Hosb, or Eiseiba, as it was known in Nabataean to Byzantine times, served as one of the most important gateways along the entire length of the Wadi Arabah, through which the Nabataeans poured into the Negev. First they came as traders and then as settlers. Conquering its wilderness with their vast energies and tremendous skills, they built villages and temples and farming communities in such numbers that their hold on it and on Sinai became unshakable for several hundred years. It became as much and as firm a part of their kingdom as had the territories of Edom and Moab in Transjordan. The techniques of settlement they displayed at such places as et-Telah and Ain Hosb and elsewhere along the length of the Wadi Arabah, and that had been developed and perfected in the highlands and deserts to the east and southeast of it, were employed throughout the Negev and Sinai with startling results. The Nabataeans and the Nabataean-ized Idumaeans whom they absorbed, ruled the Negev firmly, with neither Maccabees nor Judaized Idumaeans from the north, nor nomads from Arabia or farthermost Sinai entering it except by their leave.

Fig. 38. This very large Nabataean cistern dug into the side of the Wadi Ramliyeh, opposite Abdah in the Negev, is still watertight and serviceable after two thousand years of use (see page 223).

FIG. 39. Roman milestones in the Wadi Raman (Machtesh Ramon) (see pages 33, 227).

FIG. 40. Interior of a Nabataean-Byzantine covered cistern by the Wadi Siq in the Negev (see page 234).

FIG. 41. Pillar of a Nabataean cistern, upon which Byzantine crosses and Greek inscription BOETHON were superimposed (see pages 224, 256).

FIG. 42. Prehistoric rock-drawings at Kilwa in the Jebel Tubaiq, Transjordan (see pages 237, 241).

FIG. 43. Nabataean rock-drawing, showing hunter with bow and arrow following his dog, which is pursuing an ibex (see pages 236-237).

Fig. 44. Nabataean-Byzantine hill city of Abdah in the Negev (see pages 271-275).

Fig. 45. Ruins of one of the Byzantine churches at Isbeita (see pages 264-269).

Fig. 46. Sculptured building stone from Byzantine Isbeita (see page 268).

The Scorpion Pass

Caravans could rest for as long as they pleased at Ain Hosb before continuing the next stage of their journey westward. To do this required them to climb the steep hills several miles away to reach the high, broken plateau of the Northern Negev. There is a somber-hued crazyquilt of bad lands to cross between the western edge of the Wadi Arabah and the base of the Negevite hills beyond. In and alongside the wadis, which crisscross this weird-looking area, a surprisingly large amount of natural forage can be found. It is sustained by underground seepage, to which Ain Hosb and some smaller springs nearby owe their existence. Among the largest of these dry stream beds is the Wadi Fiqreh. A large oasis exists in it, nourished by the spring of Ain Fiqreh. It seems like a dream to find numerous palm trees and masses of green shrubbery growing there.

It was even more surprising to find a fair amount of water in sizeable crevices in the bed of the wadi, remaining as late as the end of the summer. It was left over from the occasional torrents which roar down these wadi beds with frenzied strength several times a year, after a few days' rain in the hills above. When not restrained by dams or terraces, the rampaging waters cut their way down to the bed rock of the natural channels, and gouge out pockets and depressions that act as miniature reservoirs after the flood has passed. The Nabataeans and many others before them must have been as grateful for this reserve supply as are the modern Bedouins. Because of the presence of the spring of Ain Fiqreh and of the water in these rills which lasts throughout the summer and fall, the Wadi Fiqreh is alive with bands of graceful gazelles and birds of many songs and colors.

The high, flat-topped, sheer-sided, rectangularly shaped hill of Jebel el-Medhra makes a strong impression on every passerby in this district, which lies between the Arabah and the beginning of the steep ascent to the Negev proper. Near its base, we found at summer's end a deeply rooted vine trailing over the hard baked earth, bearing a fruit that looked like a wild melon.

The Jebel el-Medhra can be seen from far and wide. It juts above the broad meeting place of many wadis, which merge together and join the Negev-born Wadi Murrah to form the Wadi Fiqreh. Like the peak of a mountain looming above masses of clouds, its striated top of hard sandstone layers rises above the chalk formations which press against its sides. They look like white robed suppliants stretching out their hands to touch the hem of the deity.

It is thought by many that Jebel el-Medhra can be identified with the Biblical Mount Hor, on the top of which Aaron died in the presence of his brother Moses and his son Eleazer: "And Jehovah spake unto Moses and Aaron in Mount Hor, by the border of the land of Edom, saying, Aaron shall be gathered unto his people; for he shall not enter into the land which I have given unto the children of Israel, because ye rebelled against my words at Meribah. Take Aaron and Eleazer his son, and bring them up to Mount Hor; and strip Aaron of his garments and put them upon Eleazer his son; and Aaron shall be gathered unto his people and shall die there. And Moses did as Jehovah commanded . . . and Aaron died there on the top of the mountain . . ." (Numbers 20:23-28; 33:37). Whether or not this identification is correct is in doubt. There has been no proof of its correctness. The scene of Aaron's death may possibly have been on one of the mountain tops northeast of Kadesh-barnea in Sinai. I have pointed out that at one time Se'ir-Edom was thought of as having been located there.

An arduous ascent of the Naqb Sefei awaited all the caravans journeying westward from el-Hosb before they reached the top of the Negev proper. The zigzag path which led up to it in sharp steep turns was known in the Bible as the Ma'aleh Aqrabbim, which means the Scorpion Pass (Numbers 34:4; Joshua 15:3). There were three way-stations alongside it in ancient times, one at the bottom, a second about half way up and a third near the top. Known today, respectively, as Rujm Sfar, Khirbet Sfar, and Qasr Sfar, they are Nabataean in origin, Roman in repair, and Byzantine in reconstruction. Others of earlier vintage probably preceded them. The serpentine windings of the modern Scorpion Pass descend a ridge a short distance to the north of the older one. Automobiles are now replacing camels and donkeys as the means of transportation. From the top of the pass there is a fine view over the bad lands below it, which slope down to the Wadi Arabah. The deep and broad rift of this Valley of the Smiths which I have dealt with before splits the earth lengthwise, and is visible in the distance, with the hills of Moab and Edom rising above it to the east, half hidden in a purplish haze.

Kurnub

Once the Wadi Arabah had been crossed and the difficult climb to the top of the Negev negotiated, the way ahead was smooth and easy by comparison. The next major stop was at Kurnub, on top of the watershed, below which the wadis turn either eastward down to the Wadi Arabah or westward toward the Mediterranean. The far-ranging caravans, coming from the east, could make a longer halt at Kurnub than at previous camping places, in order to replenish stocks of food, repair gear, and give men and beasts more than a cursory opportunity for rest. Kurnub served as an important market place for the interchange of goods from the east and the west. Heavily resinated Aegean wine was offered in return for Arabian spices and incense. Heaps of ivory, bolts of silk, exotic goods of many kinds, piles of tools and weapons and pottery, and sacks of grain and of dried fruits were the center of furious, multilingual barter. Kurnub was the terminal point for some of the itinerant merchants, while for others it was either the entrance to the Northern Negev and thence to the lands of the setting sun, or the jumping off place towards Arabia and the kingdoms that bordered it or beckoned beyond it.

The Nabataeans were by no means the first ones to seize and enlarge upon the natural advantages of Kurnub's favorable geographical position. Shepherds of the Upper Palaeolithic period, who left their characteristic flint instruments behind them, and others of more advanced cultures knew it well. The spring in the wadi bed below Kurnub made it a natural halting point and dwelling place from earliest times on. The nature and size of the city established by the Nabataeans and massively rebuilt by the Byzantines seem to have resulted in the obliteration of the pottery remains left on the surface by earlier inhabitants. Nearby, however, we found villages of the Chalcolithic period of the fourth millennium B.C., followed by others of the Abrahamitic period of the beginning of the second millennium B.C., and in due course by fortresses and camps of the Judaean kingdom.

The massive ruins of Kurnub (Mampsis) stem from the Byzantine city which rose over the Nabataean foundations. The town was surrounded by a great wall, with a double thickness on the west side, where the outspur on which it stood was connected with the mainland. The Byzantines raised up elaborate churches in place of the Nabataean temple and Dushara niches which had existed there. Where plaques in relief of Nabataean gods had adorned public buildings, the Byzantines employed architectural features decorated with the typical Christian crosses of their day. The lively Byzantine mosaics, characteristic both of church and synagogue construction, replaced the flashing murals that brightly colored the plaster coatings of so many Nabataean buildings. We found innumerable fragments of the unmistakable Nabataean pottery among the masses of Byzantine sherds which littered the ground.

But rather than poking about in the bewildering maze of

destroyed Kurnub with its acres of tumbled-down walls, streets obscured by fallen debris and cisterns usually concealed under a cover of dirt and stones, go down with me to the bottom of the canyon below it on the south. Here we can look with admiration at the dams thrust across it. Built in all probability by the Nabataeans, kept in excellent condition by the Byzantines, and repaired in modern times by the British, they have been able to resist the vandalism of passing shepherds and the violence of nature. Upstream from them are the remains of several others of smaller size, which, however, have succumbed in varying degrees to the onslaught of the centuries.

The dams served the purpose both of soil and water conservation. A considerable body of water is still captured each year behind the two intact ones, lasting for months after the end of the rains. Pools from the overflow in the wadi bed farther downstream nourish the growth of clusters of papyrus. I like to think that some traveler of long ago transplanted the original ones from the land of Goshen or from the fields of Lebanon. As the flood waters caught behind the two intact dams lessen from Bedouin use and natural evaporation, the surface of the silt exposed at the bottom becomes baked under the heat of the sun and cracks into myriad pieces. Like impressions in wet cement, they hold fast the imprints of the hooves of gazelles that tread daintily across the still wet clay to drink their fill of the diminishing waters.

Ancient history is being repeated in the modern Negev. Another dam of even larger size than the main Kurnub one has been erected across the Wadi Rekhmeh, several miles to the west of Kurnub, as I have already said. The result is the miracle of a large body of water gleaming in the grayish-brown setting of the desert, and lasting all year long. Several recent new settlements are already largely dependent upon it. About two thousand years have elapsed between the construction of the Kurnub and Rekhmeh dams. Human foresight and energy have made this possible. The climate has changed not a whit in the interval, so far as we can ascertain. Once again, it has been demonstrated that the decisive factor in the rise and fall of civilizations is the human one.

The Kurnub dams were not the only ones that the Nabataeans and Romans and Byzantines built in the lands of their dominion in the ancient Near East. Some of these structures have been found in the most unexpected places. We came across one of them in the Wadi Dhobai, far out in the eastern desert of Transjordan, remote from any settlement of the past or the present. Holding back the rare flash floods that surge through the Wadi Dhobai, this dam exacted a tribute of water sufficiently large to satisfy the needs of numerous flocks of sheep and herds of goats and camels for many months of the year.

If one visits the desolate and forbidding districts of northern Transjordan and southern Syria, one is amazed at the ruins of sizeable towns established there by the Nabataeans and rebuilt or expanded by the Byzantines. Each of them possessed one or more reservoirs of considerable dimensions. In addition, every one of their houses had a cistern of its own, hewn out of the solid rock and at least ten feet deep and square. Walking through the dark, basalt ruins of the Nabataean-Byzantine emporium of Umm el-Jemal, near the border between the two countries, one looks with astonishment at the largest of its reservoirs, which is still serviceable after the passage of millennia.

Wonder Workers

However important and indeed inexpressibly precious water is, particularly in the desert, man cannot live on water alone. The question of adequate food supplies became increasingly pressing as the Nabataeans began to establish ever larger numbers of permanent settlements in the Negev. Their paramount problem was to find sufficient land for farming and sufficient moisture to sustain crops. As their economy expanded in the Negev, it became obvious that they could maintain themselves and continue their trading activities only in closest conjunction with agricultural activities. The comparatively fertile plains of the Northern Negev were soon utilized to the fullest possible extent. New acreage had to be found or created, in which wheat could be grown and grapevines planted. The Nabataeans did not have to go far afield in their search. Their fortune lay literally underneath their feet.

Turning their attention to the almost endless number of wadis or dry creek beds and their branches, which veined the entire surface of the Negev, they commenced and doggedly completed the herculaean task of creating cultivable fields in the beds or on the banks of most of them. No difficulty seemed to be too great, no engineering problem too involved, no patch of earth too insignificant for this formidable enterprise. In the end and after the passage of numerous generations, many thousands of additional acres were made available. Several hundred Nabataean agricultural villages sprang up and flourished in the Negev, many of them in places which previously had never been able to sustain civilized life. The earth became adorned with ribbons of green during the growing season. Temples were constructed, in which the inhabitants of the land worshipped their gods and goddesses of fertility. In physical fact and in appearance and spirit, the Negev became thoroughly Nabataean.

The secret of the ability of the Nabataeans to live and thrive there lay in their mastery of the science of soil and water conservation. Their agriculture and their commerce complemented each other. Wherever possible, the Nabataeans superimposed upon every wadi, including its beginnings in the uplands, a framework of terraces, dams, spillways and aqueducts. Their cisterns and reservoirs stored millions of gallons of water. The techniques of water-spreading devices became second nature to them. The few flash floods which tore down through the wadi beds during the winter and spring became welcome and profitable rather than pernicious and feared.

The ever-present concern of the Nabataeans was to trap as much of even the lightest rainfall as possible. It was because of this that they were able to push the boundaries of the Sown farther into the wildernesses of Syria, Transjordan, Arabia, the Negev and Sinai than had ever been done before. They bound mountain tops and slopes to their purposes and put tight checkreins on riotous, runoff rainwaters. The prospect of carving temples and tombs and dwellings out of solid rock and a livelihood out of seemingly waterless deserts daunted them not at all. They advanced far in art and architecture and commercial enterprises. They were, however, not superior to other peoples in these respects, and were definitely inferior to some. In water engineering and agriculture, however, the Nabataeans have never been surpassed in all the annals of history.

The terraces they constructed almost everywhere formed the chief, although by no means the only tool of their trade. East of Kurnub, the canyon which imprisons the wadi of that name flattens down and spreads out till it merges with a small plain, which is several miles long and from half to a quarter of a mile wide. This entire area was carefully divided into great, rectangular fields, which were fenced in on all sides by massive stone walls. They are reminiscent on a magnified scale of the checkerboard arrangement of the wall-enclosed gardens of et-Telah in the Wadi Arabah. Closer inspection reveals that these walled divisions form a succession of broad steps.

They descend with the slope of the plain and of the narrow wadi which loops its way through it, until it is lost from sight as the hills to the east press in against it once more. Constructed like dams with stepped back rows of large, roughly shaped limestone blocks, many of these terraces still stand to their original height of four to six courses, and have remained intact during the approximately two thousand years of their existence. Neither time nor floods have put them in disarray. It is noteworthy that the earth of each field is flush with the top of the terrace wall at its lower end. Had the terrace walls not held up, the earth would have been washed away. Picked clean of stones many centuries ago, these large plots of ground could be cultivated as readily today as they once were by the industrious Nabataeans and their Byzantine successors and others before them.

In the case of the Wadi Kurnub, the winter and spring freshets were tapped upstream and diverted from their natural channel to cascade over the entire series of terraced plots in the plain through which the wadi coursed. Each terraced area would capture some of the passing water and receive also from it a deposit of some of its suspended soil and organic material. When crops were planted then on these fenced-in plots, they would find that the sponge of the enriched earth had absorbed sufficient moisture to nourish them to harvestable maturity. Frequently, when a wadi bed was sufficiently shallow, the flood waters were permitted to flow directly over the terraced fields, which lay directly in the path of their natural flow. Widely separated lines of shrubbery can be seen stretching across many wadis, indicating the presence of intact terrace walls of ancient origin. The Nabataean *fellahin* used to plant tamarisk bushes along the inside faces of these walls, as yet another means of forcing the annual floods to enrich the earth with their freight of sediment and to bring into being or to restore the crucially important, underground water level. Upon its sure existence, their lives depended.

A Hidden Valley

We stumbled across several fields of ripened barley one day last summer, as we made our way through the completely terraced Wadi Raviv. Its Nabataean crosswalls are marked by lines of perennial bushes. There was not a single village or tent encampment to be seen along the entire length of the wadi or in the hills above it. We seemed to be completely alone in a hidden valley in a deserted world. Yet it was obvious that some Bedouins had been there before us. They had arrived in the springtime, and had plowed shallow furrows and scattered seeds in them, and had then flitted away like birds of passage. To Allah they entrusted the welfare of their crop, with the prayer that He might prosper its growth, until they managed to return. My hope was that, somehow, they did get back to reap the reward of their labors, such as they were. They would have found that, like Topsy in Uncle Tom's Cabin, the barley had just "grow'd" without any care whatsoever.

As a matter of fact, almost all of the Wadi Raviv could again be put under cultivation as successfully today as it was in remote yesterdays. And this applies to its numerous branches, as well as to many miles of other, similarly terraced wadis in the Negev. All the groundwork was done systematically and thoroughly by the Nabataeans ages ago. The terraces they laid out, the supporting walls they built, the dams they erected, the deflecting channels and spillways they engineered, the cisterns they dug and the water-spreading techniques they developed, enabled them to thrive in considerable numbers where only a few are eking out a miserable livelihood now. Most of their handiwork has endured, however. It can be taken full advantage of again by those sufficiently enterprising to do so, and indeed can be extended and improved upon. The prerequisite is the expenditure of tremendous energy and the establishment and maintenance of firm, public security.

We discovered that many Nabataean settlements were clustered along the sides and in the neighborhood of the Wadi Raviv. That did not surprise us at all, who had learned to associate the appearance of terraced wadis with the existence of nearby Nabataean villages and pottery. What did surprise and excite us was to discover how important this valley also was in pre-Nabataean times. In front of us, as we stood among the swaying stalks of stunted barley, there were visible the remains of a Judaean fortress and of a much earlier Abrahamitic village. The one crowned an adjacent hill. The other was spread over the slopes and top of the hill beyond, with suburbs extending over connecting ridges. Other sites, too, belonging in time from the Abrahamitic to the Byzantine periods, crowded the slopes of the more than ten mile length of the Wadi Raviv and of the deeply scarred uplands on either side of it. Judaean strongholds commanded both its entrance and exit. It is certain that already in Judaean times and perhaps also in the Abrahamitic period, the art of terracing wadi beds was practiced, although much less extensively than in the Nabataean and Byzantine periods.

This Wadi Raviv proved to be an important link in the famous Biblical highway that you will remember led from Kadesh-barnea in Sinai to Beersheba or Hormah in Canaan. Later on it served to connect the great Nabataean to Byzantine emporia of Isbeita (Subeita) and Nitsanah (Nessana) with each other. A different route might have been chosen through other wadis, which would have lessened the distance between these two points. None, however, which came within the range of possible choice, could compete with the good soil and the plentiful underground water supply of the Wadi Raviv. It had been cultivated intensively, as I have already said, as far back as Abrahamitic times. Among the circular foundation ruins of the houses of this period, we found numerous fragments of the easily recognizable pottery of approximately the twentieth century B.C. It was the kind used from the border of Egypt to the border of Asia Minor.

"Bring Forth to Them Water Out of the Rock"

The Nabataeans were apparently prepared to go to any lengths to collect every possible drop of water. Not only were entire wadi-systems terraced, but great lateral walls were built above them on the slopes leading down to them. Such walls protected the terraced fields in the wadis below against washouts from above and were angled to deflect the runoff rain water into cisterns or onto designated lands. The will of the Nabataeans and not the vagaries of the floods was the determining factor. In effect, various sections of each terraced wadi bed were located at the bottom of roughly rectangular, walled troughs. The beneficial effects of the rainfall were carefully husbanded; the harmful ones were equally carefully warded off. Erosion dams and terraces were constructed by the Nabataeans even at the thread-like beginnings of watercourses.

One of the most amazing engineering feats executed by the Nabataeans in their search for water was to use fairly level hilltops as catchment areas. I have come across some of them in the southwestern part of the Negev near the Sinai border. They were completely surrounded by low, well-planned stone walls, which seemed to serve no sensible purpose. The truncated hilltop of Site 367 is one of them. It is enclosed by such a wall, which is more than a mile in circumference. Not far from it in the same Bir Birein area is a massively fenced-in mesa of smaller size, which is ellipsoid in shape. It measures some five hundred and fifty by two hundred and twenty yards at its greatest dimensions, and appears as number 346 on our map. It may have been employed in Judaean and Abrahamitic times as a sacred burial and assembly place. Otherwise, both sites represented nothing more than desolate stretches of barren land, carpeted with innumerable stones.

The construction of such elongated stone walls around these hilltops was a tremendous task. It required months of effort, legions of workmen and the expenditure of the equivalent of great sums of money. The building stones had to be fetched from the slopes and wadis and hills round about. That in itself was a considerable undertaking. Dry built by experts and capped with flat boulders, the walls of Site 346 were about four feet high and nearly two feet thick. For all the effort involved in erecting them, they seemed to have little utilitarian use. They could not have prevented the entrance of human beings, nor served as a barrier against sheep and goats, which could easily have clambered over them. I believe that these walls, built perhaps in pre-Nabataean times, marked off an age-old sacred enclosure—a "holy mountain."

As I examined and reexamined the walls around Site 367, however, it appeared likely that they were Nabataean in origin and could not be earlier. They were closely related in form and manner of construction to some of the lateral walls which protected innumerable, horizontally terraced wadis. It was while considering this fact that the answer to the meaning of this particular enclosure came to me. The slightly inclined expanse of this wall-enclosed hilltop was used as if it had been the flat roof of a man-made building, which is commonly employed in semi-arid countries to collect the occasional rainwater, funneled then into cisterns beneath the building. The large cisterns underneath the buildings of the American School of Oriental Research in Jerusalem were filled each year in this fashion with a precious supply of soft water. On numerous occasions in past years, when the Jerusalem Municipality was unable to pump water to the Bab ez-Zahari Quarter of Jerusalem, in which we lived, we turned with equanimity to our cisterns, filled with fine water gathered in good time from our rooftops.

Airplane views of the top and slopes of Site 367 confirmed this explanation. They showed, furthermore, that this wall-enclosed mesa still serves its original purpose in part. Its natural runoff, stemming from the few annual rains still follows channels which were originally laid out probably by the Nabataeans. Flowing into small watercourses, which rise farther down the slopes, the water is brought down in turn to the terraced wadi below. The intricate relationship between walled hilltop and channels leading from there to tributary stream-beds, which join the terraced wadi bending around the base of its hill, becomes clear enough if one takes the trouble to follow it through from beginning to end. The Nabataeans did. They established the relationship. The water collected this way percolates into the soil of the terraced plots, and remains there many months a year. It enables even untended bushes and plants which grow in them to remain green during long periods of absolute drought.

But this by no means exhausted the ingenuity and indefatigability of the Nabataeans in collecting rainwater wherever it fell and cultivating the soil however inhospitable it appeared to be. They sought out drops of moisture with the same eagerness that hunters display when stalking game. They were motivated by the drive to survive in difficult surroundings and under the most inclement conditions. They knew how to take nature at its worst and make it yield blessings for mankind. Their endless effort, crowned more often than not by success, was to make wheat or barley or grapevines grow where none had ever been planted before and to tap or to collect supplies of water where none was known previously to exist. It has not always been easy to fathom the reasons for all their undertakings.

For generations, people have been baffled by the thousands of rows of low mounds of small stones heaped up by the Nabataeans in various places in the Negev. The proximity of many of the mounds to the half dozen Nabataean-Byzantine cities there have brought them to general attention. Best known are the ones on the slopes of Mishrefeh on the way to the Nabataean-Byzantine site of Isbeita. On the lower slopes of the above mentioned, great wall-enclosed mesa of Site 367, we noticed hundreds of rows of these small stone mounds. They are called *teleilat el-anab* in Arabic, which means "the hillocks for grapevines." That name is derived from the popular notion that they served to collect the dew, and reduce evaporation from the soil, and that grapevines were therefore trellissed over them to obtain the maximum amount of moisture. No proof of this has ever been adduced, and we doubt whether it can be.

Certain characteristics of these small mounds can now definitely be listed, which on the one hand militate against the theory that they were once employed to facilitate viticulture, and on the other hand point to the use which we think was made of them. They are always on slopes; always, so far as our experience goes, on stretches of land completely covered with pebbles of flint or limestone or sandstone; and, most significantly, they are always located above wadi beds which were elaborately terraced by the Nabataeans. Although the Nabataeans, and the Byzantines after them, were very much and very successfully concerned with the growing of grapes in the Negev, it is impossible to believe that they preferred for that purpose the poorest of soils on slopes which were thickly carpeted with pebbles. The only other possible answer lies in the connection of these *teleilat el-anab* with the terraced wadis below them, as Evanari and his colleagues in Israel were the first to point out.

The purpose of the rows upon rows of the *teleilat el-anab* was to deflect every possible drop of rainwater on and between them to predetermined goals. The idea was to permit the minimum of rainwater to sink into the pebble-covered slopes on which nothing could be grown anyway, and to channel the maximum of it to the cultivable wadis below. Smooth paths were cleared thus for the free flow of the rainwater, much of which would otherwise have clung to the myriads of small stones spread over the surface of the ground. Piling them up into long rows of small mounds was much simpler, cheaper and more practicable than grooving the hillsides in order to catch the water. Had that been done, there would have been danger of both stones and soil being washed down from the slopes and deposited on the terraced fields in the wadis below. It was to safeguard against such contingencies, that the great lateral walls were almost always constructed paralleling the banks of the terraced wadis.

The rows of *teleilat el-anab* can be understood only as another means in the full list of numerous methods employed by the Nabataeans to attain their goal of diverting as much runoff rainwater as possible onto and into their terraced fields. Sometimes, in their stead or also in conjunction with them, continuous rows of piled-up stones were used for the same purpose. Meticulously arranged in accordance with the contour lines of the hilltops and slopes, they converged on collecting channels which brought the water to the cultivated fields in the wadi beds. On the slightly rolling hilltops south of Qetsiot near Nitsanah, close to the Sinai border, we found several square miles of these water-gathering devices.[1] Many years, if not generations of carefully planned labor must have gone into their construction. One stands in awe of the Nabataeans and Byzantines, who thus impressed whole ranges of utterly barren, pebble-covered hilltops and slopes into service as catchment basins, to help collect as much as possible of the extremely limited annual rainfall and bring it to the terraced wadi beds and banks below them.

It is only when they are seen as serving as channels for the collection and diversion of rainwater,[2] that the *teleilat el-anab* on the slopes below Mishrefeh or the hill of Site 367 make any sense. As such, they do make abundant sense, because it can be clearly seen that they are located on the pebble-strewn slopes directly above the terraced wadi bed. A series of clearly defined conduits is visible, especially from the air, which collected water from the rows of *teleilat el-anab* and conveyed it through master channels to the terraced fields in the wadi-bed. The end sections of the master channels no longer exist, but could be retraced through surveying efforts.

[1] Palmer in his *The Desert of Exodus*, 1872, pp. 286, 304, 312, has made mention of them in this area.
[2] Proof for this was first furnished by Tadmor, Evanari, Shanan and Hillel in 1957, in their article "The Ancient Desert Agriculture of the Negev," KTAVIM 8:1-2, pp. 127-151.

THE NABATAEANS

These *teleilat el-anab*, however, formed only a single part of the grandiose, water conservation scheme perfected by the Nabataeans and maintained by the Byzantines to enable them in larger numbers than would otherwise have been possible to live in and off the Negev. At Site 367, this scheme manifests itself in descending order from the top of the hill down, as follows: a) walled hilltop serving as major catchment area; b) minor tributaries on slopes immediately below it, to which its runoff water was led at first; c) *teleilat el-anab;* d) terraced wadis; e) interconnecting channels leading from the top to the bottom and tying them all together.

You can see how much thought and care and work had to be expended before even a single, comparatively small, but nevertheless quite complex water and soil conservation scheme such as the one centering about hill 367, could be completed. There was much that had to be done before the work itself could actually be started. A master plan had to be drawn up, in which each part of the entire scheme was given its appointed time and place. The hilltops and slopes had to be contour mapped or studied, a comprehensive knowledge of the frequency and force of the winter and spring rains and floods had to be acquired, and a solution of all the engineering problems involved, dealing with everything from angles of slopes to widths and heights of terrace walls, had to be arrived at. Long experience was required to establish whether or not the soil was fertile enough for crops or whether or not it could retain underground moisture. The Nabataeans and Byzantines apparently never built dams over porous rock and completely permeable soil, although as much cannot be said for their modern successors.

When the soil and water conservation scheme centering about hill 367 was completed, it helped bring water to a limited section of the terraced bed of the Wadi Hafir below it, which was about a mile and a half long and a third of a mile wide. I estimate that in order to supplement the water obtained from the few annual freshets which rushed down the natural channel of the wadi bed each year, and which were forced to deposit tribute on each terraced plot, the Nabataeans tapped an area around this particular wadi section of some sixteen square miles. This included terracing every branch wadi which led down to it, and utilizing the top of hill 367 as a catchment basin. One can understand, therefore, how an agricultural civilization could flourish in Nabataean and Byzantine times in the Negev, in spite of the fact that only several miserly inches of rain fell there each year.

The labors of the Nabataeans in this instance and in countless others in the Negev and elsewhere created survival values, which enabled long generations of human beings to wrest a hard living from the reluctant soil.

"He Built Towers in the Wilderness and Hewed Out Many Cisterns"

The power of Judah in the Negev from the time of Solomon on depended upon the fortresses it built there and upon the cisterns it dug. The fame of Uzziah, under whose energetic rule Judah regained much of the glory, the territory and the military and economic strength it had enjoyed under Solomon, rested upon the fact that "he built towers in the wilderness and hewed out many cisterns, for he had much cattle . . . and he loved husbandry" (II Chronicles 26:10). But for every cistern dug by Judaean kings in the Negev, the Nabataeans must have dug half a hundred or more. There is no counting their number, because they bent the entire landscape to their purpose of collecting and storing water. Everywhere we roamed throughout the Negev, we found whole ranges of hills garlanded with channels to help capture the water of the brief rains and store it in underground treasure chambers. Sometimes, like a pendant jewel suspended from a necklace, we would find a great cistern lying in the bosom of a hill, with two channels curving down to it from opposite directions.

The cisterns were legion in number and of various sizes and shapes. Some, of impressive dimensions, were covered over. Their roofs rested on arched supports to prevent evaporation under the desert sun, whose rays beat down unimpeded through a moistureless atmosphere. Others nestled in natural hollows, with the inner topsides of their stone facings showing wrinkles of usage, worn deeply by the ropes of the drawers of water. Large and small cisterns and reservoirs hewn out of impermeable rock were common, too. There were also numerous others, whose sides were coated with layers of plaster, firmed with bits of pottery, and sometimes overlaid with stone block or pebble facings. Numerous natural caves were enlarged into subterranean reservoirs, with free-standing pillars being left to support the extended roofs. And almost always, by the sides or in the vicinity of these cisterns and reservoirs can be found fragments of pottery, testifying to the periods of their employment.

Much of the length of the Wadi Ramliyeh (Abdah) is pitted with the remains of great cisterns gouged out of the chalk rock of its sides, and swiftly filled when intact from the freshets that on occasion race through it. One of them is as serviceable today as it was in Nabataean times. It is refilled each year by the annual floods, and is made use of daily by the Bedouins of the district to water their flocks. It is directly opposite the great Nabataean-Byzantine city of Abdah. When we first came upon this cistern, a Bedouin girl was drawing water through an aperture in the rock slope above it, which formed its roof, just as her sisters in service had done some two thousand years ago. The main access to the cistern was through a front portal to the top of an inside staircase, which led down into the water. Standing on the top step, we could discern, as our eyes became accustomed to the gloom, a great, supporting pillar rising out of the water and bearing the weight of the ceiling. On its front side was embossed a representation of the Nabataean deity Dushara (Dionysus). It resembled one of the two tablets of stone, such as those on which the Ten Commandments are commonly inscribed. This is the god who was worshipped by the Nabataeans at Petra in the form of an unhewn, four-cornered, black stone, as I have already said, and is reminiscent of the one which is still the object of Moslem adoration at Mecca.

A Greek cross, with part of a Greek inscription on either side of it, was superimposed upon a Dushara relief on a pillar in a cistern of similar type to the one above. There was another cistern of much the same size almost immediately next to it. The whole sense of the sacred, connected with water as the source of life, was caught in the six letters of the single Greek word, whose syllables were separated by the Christian symbol. It read BOEΘON (Boethon), which may be translated as "the Savior" or "the Helper." There were other inscriptions, too, on this pillar, some in fairly modern Arabic, but none of comparable importance. The miracle of water and the pathos of man's struggle for survival and the nature of his relationship to God as the fountainhead of all being, are caught up in that single word of Boethon. It is resonant with the confidence of a passage in the New Testament, which reads: "So that with good courage we may say, the Lord is my Helper [Boethos]; I will not fear. . . ." (Hebrews 13:6).

The necessity of hewing out cisterns or at least of cleaning out and repairing and replastering many of the ancient ones, is being ever more fully appreciated by the modern inhabitants of the Negev. Experience has already taught them that they cannot maintain themselves otherwise. We came across an excellent one, which was still comparatively intact after the passage of centuries, but had been almost completely choked up with deposits of silt. The young settlers of nearby Sedei Boqer were removing seemingly endless numbers of buckets of debris from it. They had already repaired the stone-banked channel twisting down to it over a chain of four connecting hills. Replastered and watertight, this cistern can easily be filled each year by the runoff of one or two rains, and will provide an excellent reserve supply of water.

We descended the rock-hewn staircase leading down into it, to find that it was much larger than we had suspected from the surface above. It had obviously been repaired on several occasions in earlier times, and seems originally to have been carved out of a natural cave. Two great pillars had been left standing to uphold the roof. Each of them bore a Dushara niche and was scored with masons' marks, Byzantine crosses and tribal *wasm* signs. A feeling of wonderment and awe overcame us as we looked about. The pillars had been transformed by the Nabataeans into altars, to which their reverence had been addressed. The young men we saw working there might have been acolytes performing ritual tasks. The steps we descended gave access to what seemed to have become a sanctuary. It was indeed proper, in this underground chamber and others like it, for the Nabataeans to affix the semblance of one of their deities and for the Byzantines to incise and hallow the name of God.

"He Led Them Also by a Straight Path"

Not every canyon could be dammed, every dry creek bed terraced, every hollow have a cistern dug into it, nor every cave be enlarged into an underground reservoir. Some of the larger wadis in the Negev, particularly on the east side of its major watershed, were of such a wild nature that not even the Nabataeans could dragoon them into the service of agriculture. Their main importance lay in the passageways they afforded for caravan traffic. One of the routes most heavily traveled from early antiquity on lay between Petra in Transjordan and the Nabataean-Byzantine city of Abdah in the highlands of the Negev. Between them lay the great chasm of the Wadi Arabah, the narrow canyon of the Wadi Siq and the weird depression of the Wadi Raman (Machtesh Ramon).

To cross them was a formidable undertaking. The journey with slow moving pack animals could easily take a week or more. Regular camping and watering places had to be available. We found a whole series of them, some of which showed clear evidence of use in the Age of Abraham and others in the period of the Judaean kingdom. All of them had been utilized in the Nabataean, Roman and Byzantine periods.

The litter of centuries marks the ragged sequence of civilizations, as they follow one another like a line of elephants, each one holding on to the tail of his predecessor. Gaps appeared in the parade when the connections between them were broken. Near the top edge of the cliff, overlooking the blotched landscape of the Wadi Raman, are the ruins of a small, Nabataean way-station, known today as Khirbet Neqb el-Hamleh. Crossing the broken uplands of the Qa'at en-Nefkh from Abdah en route to the Arabah, we paused there, as had countless other caravans before us in the ancient past. Among the tumble-down building-stones were scattered thousands of fragments of exquisite Nabataean pottery and glassware. To an almost constant stream of transients food and drink must have been served in the original vessels of which they were parts. From the vantage points of the *khirbeh,* one has a wonderful view over the great crater of the Wadi Raman (Machtesh Ramon), which lies several hundred feet farther down. Its mottled beauty of vivid browns and purples, of reds and blacks makes it look like a tremendous palette, upon which large blobs of sharply contrasting colors have indiscriminately been squeezed out.

Using a steep, zigzag path leading down along the face of the nearly sheer cliff wall, we reached the corrugated floor of the brilliantly hued basin. No crops have ever been planted there. Its primeval virginity has never been disturbed. A narrow track, pounded smooth and clean by the footsteps of many generations, leads through its wilderness. We followed it without hesitation, being certain that if we continued with it southeastward, we would find ourselves in the Wadi Arabah. Furthermore, it stood to reason that it would bring us to forgotten and, frequently, completely razed sites of distant years, where passersby had halted in the course of their journeys. The direction of this trail, which sometimes splits in two, only soon to draw together again, was determined by the topography of the land. There could be no other travel route in this area. Its course had been predetermined ever since the earth, eons ago, cooled into its present folds and creases.

"He led them also by a straight path that they might go to a city of habitation" (Psalms 107:7). We moved along the narrow catwalk of the path which knifed its way across the desolate, stony plain. Before we were fully aware of what was happening, we found that we had reached the remains of an ancient settlement, whose existence seemed completely incongruous in this strange environment. What we saw on the top of a low hill was the sorry debris of a former hostelry that had been abandoned so long ago as practically to have merged with its surroundings. Three things proclaimed why and when this disintegrated inn had first been called into existence. The first was the almost unbelievable presence of several water holes. The second was the existence of a widely strewn mass of Nabataean potsherds. The third was the presence of a forlorn group of weathered and broken milestones, that reminded one of some tattered castaways on a deserted island.

The empty socket in the base of one of them gave it the appearance of an eyeless creature. It stared at us with the unseeing gaze of vanished glory. The pivot of lead in it originally, which bound it to the pillar drum above it, had been removed by passing Bedouins to be melted down into bullets. Yielding to a whim to reverse for a moment the effect of tidal forces of the past, we put one of the fallen milestones back again into an erect position. Almost a millennium and a half had passed since it had fallen or been knocked over. Some miles farther on, we came across another collection of these disfigured and dislodged road markers. They seem to have gravitated together to share their common misery. Originally serving the needs of heavy caravan traffic, they became tombstones of an empire that passed away like a desert mirage.

It was obvious that we were on the Roman road leading from Beersheba to Abdah and thence via the Wadi Raman and the Wadi Arabah to Aila on the Gulf of Aqabah. Remnants of the curbstones on either side of the wide roadway were discernible. The Bedouin path we were following bisected it lengthwise as if it were a dividing traffic line. Occasionally, it bent away from it, but always returned to it sooner or later. The forces of topography have compelled the roads of all periods to follow the same directions. For all practical purposes, they may be thought of as having been built on top of each other. For example, the main, central trunk road along the length of Transjordan deviates little from Trajan's highway which led from Damascus to Aila. In earlier, Biblical times, the Royal Road, which the Edomites and Moabites forbade the Israelites to cross, had much the same alignment. And the Kings of the East of Genesis 14, in their journey from Syria to Sinai and back again, undoubtedly followed the same general track. We found the ruins of villages they had destroyed alongside of it, which were never again reoccupied.

Witness Mounds

Sometimes, a track which may have been of minor significance in one period, assumes major importance in another. That proved to be the case in the Negev with regard to the Darb es-Sultani (the Road of the Sultan). Of secondary rank in Nabataean to Byzantine times, it came into its own for reasons we cannot fathom when Turkish rule extended from Asia Minor to Arabia and Egypt. Crossing the uninhabitable hill country between the two deep faults of the Wadi Hathirah (Machtesh Gadol) and the Wadi Raman (Machtesh Ramon), it connects the spring of Ain Wehbeh (Ain Yahav) in the Arabah with the modern settlement of Sedei Boqer, several miles north of Abdah, in the Central Negev. It was a shorter and more direct, but even less pleasant route than the Kurnub-Beersheba one to the north of it and the Wadi Siq-Wadi Raman-Abdah one to the south of it. The eastern ends of both of these latter routes terminated in the Wadi Arabah, the northern one at the spring of Ain Hosb and the southern one at the well of Moyet Awad.

At several places along the Darb es-Sultani, there are mounds of stones, which are related in kind to the "witness heaps" erected by the Israelites to commemorate their entry into the Promised Land. It is still common practice for Bedouins or pilgrims to raise up such mounds when they arrive within sight of their goals or when they complete various stages of their journeys. The passers-by hurl stones at given points as thanksgiving offerings or, at times, as a means of warding off evil spirits that might impede or prevent their further progress. Such cairns, however, are not to be confused with the Nabataean *teleilat el-anab,* which, as we have seen, were water-gathering devices. Larger stones are generally used for the "witness heaps" which have greater dimensions than for the *teleilat el-anab* mounds and are never arranged in symmetrical rows. It must be a wonderful thing to release feelings of joy or of fear by flinging a good-sized stone at something and helping thus raise a monument to one's sentiments.

Then and Now

The highway through the Wadi Raman was heavily traveled in Nabataean, Roman and Byzantine times, as well as in earlier Judaean and still earlier Abrahamitic times. It was used in the dim recesses of prehistory, too, to judge from our discovery in it of worked flint tools of the Neolithic and even remoter Palaeolithic period. There is therefore no inconsistency in the presence of Nabataean sherds and Roman milestones at the same places in the Wadi Raman. Actually, their relationship is that of older and younger contemporaries. The independent kingdom that the Nabataeans had so capably sculptured out of the raw materials of favorable circumstances, was, as we have seen, conquered by the Romans in A.D. 106. It was absorbed then into the new Province of Arabia, which included also the Cities of the Decapolis beyond Jordan and parts of Syria as far north as the mountains of the Jebel Hauran. But the Nabataeans did not forthwith disappear off the face of the earth after the eclipse of their political autonomy. It took another hundred years and more, before the stream of their cultural distinctiveness merged indistinguishably with the sea of their general Hellenistic-Roman environment.

The Nabataeans continued to fashion their own distinctive pottery, from statues of their gods, build temples to house them, call into being dams, terraces, cisterns and reservoirs, and carry on intensive agricultural and commercial pursuits. At the same time, the Roman rulers instituted certain changes. Among them was the incorporation of the Nabataean travel routes into the far-flung network of their own road system. They set up milestones at regular intervals alongside them. Otherwise, they were content to let well enough alone, provided that peace was maintained and Roman economic and imperial interests were served, or at least not interfered with. They permitted the peoples they subdued to cultivate their regular pursuits and languages and deities. They even suffered them at times to continue with their own political systems, as long as they remained faithful to Rome.

The main halting place for caravans passing through the Wadi Raman during the Nabataean to Byzantine periods was at Qasr Muheileh. It is located on a low hill, which is completely encircled by converging wadis. It commands the approaches to the outlet of the Wadi Raman through the narrow and tortuous Wadi Siq. This, in turn, leads down to the perennial water of the Moyet Awad and to the large Nabataean site of Moa near it on the west side of the Wadi Arabah. The importance of Qasr Muheileh is emphasized by the fact that it is almost exactly midway between Moa and the imposing Nabataean-Byzantine hill city of Abdah. Although, at first glance, Qasr Muheileh seems to be just a mass of crumbling, sandstone blocks, piled indiscriminately on top of each other, the outline of this collapsed caravanserai can still be made out. It is about forty-five yards square, with blocks of rooms facing an inner court. The south side is the best preserved one.

The chief reason for the existence of Qasr Muheileh was the presence of water in the wadi bed below it. The underground moisture, even in the dry season, still nourishes along its sides clumps of reeds and shrubbery. Seen from the air, they protrude like fringes of hair on a bald man's head. The entire spread of minor creek beds throughout the length and most of the width of the Wadi Raman merges with the beginning of the Wadi Siq that commences below the base of the hill of Qasr Muheileh. The slight rains of the deep crater are thus drained to this particular point. They form a subsurface reservoir there, that the ancients learned early to tap. There can be no question but that this meeting place of wadis and of water was frequented long before the advent of the Nabataeans by Judaeans and by still earlier Canaanite shepherds and travelers, although no trace of their presence remains.

When we arrived on the scene, we saw that water was being drawn from one of several crude wells. Around it, waiting their turn to drink, in casually disciplined order, were numerous sheep and goats. A dozen or so Bedouins squatted in a circle, preoccupied with their endless chitchat, while several ragamuffin children and one woman in black did the work. A couple of men arose to greet and join us, as we examined the ruins and general area and collected quantities of the Nabataean and later sherds strewn on the surface. We tried to explain their significance to them. They and their families live meagerly in the recesses of the Wadi Raman, almost completely dependent for their sustenance upon their herds and flocks. Given their daily meed of water, these animals thrive on the hard crusts of tough bushes that flourish during the exceedingly infrequent and brief rains and outlast the long intervals of dryness in between. More succulent is the shrubbery sustained by the underground moisture in the wadi beds. The art of making graceful water jars out of clay turned on a potter's wheel and fired into permanent shape in a kiln, which was practiced so expertly by the Nabataean and Byzantine occupants of this site, is completely foreign to the modern Bedouins who have inherited their places.

Near the water hole, we saw what seemed to be a small group of goats lying on the ground, huddled together in strange stillness. A few steps in their direction, and it quickly became apparent that although their bodies were full and even swollen, there was no life in them. When they had been slaughtered, their skins had been stripped off and sewn together again, with only the aperture of the neck left open to be tied closed at will. As inert containers, they served their masters even in death. A piece of burlap thrown across their bodies to protect their fill of living waters against the burning sun, was their constantly replaced shroud.

Pathway and Portal

After one leaves the Wadi Raman, the ancient highway leading east-southeastward from Qasr Muheileh toward the Wadi Arabah can be traced through the narrow canyon of the Wadi Siq. It has been hewn into the earth by the occasional flash floods of countless years. The abundance of its underground moisture explains the unusual greenery and thickets of shrubs and bushes that appear in it. Several springs are conveniently spaced along its length. At each of them, the Nabataeans, and others both before and after them, halted in the course of their journeys. There were ruins of ancient caravanserais at two of them, where colorful Nabataean sherds were particularly prominent. The first spring we encountered, half-choked by wild plants, had once been excellently housed in a basin of smoothly cut limestone blocks, some of which were still in place.

Further surprises were waiting for us in the Wadi Siq. Chief among them was the important way-station of Qasr Wadi Siq. It is some seven miles away from Qasr Muheileh. As we studied its remains, we were lost once more in admiration of the Nabataeans, whose presence and initiative here were documented by thousands of Nabataean sherds. It is a small, square, fairly intact sandstone block structure, located on a tongue of high ground, overlooking the confluence of five separate wadis. The largest of the wadis is known as the Wadi Qreiq, which comes from the south. Smudging the earth, a short distance in front of it, are the outlines of a larger, completely dismantled caravanserai. To this day, the Bedouin track leads as directly and clearly to it, as did the Nabataean and Roman one before it.

Across the way to the east, and separated from it by the junction of several small wadis, rises a razorback ridge, on whose highest point stands a small, stone watch-tower of uncertain origin. It commands a view of the approaches to Qasr Wadi Siq from all directions. Qasr Wadi Siq represented not only a fixed station on a heavily traveled caravan route, but also a permanent military post, which was located there to regulate and protect the flow of traffic. A small garrison must have been stationed there all the year round. To furnish it with an extra source of water, other than could be obtained by digging in the wadi bed, the Nabataeans built for its occupants an above-ground, covered cistern. Nobody but they or the Byzantines would have had the skill or temerity to do it.

They constructed it on a bench above a side gully, immediately south of Qasr Wadi Siq. Located at the bottom of a hill slope there, it caught and held the precious runoff rainwater that the Nabataeans channelled to it. A well built aqueduct, formed in part of blocks of stone and in part hewn out of the native rock, conducted the seasonal flow into the cistern proper. From the outside, the cistern looks like a regular house. Its walls are from five to seven courses of limestone blocks above ground and vary in height from about eleven to fourteen feet. The roof, which is still largely intact, is made of long stone beams, and rests on three strong, stone vaults. An entrance way opens to the remains of a staircase, which led down to the water. The inside of the structure was completely plastered over. Some of the plaster is still visible, several layers thick. The passage of the centuries has not changed the capacity of this small reservoir to store water. When we visited it late one summer, the last of its yearly renewed supply had just been used up, leaving the silt soggy wet at the bottom of it.

Farther east, the Bedouin track abandons the growing discomfort of the increasingly precipitous Wadi Siq, and takes to the top of the rolling and split-up highland. For deceptive distances there are smooth stretches, which are completely blanketed with thin covers of myriads of dark-hued pebbles of various kinds. The track picks its way almost knowingly across them, as if with the inborn assurance of a homing pigeon. We clung to its smoothness as to a guideline, avoiding the sharp pointed stones that made walking on either side of it for long a trying experience. Soon, it led us to a T-shaped group of buildings, called Qasr Umm el-Qeseir by the Arabs, which means "the Castle Mother of Little Castles." They are planted at the very edge of the plateau. Below it, the landscape caves in, falling away in wild disorder down to the great cleft of the Wadi Arabah.

The buildings of Qasr Umm el-Qeseir were Nabataean in construction, having been added to and used until the end of the Byzantine period. After that, with no one seeing fit to keep them in a state of constant repair, they began to fall apart. No cisterns were visible, but some of them must exist under the debris of the collapsed walls. The original structure, enlarged subsequently by three sizeable additions, was much the same as Qasr Muheileh in the Wadi Raman. Depending on the direction of the journey, this was the first or last station of this particular travel route across the top of the Negev. Here one girded one's loins anew for the hard trip northwestward to Abdah and beyond, or for the no less difficult journey southeastward down to Nabataean Moa and Bir Madhkur on opposite sides of the Wadi Arabah, and then up to Petra in the eastern hill-country on the route to Arabia.

Gone are the shouting and smells of the caravans that once halted at Qasr Umm el-Qeseir. The pathway leading past it will, however, always be sought out as long as human beings live and travel in this part of the world. Some of them may be as energetic and creative as the Nabataeans, and others as unwittingly durable as the feckless nomads who tent beside their ruins. Much of the story of the creation of the earth and of the strivings of mankind can be read in the fossil-laden building blocks of this site and in the fragments of fine Nabataean and later pottery that can be found among them. The petrified conglomeration of primeval matter and sea creatures out of which buildings were constructed and the earthenware formed and fired by mortal men, bear a relationship to each other that is established in the wonder of the divine order.

They Drew on Rock

The artistic temperament of the Nabataeans did not always express itself with equal excellence, which is in accord with the normal order of things among any people. The high quality of much of their architecture, pottery and painting could naturally not be maintained by every section of the population. Apparently, however, even the lowliest Nabataean villager and shepherd and the roughest caravaneer often paused to translate the images of their concern into visible form. Occasionally, they scribbled a few words of prayer or memorial. Rock drawings or petroglyphs were their forte, blackened sandstone surfaces their medium and flint burins their tools.

It is not surprising, therefore, in view of the thickness of the settlement of the Nabataeans in the Negev and the constant passing of their caravans through it, that we and others should have found hundreds of Nabataean rock drawings and occasional inscriptions. Some of their writing was in Greek and Latin. There were numerous later rock drawings and inscriptions too. Some of these permanent and striking Nabataean billboards helped determine the location of several Nabataean sites and more particularly the direction of their travel routes. Experience taught us that the petroglyphs were usually to be found on outcroppings of dark sandstone. As a result, whenever we came across such formations, we stopped to examine them, and frequently found that they had been used as canvases for this folk art. It seems to have flourished especially in certain areas of the Negev.

One such area consisted of a long, narrow stretch, only a few miles wide, on either side of the much-traveled track that leads west-southwestward from the Nabataean metropolis of Abdah in the Central Negev highlands over an intervening watershed to the well of Bir el-Hafir and thence to the spring of Ain el-Qudeirat (Kadesh-barnea) and to that of the nearby Ain el-Qadeis in Sinai and beyond them to the Egyptian border. In Sinai, too, we know of the existence of many rock drawings reaching back from the present to Nabataean times.

There was another amazing concentration of rock drawings

photo: S. J. Schweig

FIG. 47. Nabataean sculptured relief of a gazelle from Qasr Rabbah in Trans-Jordan (see page 240).

FIG. 48. Part of mosaic floor of synagogue at Nirim in the northwestern Negev, showing lion and lioness flanking candelabra, with *lulav, ethrog* and *shofar* symbols visible below, and part of an Aramaic dedicatory inscription above (see pages 279-280).

FIG. 49. Canyon wall of Wadi Umm es-Sedeir in Sinai, near Elath, showing inscriptions AKRABOS and VICTORIA AUGC (Victoria Augusti Caesari), and candelabra with *lulav, ethrog,* and *shofar* symbols incised on it (see pages 282-283).

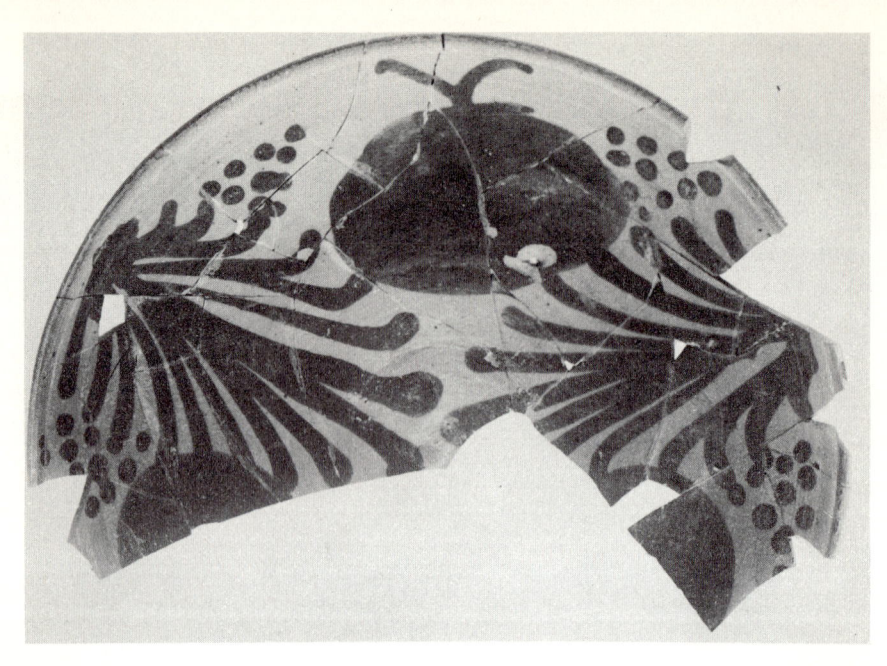

photos: S. J. Schweig

FIGS. 50 (a) and (b). Nabataean pottery from Khirbet Tannur, with palmette, pomegranate and grape designs in dark reddish-brown paint (see page 200).

photo: S. J. Schweig

Fig. 51. This relief, found at Khirbet Tannur, represents Tyche as guardian goddess of the city. She wears a crown representing a turreted wall, and is surrounded by a clockwise and counter-clockwise zodiac panel (see page 196).

photo: S. J. Schweig

FIG. 52. Nabataean Atargatis from Khirbet Tannur, with a veil of leaves covering her face and forehead (see page 197).

photo: S. J. Schweig

FIG. 53. Atargatis as fish goddess of fertility, from Khirbet Tannur (see page 196).

photos: S. J. Schweig

FIGS. 54 (a), (b), and (c). Grape and vine motif in Nabataean sculpture from Khirbet Tannur (see page 199).

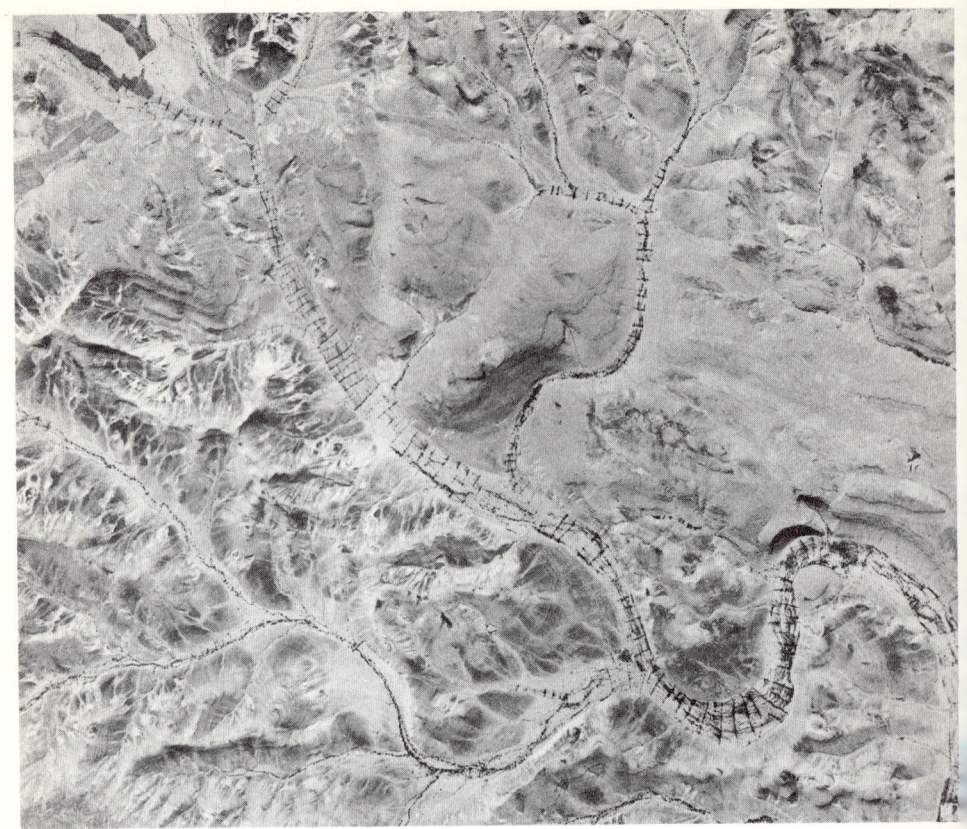

photo: Israeli Air Force

FIG. 55. Nabataean and Byzantine terracing in the Wadi Raviv and its tributaries, which incorporated earlier Judaean terracing. On a hilltop in the upper center are visible the remains of a rectangular Judaean fortress which commanded the junction of the Wadi Raviv with one of its branches (see pages 202, 214-215).

farther south in the Negev on the slopes and tops of the almost hopelessly barren range of high, truncated hills, called the Jebel Ideid (Har Geshur). A much used trail, employed from early antiquity on, passes below its west side. It is a continuation of the great north-south route, which, commencing at Beersheba, touches Abdah, links the wells of Biyar Ideid Umm Salih with those of Biyar Ideid es-Samawi, and skirts the hills of Jebel Ideid to the water holes of Thamilet es-Suweilmeh (Gerasa) in Sinai. Numerous trails converged there from southwestern Sinai and from the southernmost Negev, which threaded both to important centers of trade and settlement.

We found numerous Nabataean rock drawings in southern Transjordan too. As in the Negev, they occurred seldom in the heavily inhabited, agricultural districts. They were particularly common along the caravan trails and near the comparatively few springs and water holes in the great desert of Wadi Hismeh, which stretches from the southern base of the mountains of Edom into Arabia proper. They have been found there, for instance, in the vicinity of the spring of Ain Shellaleh in the Wadi Ramm, where a Nabataean temple devoted to the goddess, Allat, existed.

Together with George and Agnes Horsfield, we discovered a whole group of fascinating rock drawings at Kilwa, among the hills of the Jebel Tubaiq. That is situated in the southeasternmost corner of Transjordan, on the border of Arabia. A number of important roads met there. One led southward from Amman, the capital of Transjordan, to the history-soaked oasis of Teima. Another passed it going eastward from Aila, on the north shore of the Gulf of Aqabah, to the great oasis of Jauf, which is likewise in Arabia. The latter place marks the southern end of the economic and military lifeline through the long and shallow and wide Wadi Sirhan, that connected Nabataean Syria with Nabataean Arabia.

In other words, these rock drawings are to be found usually, although not exclusively, at sites along travel routes, and at burial places, way-stations and crossroads. The position and prominence of Jebel Ideid (Odeid), which of old may have had a certain sanctity attached to it, may explain why so many of them, together with occasional inscriptions, were chiseled into the blackened surfaces of its large sandstone boulders and smooth rock faces. There is, we think, a certain religious feeling reflected in them. It may be related to the fact that the shepherds, hunters, raiders and travelers, to whom most of them are to be attributed, did not have ready access to the fixed shrines and temples of their gods in lusher surroundings.

The basic, if not always conscious purpose of the homespun artists may have been to propitiate the spirits or gods, upon whom they felt their welfare depended. They turned to them for safety in travel, success in the chase, victory in battle and the blessings of fertility. That may explain why one generation after another persisted in chipping out their pictographs on the very same surfaces that had been used and reused many times before. Frequently, they were actually superimposed upon each other, resulting in a jumble of lines which are difficult and sometimes impossible to disentangle. The saving grace is that various periods of these rock drawings, even without accompanying inscriptions, can be separated both stylistically and by the different degrees of the darkness of the patina they acquire through centuries of weathering.

Many themes are treated in these rock drawings. There are helmeted warriors on foot with drawn swords. There are spearsmen mounted on camels and less often on horses, riding off to the *ghazzu*. Some of them are depicted hunting heavily antlered ibexes or short-horned gazelles, animals that can still be found in the Negev and in the eastern desert in Transjordan and Arabia. Extinction threatens them there because of modern hunting methods, but fortunately, their number in the Negev is increasing because of rigid game laws. The Nabataeans, and others before and after their time, must have encircled entire districts frequented by these animals and driven them ahead until they could kill them with their spears and arrows when they were half exhausted. The huntsmen of our own day, if that is what they should be called, adopt the same general method in remote desert areas, except that they are armed with high-powered rifles and ride the game down within narrowing circles of fast-moving jeeps.

A recurrent theme in the drawings is that of the nimrod with drawn bow and arrow, following his dog in hot pursuit of an ibex. One spirited scene shows a hunter on a galloping camel throwing his spear at an ostrich fleeing before him. This is not astonishing to one acquainted with this part of the world. As late as the nineteen thirties, ostriches were still being hunted in eastern Transjordan, where they now no longer exist. The physician of our expedition was given a pierced ostrich egg by a Bedouin as a gift for taking care of his broken finger.

There are other themes too. Among them is that of couples engaged in vigorous dances. They are represented with a simple skill that conveys a sense of passion and abandon, rather than being merely an expression of *joie de vivre*. In what seem to be chiefly post-Nabataean drawings, the male partner is drawn with a grossly exaggerated genital organ. This must be viewed from the relevancy of prevailing fertility ideas, rather than from the specious sophistication of related representations in such places as Roman Pompeii. There were also fairly numerous but invariably brief Nabataean, Thamudic and Arabic inscriptions, as well as some Greek and Latin ones. We also found petroglyphs of hands and feet, of games and tribal signs. Some of them belong to most recent times, as one can tell from the whiteness of their lines. Almost invariably, however, they are to be found on the same rock surfaces, on which much older drawings were originally incised.

The Chain of Connection

As one moves from the Nabataean period to modern times, there seems to be an almost steady decline in the composition and nature of the rock drawings. The best of them cannot, of course, be compared to the magnificent Nabataean murals in the lovely chapel of the "Painted House," which was hewn out of a canyon wall at Siq el-Bared, a suburb of Petra. A formidable and highly developed talent was in evidence there in the tapestry-like paintings of grapevines, flowers, birds, and graceful mythological figures of Eros, Pan, or either Cupid bearing off Psyche or Zeus carrying off Ganymede. By the same token, it would be folly to place any one of the Nabataean or later petroglyphs of ibexes or gazelles alongside the exquisite, sculptured relief of a gazelle from the Nabataean temple of Qasr Rabbah in Transjordan.

They are worlds apart, representing opposite poles of artistic ability and cultural attainments, yet they definitely belong to the same civilization. Its influence can be traced imperfectly through many succeeding centuries. One recalls the sculptures of Khirbet Mefjer, north of Jericho, and the paintings of Qeseir Amra in the eastern desert of Transjordan, both of which belong to the Omayyads of the eighth century A.D. There is a distant relationship between them and the sophisticated forms of Nabataean art of the first and second centuries A.D. The Nabataean rock drawings, however, were of a very different order. There is little connection between them and the lusty paintings, professionally executed, of buxom nudes and of dancing bears playing musical instruments, which titillated the effete Omayyad princes in their desert hunting lodges.

The untutored Nabataean rock drawings are by no means the earliest ones of their kind in the ancient Near East. On the sides of a small, Nubian sandstone hill in the Jebel Tubaiq in southeasternmost Transjordan were chiseled early prehistoric rock drawings, as we have mentioned above, which must have been familiar to thousands of Nabataean travelers. They, themselves, and their Thamudic and later successors, used the very same surfaces for their own pictographs, superimposing some of them on the very much earlier ones that they found there. One of the oldest Kilwa pictures, done about ten thousand years ago by some untrained wayfarer who passed this apparently sacred hillock, rivals in artistry the second century A.D. relief of the gazelle from Nabataean Qasr Rabbah.

It is a faithful and beautiful representation of a wounded ibex in flight. The burin marks are clearly visible, with the lower end of each stroke being slightly deeper than the upper end. The full gracefulness of the delicate animal has been caught with a few simple lines. Nostrils and neckline, horns rising and curving back to tapering points which almost touch the back, and a foreleg delicately uplifted, are among the features depicted. It is done in so excellent a fashion as to give the drawing a sense of vibrant reality. The head of the ibex is raised, and from its mouth stream two lines of blood.

Another of the most interesting of the rock drawings at Kilwa represents a hunting scene or possibly an animal being sacrificed to one of the gods. There is an elongated, narrow-headed, horned ox, superimposed over several smaller and previously incised drawings of some ibexes. Squatting beneath it is the highly stylized figure of a man, who is thrusting a spear into it. The squatting figure resembles one of the prehistoric, Fezzan rock drawings in North Africa.

And so the chain of connection can be traced from land to land, from continent to continent, and from age to age. The bleak surroundings of Kilwa were typical of the Arabia from where the Nabataeans had come. Even Arabia, however, was never an island isolated to itself. Many cultural influences from abroad left their impress upon its peoples. The rock drawings which the Nabataeans encountered there must have impelled them to copy them after their own fashion. One of the recurrent miracles of history is contained in the fact that stemming from this bleak background, the Nabataeans were able at a favorable juncture of events to create a unique civilization, full of achievement and color. When it was overwhelmed in due course of time by forces stronger than it could cope with, it did not just fade away. It transmitted not only its wealth of possessions and accomplishments but also its warmth and creative spirit to those who took over its inheritance. Much of the brilliance of the Byzantine civilization in the Negev may be attributed to the legacy left it by the pagan Nabataeans. Indeed, as we shall see, their successors in the Negev were predominantly their own, Christianized descendants.

CHAPTER VIII

THE CROSS AND THE CANDELABRA

The Turn of the Wheel

The changes resulting from the absorption of the Nabataean kingdom into the Roman Province of Arabia were drastic in their ultimate effect, although hardly noticeable at first. This does not mean that the Romans were unappreciative of the importance of the Negev. Nothing could be farther from the truth, as attested, for instance, by the fine Roman highway that led from Beersheba, via the Wadi Raman, to Aila on the Gulf of Aqabah. As late as the end of the third century A.D., they transferred the Tenth Legion (Legio X Fretensis) from Jerusalem to Aila, the better to guard against the unceasing danger of nomadic incursions from the south. On the whole, as I have pointed out before, the new overlords interfered as little as possible in the affairs of the Negev, leaving them largely in the hands of its former masters. Nevertheless, things could not remain the same, as they had when the Nabataeans were determining the overall policy that governed the various regions of their kingdom.

Imperceptibly, a decline set in, resulting from innovations established by the Romans elsewhere. Far-ranging imperial interests necessarily took precedence over the welfare of the Negev. No other city there would ever again be named after a Nabataean king, as was Abdah after Obodas. In deified form, he may have been worshipped in the temple which was raised there probably over his tomb. Stephen of Byzantium, of the early sixth century A.D., refers to an Obodas cult in this Nabataean city of the Negev. Which one of the four Nabataean kings called Obodas served as the eponym of Abdah, is still uncertain, as I have already said. Perhaps either Obodas III or Obodas IV.

With the extension "of the immense majesty of Roman peace" to the borders of Parthia, the capital of the new Province of Arabia was established at Bosra in southern Syria. As a result, the cultural and commercial importance of Petra gradually dwindled and finally disappeared. Other market centers rose to compete successfully with it for the rich caravan trade that had brought prosperity to it. The entire Negev suffered as a consequence, losing much of the transit traffic that flowed across it between Petra and the Mediterranean. No longer were the precious imports from the Persian Gulf, Iranian plateau, India and even far-off China sent mainly through Arabia to Nabataean entrepreneurs for further distribution, with much of it following various routes through the Negev.

Instead, many of the valuable commodities of the east were assembled at Ctesiphon on the Tigris River. From there, they were dispatched ever more regularly to Dura on the Euphrates River, or in an almost direct line west-northwestward to the mushrooming emporium of Palmyra (Biblical Tadmor). Situated at an oasis in the central desert of Syria, Palmyra reached full bloom in a very short time. Like an iris after the spring rains, it shot up suddenly to mature beauty. It faded fast, too. While its glory lasted, great caravans fanned out from its gates, bringing the eagerly sought-after products of the east to Emessa, Damascus and Bosra in Syria, and to Gerasa in Transjordan, and from these and other distributing centers to many places along the Mediterranean coast to Phoenicia and Palestine.

The gradual eclipse of Nabataean rule and civilization was an attendant phase of many shifts of power, which at first advanced the growth and then contributed to the eventual disintegration of the Roman empire. The entire Hellenistic Orient was surging forward to renewed strength. The process of recapturing much of its ancient glory was furthered by the weakening of the moral fiber and of the economic and military power of Rome in the west. Many factors over a period not of generations but of centuries heated the furnace of events, in which history was being fashioned into new shapes. Parthians from the east, barbarians from the north and nomads from the south pressed unremittingly against the flanks of Roman dominion. The contagious fervor of the new religious movement centering about the person of the gentle Jew, Jesus, came increasingly into conflict with the sophisticated paganism of the Mediterranean cultural area, and proved in the end to be more than a match for it.

A New Constellation in the East

Affairs of world-shaking importance, directed from the citadel of authority on the banks of the Tiber, were immeasurably influenced by developing Christianity. The convictions of its founders, who had been baptized in the purifying waters of the Jordan, penetrated into the strongholds of many countries and into the fastnesses of innumerable hearts. The day came when the emperor of Rome accepted the new faith not only for himself but as the official religion of his entire realm. Seeking a new atmosphere for the growth of the Church and keenly mindful at the same time of a multitude of mundane advantages which had nothing remotely to do with religious interests, he moved the capital of his government to Byzantium. By this act, Constantine I, as he was first called, or Constantine the Great, as he was later known, profoundly affected the course of history. Henceforth, Constantinople, as it soon became known, assumed a position of importance in the annals of civilization comparable to that of Athens and Rome. None of them, however, could ever really dispute the abiding supremacy of Jerusalem.

The elevation of Byzantium to a position of preeminence inaugurated an economic and cultural renaissance in the lands extending from Asia Minor to North Africa. It was accompanied by glittering opulence and unbridled despotism. Absolutism of authority was advanced and practiced as being divine in origin. The impact of the Church manifested itself in every phase of activity. Indeed, it became difficult and even impossible to determine where temporal power ended and religious rule began. Economic and ecclesiastical interests were inextricably interwoven. Bishops acted as governors, priests resided in palaces, and kings assumed that they were the elect of the Lord. And once again, as on repeated occasions in the past, there were those who could not abide this confusion of man's presumptions and God's will, and who rebelled against the fatness and profligacy that were characteristic of public and private life. Many of the truly pious fled to the simplicity and rigors of the desert, or immured themselves behind the walls of self-imposed privation.

It was also an epoch of intellectual ferment, artistic accomplishment, and material gain. Great riches were amassed by a redoubtable few, among whom the clerical garb was common. The rise in the fortunes of the Roman east, which commenced with the reign of Constantine I, A.D. 288-337, reached its climax in the reign of the wise and able and harsh Justinian, who ruled from A.D. 527 to 565. These dates need to be noticed. They mark the beginning and end of a period of high achievement, much of it on a grandiose scale. It exercised an enduring influence upon the art and literature and religion of the western world.

Subsequently, it became the inevitable turn of the rejuvenated state to be again on the wane and to sink forever below the horizon of the past. Sasanian Persia struck again and again with body blows that were increasingly hurtful. And not long thereafter, early in the seventh century A.D., the restless and constantly probing Arabs of the desert swept into the lands of the Sown, with Byzantium no longer strong enough to ward them off. It was the repetition of an old story. Fused together, furthermore, into an irresistible force by the fires of Islam, the Mohammedan armies planted the standards of their power and faith upon the embattlements of Christian government and worship, stopping at first at the edge of the Mediterranean. Then, after a lull of centuries, the fury of their evangelism by the sword swept them as far east as India and as far west as Spain. Ultimately, they were driven back to narrower confines, which, however, still remain continental in scope.

Renewal and Efflorescence

The very prosperity achieved by Byzantium and the empire it adorned made it the envy of its neighbors and the object of attack at the slightest manifestation of weakness. It collapsed before the sweeping imposition of the peace of Islam. While it lasted, the flowering of the Byzantine civilization may be attributed to many factors, aside from the burgeoning of Christianity. Among the most important of them was the intensification, and in certain areas the restoration, of commerce between the east and the west to their mutual enrichment. Constantine's new capital and other cities of his domain as far south as the Negev became the beneficiaries of Palmyra's eclipse at the end of the third century A.D.

The spectacular rise of Palmyra to great wealth and power,

after replacing Petra as the greatest trade emporium of Syria and Arabia, misled its rulers and merchant princes to attempt to carve out an empire of their own. They chose the wrong period, for they came into conflict with a resurgent Rome. In the end, Palmyra was so completely destroyed by the Roman emperor, Aurelian, that it never again recovered the high estate it briefly enjoyed, although it was restored in part on several later occasions. Palmyra's loss soon redounded to the Negev's gain.

In the course of the further expansion of Byzantium's authority and interests, the Negev experienced an upsurge in its fortunes. The decline it had suffered following the conquest of the Nabataean kingdom near the beginning of the second century A.D. by Trajan had not been of sufficient intensity and duration to change the face of the land. The terraces and dams and cisterns and other water-gathering devices had remained intact. The population had dwindled little, if at all, and the cultivation of the soil had been continued intensively. The chief difference now was that once again heavily laden caravans traversed its ancient roads. If anything, the density of the permanent population in the Negev became heavier in the Byzantine than in the Nabataean period. The height of the renaissance occurred especially during the fifth and sixth centuries A.D.

Throughout the eastern Roman empire, from the time of Constantine I on, there ensued a hubbub of productive activity that supported the elaborate structure of the Byzantine economy for several glowing centuries. The lively interchange of goods and services was leavened by the zeal of churchmen in promoting their own interests, in addition to those of the kingdom of God. Silks, silver, gold, ivory, ebony, teakwood, precious stones, incense, perfumes, cosmetics, spices and salt were exchanged for tools, weapons, base metals, cloth and foodstuffs. The latter included everything from oil and wine to barley and wheat. Merchants and royal messengers, soldiers and missionaries and pilgrims, itinerant smiths, artists and musicians passed busily to and fro with their goods or instruments along the travel-routes that bound the Byzantine world together. The exotic products of Arabia Felix, Ethiopia and other eastern lands were in especially high demand, and in very considerable measure were transported across the convenient crossroads of the Negev.

Depots and shops, camping places and fortresses, industrial and agricultural communities sprang up to minister to the needs of the settlers and travelers, or took a new lease on life. Completely new cities were built, and the appearance of old ones was radically altered. In addition, a veritable flood of churches and monasteries inundated the Negev. They were established in every place of sizeable habitation, with all of them being of relatively large dimensions and commanding appearance and importance. They were by no means limited to the half dozen Nabataean-Byzantine cities of the type of Abdah and Isbeita. The prominent ruins of these places have long attracted attention to themselves, to the exclusion of literally hundreds of smaller sites, the very existence of which was previously unsuspected.

Some of the churches were erected on the foundations of Nabataean temples, and often out of stones quarried from their ruins. Religious retreats were built in hidden nooks and corners. The Byzantine crosses of early Christianity were emblazoned in countless places. Nowhere else can earlier ones be found. They were of no avail, however, in preventing dissension among the believers in the new dispensation or in staying the persecution of nonconforming Monophysites and Jacobites. In fact, so cruel were the disabilities they suffered, that they welcomed the Moslems with open arms when they burst upon the scene.

The Epicenter of Christianity

It was as natural as the singing of birds for special attention to be paid in the Byzantine period to the Holy Land. For the Byzantine Christians, as for all other Christians after them, it became the epicenter of Christianity. Jesus had suffered and died in Jerusalem, and there were witnesses who testified that they had returned to find the door ajar and the tomb empty, in which the Rabbi's body had been buried. No wonder that churches were planted like roses on both sides of the Jordan, to flourish in the Garden of Gethsemane. At Gerasa of Beyond Jordan, a whole series of splendid churches was constructed, which clocked the passage of the late fifth to the beginning of the seventh centuries A.D. To list their names is to recall much of the story of the appearance and expansion of Christianity and the contributions of many of its foremost sons. These are they in this one place alone: the church of the Apostles, Prophets and Martyrs; of St. Theodore; of St. George, St. John the Baptist and Saints Cosmos and Damianus; of Saints Peter and Paul; and the church of Bishop Genesius of A.D. 611, which brought the period to a close. There were also several other churches, whose names could not be ascertained, and one of which had been constructed over the ruins of a Byzantine synagogue.

Of particular sanctity to the Christian world is the Church of the Holy Sepulcher in Jerusalem. Originally built by Constantine I in place of Hadrian's Temple of Venus, it was demolished by the Persians, and was restored by the Crusaders. Justinian's sixth-century basilica of St. Mary was transformed by the Moslems into the Aksa Mosque, which is one of the most sacred of Islam. It would require a large catalogue to compile the names and dates and locations of all the Byzantine churches in the Holy Land, if that were possible, and a whole library to include all those that sprang up throughout the Byzantine world. It was above all natural that large numbers of them should have been erected in the Negev, which from earliest Biblical times on proved to be a haven for the spiritually hungry.

The love and skill and labor and wealth poured into the

construction of all these churches in and outside of the Negev and Palestine defy description. The loveliest interior of them all, to my way of thinking, is that of the Church of the Nativity in Bethlehem, which was built originally by Constantine I in the fourth century A.D. and replaced by Justinian two centuries later. All of these churches were tied in with the economy of the times and reflect in general the flourishing conditions of the Byzantine period. This is true of the Negev, where no Christian need have traveled far in the fifth to seventh centuries A.D. to have found a sanctuary in which to pray. Contemporary synagogues existed there too, for the benefit of its considerable Jewish population. Indeed, although they were far fewer in number, they were to be found throughout the entire Byzantine cultural world.

The spate of churches and monasteries that flooded the Byzantine world in the springtime of Christianity brought into being new forms of art and architecture, many of which were adopted by the synagogues of the time, too. Distinctive, Corinthianized capitals were developed from classical patterns. All the color and verve of Hellenistic mosaics were caught in the ones that covered the floors and at times even the walls of these edifices. Their themes vary greatly, ranging from the miracle of the loaves and fishes to the seasons and months of the year and to the fruits of the field and the birds and beasts found there. The zodiac was one of the most common of the representations both in churches and synagogues, and Biblical scenes were often depicted.

Pagan motifs were often woven into these stone drawings, and pagan sculptures were employed for ornamental purposes even in such a place as the synagogue of Capernaum on the Lake of Galilee. The variegated subject matter of the mosaics and sculptures in church and synagogue emphasized the vitality of these institutions. They sought to subordinate but not to sacrifice the robustness of familiar art forms and of everyday reality to the striving for spiritual redemption and to the hope for near salvation. The aim was to bring about a natural and general harmony of felicitous conduct and prayerful worship of God.

Old Wine in New Bottles

The Byzantine Christians of the Negev were not new immigrants. They were by and large the descendants of the old inhabitants of the land, who apparently gladly adapted themselves to the new conditions. The recovery of the Negev from the recession it experienced with the downfall of the Nabataean kingdom coincided, as we have seen, with the rise of Byzantium and the enrichment of the lands under its control. With the resumption of the intensive transport of much of the precious freight of the Orient across the highways of the Negev, and the rebuilding of old and the construction of new cities and the expansion of all kinds of public works, the prosperity of the entire Southland reached and even surpassed that which it had enjoyed when it was an integral part of the Nabataean kingdom. Some of the finest and most cultured cities of all of Christendom developed there, all of them on the foundations of earlier Nabataean towns. The cultural accomplishments of some of them enjoyed international repute.

It soon became necessary to change the backward position to which the Negev had been relegated by the Romans, when they made it a part of their Provincia Arabia. The safeguarding of its frontiers, the direction of its internal affairs and the integration of its booming economy into that of the rest of the empire, could no longer be entrusted to the remote control of the relatively distant, provincial capital of Bosra in Syria. Consequently, in the fourth century A.D., the Negev was incorporated into a district of its own, called Palestina Tertia. This reevaluation of its economic and political importance was underscored by a related move in the sixth century A.D. Arabia had been assigned in the meantime to the Patriarchate of Antioch. The emperor,

Justinian, found it desirable, however, to change that jurisdictional set-up, and in A.D. 553 he transferred Arabia to the Patriarchate of Jerusalem. Princes of the Church were also rulers of the land, with the emperor arrogating to himself the authority of supreme religious functionary. The Negev was governed by its bishops, who were responsible, in the final analysis, to the king of Byzantium.

By the time of Justinian, the Negev was in the fullest bloom of its renaissance. Every single Nabataean settlement there had been succeeded by a Byzantine one, with new villages springing up in addition. The intensive cultivation of the soil in carefully terraced, dry creek beds, and the meticulous husbanding of every possible drop of rainwater behind dams and in cisterns and in the sponge of the earth, were continued by the Byzantines. They adopted all the methods and techniques of water and soil conservation that the Nabataeans had perfected. This is not too surprising, because the Nabataeans and the Byzantines after them in the Negev were essentially one and the same people. The chief difference was a drastic change in religious persuasion and practices. Otherwise, it was definitely an instance of old wine being poured into new bottles.

The Nabataeans, as we have already seen, were neither destroyed nor driven away when the Romans took self-government away from them. The people of the land remained in their places, erecting or repairing stone terraces, building or maintaining dams, tapping catchment areas with intricate arrangements of solid lines of heaped-up, small stones or of long rows of separate mounds of them, plastering cisterns, tending their flocks, tilling the soil, speaking and writing their Aramaic dialect and making much use of the Greek tongue, and worshipping their pagan gods in their old or even in newly constructed temples. Most of them were little concerned with political changes as long as they were permitted to pursue their customary way of life. It was of little moment to them whether they owed allegiance to Petra or Rome or Byzantium, provided that they were left alone—which they were. The modern concepts of nationalism and patriotism never occurred to them even in their nightmares. If they had reflected about them at all, they might well have proclaimed: *ubi bene, ibi patria.*

Even during the economic recession following the diversion of trade from Petra to Palmyra, the largest part of the population remained rooted to the soil. The major task of preparing it for cultivation and preventing erosion and securing dependable water supplies had already been accomplished by then. The labors of the fathers benefited many later generations, including the modern Bedouins, who still plant crops on lands made cultivable by their distant Nabataean predecessors. The Nabataeans did not lightly abandon their inheritance because of a serious diminution of their caravan commerce, but clung to it with the tenacity that has always characterized the relationship of the peasant to the land.

They continued strong enough to ward off the forays of desert nomads, being aided in this by Roman troops. As the currents of trade by-passed the Southland ever more completely, there is no question but that their cities and villages which were dependent upon it to a considerable degree, experienced increasing economic hardships. Had the tide of their misfortune not been arrested and reversed by the radical improvement in the affairs of the entire Roman Orient, beginning early in the fourth century A.D., it is doubtful if they would have been able to hold out much longer. However, the increase in trade and the building boom that accompanied the advance of the Church into Negev, radically altered the course of events there. Otherwise, the periodic eclipses of the past would have been visited upon it, with emptiness enthroned, dwelling places become piles of debris, gardens gone and civilization effaced.

This had not happened. On the contrary, as we have seen, reinvigorated life was restored to the Negev, paralleling the economic efflorescence of the Byzantine empire. And, as Christianity became ever more deeply rooted and widespread, the paganism of the Nabataeans yielded increasingly to its appeal. Priests and monks and pilgrims became familiar sights in the Negev. And soon, in the natural course of events, churches, many of them of magnificent architecture, replaced the Nabataean temples, rising up frequently out of their ruins and on their foundations. The worship of God, whom the Jews had acknowledged from the beginning of their separate history, and the worship of Jesus, whom the Jews could not accept as the Son of God, became the central habit of the religious life of the Christianized Nabataeans. Their religion experienced a radical change, but their role as gifted and energetic cultivators and merchants remained the same. Their cultural horizon expanded, but their attachment to the soil of the Negev remained unaltered.

Abandoned and soon buried under a blanket of debris was the pantheon of fertility deities, to which the Nabataeans had dedicated sanctuaries such as the one at Abdah in the Negev and that of Khirbet Tannur in Transjordan. Incense was still burnt and censers were swung, but now in churches rather than in pagan temples, and to the accompaniment of sacred litanies rather than in connection with the bleatings of sacrificial animals. What Roman rule had not accomplished, Christian faith now achieved—namely, the disappearance of the Nabataeans as a distinctive people, with a unique culture of their own. The exquisite Nabataean pottery ceased to be manufactured, and the singular Nabataean script to be written.

Losing their own identity completely, the Nabataeans contributed their creative genius to the expansive, Byzantine civilization, in whose embrace the Negev found new and fruitful life. Henceforth, the Negev was occupied for the most part by Christians. There was also a considerable number of Jews who remained faithful to their ancient heritage. Art and architecture and literature of considerable importance flourished in the Negev of the Byzantine period, exercising a cultural influence that extended far beyond its borders. The end of the upsurge in the Byzantine annals of the Negev came with the advent of the overpowering forces of Mohammedanism. What continued was pitiful by comparison with the life that the Nabataeans and Byzantines had created there. So excellent was their handiwork, however, that much of it has endured to our time.

The Sign of the Cross

Wherever one goes in the Negev, one can find the symbol of the Christian cross. It is the religious sign of the spectacular rise of the Byzantine civilization. Its dramatic development and tragic disintegration can be illustrated by the remains of any one of half a dozen cities that flourished there during the Byzantine period, or by scores of smaller towns and monuments of comparable significance which existed there then. From five to twenty thousand souls lived in some of these urban centers. Never before in the history of the Negev, not even in the heyday of the Nabataean kingdom, had the size of the total population, the amount of trade, the intensiveness of agricultural pursuits and the utilization of the physical resources of the land been surpassed. Starting from the advanced position of Nabataean accomplishment, the Byzantines throve mightily under the immensely difficult conditions of the Negev. Of incalculable advantage to their physical wellbeing was the economic impact of ecclesiastical interests which were interwoven with many matters of profitable mundane concern.

Churches were constructed in the Negev throughout the entire Byzantine period in almost feverish haste and with lavish furnishings. Monasteries which looked like fortresses and possessed their defensive qualities mushroomed on high hills and in hidden clefts. In a practically treeless land, great structures had to be fashioned completely out of slabs of stone. Food and raiment and shelter had to be provided for multitudes, and incense and spices for religious services and robust appetites. Merchandise from far-off marts was assembled and sold, with the emblems of sanctity appearing on the coins of exchange. The exercise of power, the acquisition of wealth and the service of God trailed each other in exuberant competition. The excitement of accomplishment was in the air. The atmosphere of the unfixed frontier, whether physical or spiritual, has always enveloped the spaces of the Negev.

PHANTOM CITIES

It is an eye-opening experience to visit the still extant ruins of the main Byzantine cities in the Negev. The despoiled wreckage of their above-surface remains testifies eloquently to the nature of their former grandeur. It appears, at first, impossible to understand how such large urban centers could have existed in view of the bleakness and emptiness of their present surroundings. It takes time and patience and absorbed interest to perceive how large groups of human beings could live permanently off a land, which seems superficially to be so ill favored. The truth is, as we have seen throughout this book, that only extraordinarily capable people, bound together in protracted effort over many generations, could create the conditions making it feasible for human beings to survive and even thrive in the Negev.

KHALASAH

One of the most important of the ruined cities of the Negev is Khalasah, which was anciently known as Elusa. It stands on an earlier Nabataean site, from which a Nabataean inscription has been recovered. It reads: "This is the place which Natairu dedicated to the life of Haretath, king of the

Nabataeans." The reference is probably to the Nabataean king, Aretas IV, the one who ruled from 9 B.C. to A.D. 40, and whose daughter, you will remember, was married for a while to Herod Antipas, the son of the Judaean king, Herod the Great. We found a very similar inscription on an altar in our excavations of the Nabataean Temple of Khirbet Tannur in Transjordan.

Under the name of Elusa, this town was clearly marked on a fourth century A.D. map of the Roman empire, which shows principal lines of communication. It has become known as the Peutinger map, from the name of the scholar who published it. Among the stations on the single road shown leading from Palestine through the Negev are Hierusalem (Jerusalem), Elusa (Khalasah), Oboda (Abdah), Ad Dianam (Ain Ghadyan in the Wadi Arabah), and Haila (Aila on the Gulf of Aqabah). Elusa was also prominently shown on the Madeba mosaic map of Palestine of the sixth century A.D. The centrality of its location is emphasized by the fact that it is on the junction of roads which led between Gaza on the Mediterranean and Petra in Transjordan or Aila on the Gulf of Aqabah and between Beersheba and Kadeshbarnea in Sinai. One of the highways from Khalasah to the Wadi Arabah led to it via Kurnub and Ain Hosb. Another, more or less paralleling it farther south, which became known as the Darb es-Sultani, reached the Wadi Arabah via the springs of Ain el-Qattar, Ain Haruf and Ain el-Wehbeh.

The track from Beersheba to Khalasah is easy to follow. It crosses a bare, wadi-cut, rolling landscape and then a wide stretch of sand dunes till it reaches the broad, shallow and still cultivable plain of the Wadi Khalasah. The main part of the town of Khalasah lies on the east side of the wadi, with one large structure on the west side. Stripped of its hewn stones for the building needs of Gaza and Beersheba, little is left of it except the skeletal outlines of its former shape. It is estimated that some twenty thousand people may have lived in the hundreds of stone houses, which were jammed into its roughly rectangular area of approximately 110 by 630 yards.

The inhabitants of Khalasah engaged in all manner of activities. They produced a wine from their extensive vineyards that was good enough to be mentioned by name in the Life of St. Hilarion, written by the great Christian scholar and Bible translator, Jerome, in the fourth century A.D. Indeed, the city, which had become the capital of Palestina Tertia in A.D. 358, was so important that it not only had a flourishing theological school, but a bishop and even a calendar of its own. An influential Jewish community resided there, too, which had a synagogue of its own. Archaeological evidence of its existence has been recovered. Further excavations may reveal that this synagogue possessed one of the picturesque mosaic floors characteristic of nearly all Byzantine church and synagogue construction of the fifth and sixth centuries A.D.

The prominence of Khalasah is recognized also in Talmudic literature. In the Targum, it is equated with the site of Bered, which is mentioned in Genesis 16:14, in connection with the Hagar story. Furthermore, the great inland route of The Way of Shur, which led through central Sinai, and which is mentioned in the same story in Genesis 16:7, is referred to in Bereshit Rabba as "The Way of Khiltsa." Indeed, there is discussion in the Talmud as to whether God's Law was enjoined at Marah in Sinai (cf. Exodus 15:23-26) or at Elusa in the Negev. From all these comments, you can see how important Khalasah was considered by the Jews of the Talmudic period, which coincided with much of the Byzantine period. The wealth and prominence of Khalasah depended upon its position as a thriving caravan station and trade emporium on a crossroads between the Mediterranean and the Red Sea and between Egypt and Canaan.

It could not, however, have been the most important city in the Negev, as it is designated in some papyri discovered in Egypt, were it not for the presence of a plentiful water supply just below the surface of the ground in the Wadi Khalasah, which can easily be tapped. One large well there, modernly cement-lined, is still used by Bedouins and occasional passers-by. There must have been other wells, too, which fell into disuse and were buried under debris. There must also be numerous cisterns hidden under the mounds of broken stones that disfigure the extensive area of the town proper of Khalasah. It also seems likely that one or more agricultural settlements of the Abrahamitic period and of the Judaean kingdom must have existed at or in the neighborhood of Khalasah, corresponding to those we have found farther south in the vicinity of the wells of Bir Birein, Bir Resisim and Bir Hafir.

There is little to be seen at Khalasah today, except the threadbare ruins, which have been picked clean of their good building stones.

Among the thousands of shattered building blocks that litter the site of Khalasah, we found only one that gave expression to some of the lusty strength and exuberant vitality and religious consciousness of this once-striking Byzantine city. Carved on the face of a broken capital was a sturdy Byzantine cross, placed in the center of a stylized leaf and fruit arrangement. The workmanship was somewhat crude, but in the very crudeness I found reflected some of the warm-blooded forcefulness of the Byzantines and of their civilization. Accepting and emphasizing the example of the Nabataeans who blazed the path before them, they succeeded in building flourishing gardens and cities in the midst of the desert. They were a credit to Christianity, whose faith was their fortress, and whose cross was their emblem of honor and mission and hope.

RUHEIBEH

From Khalasah we followed the once-thronged caravan ar-

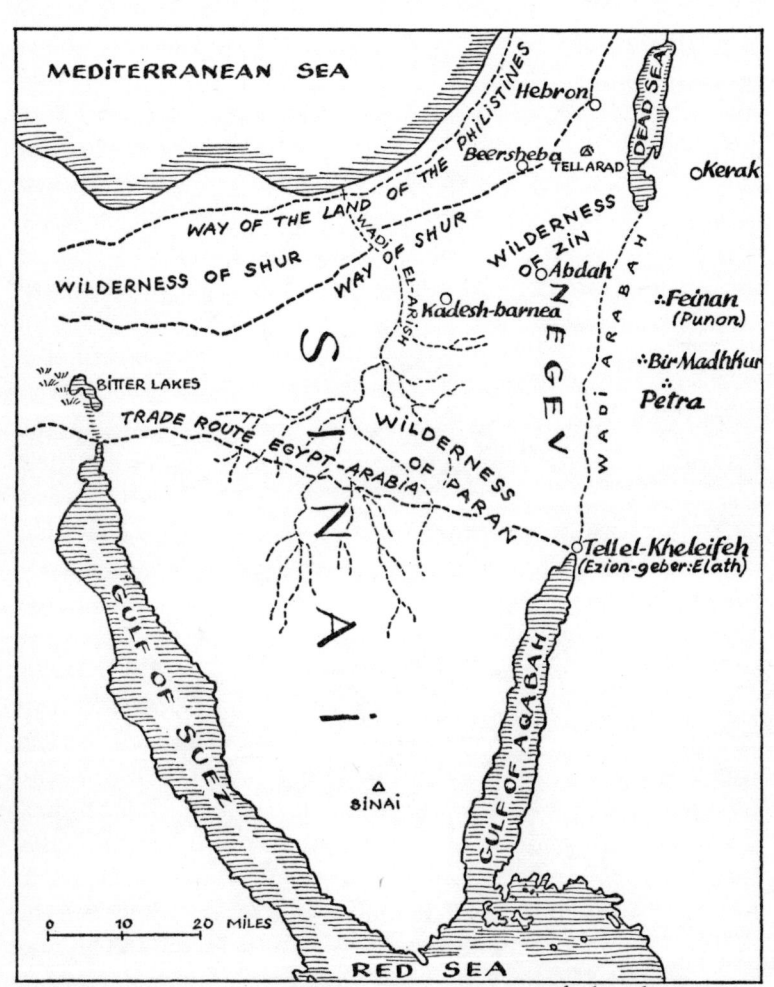

THE WAYS OF SHUR AND THE PHILISTINES

tery of the Way of Shur (Genesis 16:7; 20:1) southwestward to the Sinai border. In Biblical times it served as the most direct route connecting Egypt and Canaan through the interior of the Negev and central Sinai. It was in the Wilderness of Shur, east of the Land of Goshen, that, after crossing the Red Sea and commencing the journey through Sinai, the Israelites first experienced the full bitterness and weariness of their desert wanderings (Exodus 15:22). They were too quick to complain, little remembering at the moment that their forefather Abraham had roamed about in this very region: "And Abraham journeyed from thence (Canaan) toward the land of the Negev, and dwelt between Kadesh (-barnea) and Shur, with his headquarters at Gerar (near the northwestern border of the Negev)" (Genesis 20:1).

The most important and most continuously used highway, which connected the lands of the Nile with those of the Jordan, was the coastal route along the Mediterranean, which was known as the Way of the Land of the Philistines. It took hundreds of years after their occupancy of Canaan, before the Israelites were strong enough to call it their own. It came into great prominence again in the period of the Crusades.

Our goal was the completely ruined Nabataean-Byzantine town of Ruheibeh. Our purpose was not only to examine its massive ruins, which had already been studied by others, but particularly to attempt to determine whether or not it was proper to identify it with the Biblical site of Rehobot (Genesis 26:22). That identification had been posited but never proved by Lawrence of Arabia, among others. Ruheibeh, which is about seven miles in a straight line southwest of Khalasah, is roughly about half its size. It is situated above the northwest side of the broad, shallow, intricately terraced, and still partly cultivated Wadi Ruheibeh. The low terrace walls which protected the fields in its dry stream bed, can still be seen. Without them, the Wadi Ruheibeh would long ago have become a badly eroded canyon.

Ruheibeh presents an exceedingly sorry spectacle today. If ruins, like professional beggars, could have been kings, then Ruheibeh deserves the distinction of this kind of royalty as much or even more than Khalasah. Ragged foundations of closely crowded blocks of houses hug the ground in almost hopeless confusion. They look as if they had been cut down and scattered by a mighty scythe. Ruheibeh has not the plucked chicken appearance of Khalasah, whose building stones had been purloined during generations for construction purposes in Gaza and Beersheba. Because of distance and difficulties of travel, Ruheibeh has been spared that particular ignominy. It survives in a state of complete collapse. Its jumbled blocks of square and rectangular structures of various sizes, separated by narrow, twisting lanes, still convey the feeling of the tumultuous activity that characterized its existence. A centrally located church of large dimensions once dominated the town, and there may well have been others too. It is certain that numerous cisterns lie buried under the mounds of fallen building stones.

Seen from a plane, the large, oval reservoir of Ruheibeh, which is located just below the gateway on the south side of the town, stands out strikingly. Excavated out of the soft bedrock and lined with rubble masonry which is no longer intact, it still manages to hold water for many weeks each year, obtaining it from the infrequent annual rains. But the inhabitants of Ruheibeh did not rely upon the uncertain supply of the seasonal downpours. They sank a well some three hundred feet deep into the bed of the Wadi Ruheibeh, until they found water in sure and sufficient quantity. The sides of this bold shaft were carefully lined with hewn blocks of stone, the uppermost ones of which were furrowed with rope marks. Still standing are the ruins of an impressive bath-house, which was built alongside of it.

At the related Nabataean-Byzantine site of Abdah (Eboda), there is also a deep well, with a fine bath-house standing next to it. There were deep wells also at Nitsanah (Auja

Hafir), about thirteen miles to the southwest of Ruheibeh, close to the Sinai border. The Nabataeans and Byzantines, and the Judaeans and Israelites before them, possessed immense skills in sinking wells to great depths to secure for themselves unfailing water supplies. This was particularly important, of course, in the arid Negev.

Large numbers of fine, painted, plain and rouletted Nabataean sherds and fragments of terra sigillata, in addition to quantities belonging to the Byzantine period, were examined by us at Ruheibeh. We found none, however, which could be dated to earlier, Biblical periods. The discovery of such fragments of pottery would have enabled us to confirm the identification of Ruheibeh with Biblical Rehoboth without any more ado, because the location itself conforms to the Biblical information as to where it should be. If, however, the identification can be made anyway, and we believe, as we shall show later on that it can, then its role in the Biblical biography of the Patriarch, Isaac, comes into clearer focus than it would otherwise.

Isaac was generally regarded as a man of the Negev. It is said of him that "he dwelt in the land of the Negev" (Genesis 24:62). We are told, in this connection, that when he was about to meet Rebekkah for the first time, he had just come from the direction of *Be'er la-Hai Ro'i* (the Well of the Seeing God), which is undoubtedly to be located in easternmost Sinai or in the westernmost Negev. It cannot be far from the spring of Kadesh-barnea, if, indeed, it is not another name for it. Be that as it may, the story is told that when the herdsmen of Gerar claimed as their own several wells that Isaac's servants had dug in the valley, "he departed from thence and digged another well; and for that they strove not. And he called the name of it Rehoboth, saying in explanation: For now Jehovah hath made room (*hirḥib*) for us and we shall be fruitful in the land. And he went up from thence to Beersheba" (Genesis 26:22-23).

Actually, Lawrence of Arabia had in his hands what I

consider to be adequate proof of the identification of Ruheibeh with Biblical Rehoboth. At an ancient watchtower, called Qasr Ruheibeh, about two miles north of Ruheibeh, he found fragments of pottery, which he correctly judged to be ancient, but which he could not definitely date. In the course of our explorations along the Wadi Ruheibeh, we found several Judaean kingdom fortresses, with pottery remains on them, similar to those discovered by Lawrence, which fixed the period of their occupancy without any question of doubt as extending from the tenth to the sixth centuries B.C., that is, from the time of King Solomon to the end of the Judaean kingdom. The largest of these fortresses that we came across is called Khirbet Umm Rujum. It is one of several forts of this period, which guarded the strategic highway that led from Beersheba to Khalasah, Ruheibeh, Nitsanah and across Sinai to Egypt, and which, as we have seen, was called the Way of Shur. The importance of these discoveries is twofold. In the first place, they demonstrate that this strongly guarded highway was indeed the famous trade artery of Shur, across which men and goods traveled between Canaan and Egypt during many periods of history. In the second place, the fortress of Khirbet Umm Rujum is located on the same range of hills on the lower extension of which Ruheibeh is situated. It is more than likely that the massive constructions of the Nabataean and Byzantine cities of Ruheibeh completely covered up and obliterated all the remains of the earlier city of Rehoboth, which existed there in the time of the Judaean kings and still earlier in the time of Isaac.

ISBEITA

The best preserved and most striking looking of all the Nabataean-Byzantine cities in the Negev is Isbeita (Esbeita, Subeita, Shivta). It owes its comparatively good preservation to the fact that it is somewhat off the major tracks and is not close enough to Gaza or Beersheba to serve building contractors as an easy source of ready-shaped stones. Coming upon it suddenly, one has the feeling of having arrived in the theatre just after the curtain has risen on a magnificent stage setting. It seems too dramatic to be real, too improbable to be more than a theatrical scene, too massive and majestic in appearance to have had any solid connection with the empty desert background of its setting.

Yet Isbeita is more revealing of the true nature of Byzantine civilization in the Negev than any other single site there, with the possible exception of Abdah. The dimensions and nobility of its basilicas, the beauty and even delicacy of line of the soaring vaults of their apses, the stern outlines of the great monastery, the remains of a large, double reservoir, the presence of numerous, well constructed cisterns, the façades of residences still elegant in their ruins, spell out in visual form the sparkling grandeur of Byzantine achievement in the Negev.

Isbeita was a comparatively small but extraordinarily attractive city. The lands round about it were terraced and tilled. Some of the barest and stoniest hilltops and slopes for miles round about it were curried and combed and contour-lined with rows of the stone mounds (*teleilat el-anab*) and the solid rows of heaped-up pebbles of the irrigation systems. This is particularly visible in the vicinity of Mishrefeh, which belonged to Isbeita and is about two and a half miles to the northwest of it. A large and isolated hermitage was located on it, which must have had exceedingly close connections with the religious community of Isbeita.

A direct track connects Isbeita with Khalasah (Elusa) to the north of it and Bir Hafir to the south of it. Its most important link with the outer world, however, was the road which led through the Wadi Raviv, and connected it with Nitsanah (Auja Hafir). We have seen that the Wadi Raviv was dotted with ancient settlements dating from the Abrahamitic to the Byzantine periods. Isbeita did not, however, flourish as a trade center. The scene of three churches and a large monastery, it undoubtedly benefited from ecclesiastical revenues. In addition, it derived much of its sustenance from agricultural pursuits.

The town was built at the eastern edge of a fertile plain, which is engraved with some of the small beginnings of the Wadi Abyad. The name of one of them, called the Wadi Zayatin, meaning the Valley of Olives or Olive Trees, which crosses below the south side of Isbeita, may reflect one of the sources of its livelihood. As a matter of fact, several olive presses have been found there. I have repeatedly come across gardens of olive and fig and pomegranate trees tucked away in the most unexpected nooks and corners of the Negev. They have to be seen to be believed. Each of these gardens is situated behind a dirt dam, which forces a sufficient amount of the water of the occasional freshets to sink into the soil to nourish the trees and vines planted there.

The existence of Isbeita and of the terraced fields in the plain it dominates, again represents the beneficent triumph of man over nature. All this was achieved in spite of the fact that there seem to be no ready supplies of water close to the surface which can be easily tapped. The Nabataeans who first preempted this town site, blazoned the way. What they thus introduced, in the Negev or in other lands of their rule, on a scale hitherto unknown, the Byzantines adopted and even expanded at times. In such fashion, the water requirements of Isbeita's population, which numbered at least five thousand in the Byzantine period, were adequately met, according to the standards of the time.

Near the outskirts of Isbeita, we examined a serviceable cistern, which even at the end of the summer still retained water from the previous year's rains. It covered the base of a massive pillar, which upheld the remaining part of its natural, stone ceiling. Every paved street and courtyard and every roof surface served as catchment basins. We have mentioned Isbeita's great, double reservoir. It was located in the center of the southern end of the town, into which the streets of its entire northern section drained. Every house seems to have had a large cistern of its own, and each of the churches and the monastery had several of them. All in all, there seems always to have been enough water for man and beast, and always a sufficiency for the fine baptismal font that was still intact when we last saw it.

Isbeita was a most elegant town of ecclesiastical structures, enclosed courtyards and gently stepped streets that shone in the brilliant sunshine. The heat of the day never penetrated the extremely thick walls of private and public buildings, whose flat and domed roofs and vaulted construction testify to the high skills of the architects and stone masons responsible for them. Even from the distance, its broken walls and gaping apses, holed by the abuse of nature and man, make an impressive appearance.

If one examines each fallen stone carefully, many of them reveal the handiwork of excellent craftsmen and artists. On one of them, three fishes stand out in relief on a raised medallion. It called to mind the mosaic floor of the Byzantine Church of the Multiplication of Loaves and Fishes in Capernaum on the Lake of Galilee. A basket, filled with loaves of bread and flanked by a fish on each side, is depicted there, in consonance with the miracle described in the New Testament. I was reminded, also, of the Astarte sculpture I described, found at the Nabataean temple of Khirbet Tannur in Transjordan, over whose head two dolphins rested. A Nabataean inscription dedicated to the Nabataean god, Dushara, was discovered at Isbeita. And there is every reason to believe that the stone masons who carved the relief with the three fishes, together with the large majority of the inhabitants of Isbeita, were Christianized Nabataeans.

We saw, scattered among the ruins of Isbeita, other architectural stones, which had been decorated with meaningful or sometimes merely ornamental designs. It was a source of regret to us that we were not equipped to transport them to a proper museum, fearing what vandals might do to them if they were left behind. On one of them was sculptured a Byzantine cross, contained, successively, within a circle, a diamond and a square. It must have taken a lot of figuring on the part of the stone mason, to get all of them accurately in place as a frame for the cross. On a stone next to it was a hexagonal design, enclosing a raised circle of deeply embossed lines, which radiated like curved scimitars from a central cone. Above it were the reliefs of two crude doves. They were similar in workmanship to those of an eagle and a little man on Byzantine capitals at Abdah. In addition, we came across capitals with geometric and floral designs, which betrayed distant Hellenistic influences. Similar ones occurred at Abdah, Kurnub, and numerous other Byzantine sites in the Negev.

The crowning glory of Isbeita was formed by its three churches. One of them was located at the extreme northeast end of the town, another a short distance below it, and a third in the south central part, just above the double reservoir. The architecture of the northeast church is more or less typical of all the Byzantine churches in the Negev, which differed from each other in size more than in general plan. Its three aisles, of which the central one was the largest, were separated from each other by rows of six columns. They led to three apses at the east end, with small rooms behind the side apses. Entrance to the church was gained through three doors in a screen wall from an atrium with side chambers. In addition, the plan included a small side-chapel and a baptistery with an anteroom. Sometime near the latter part of its history, a strong revetment or heavy talus was constructed around almost all of this building complex, except on its south side, where a large monastery had been attached to it. The talus converted the church in appearance and purpose into a stronghold, which proved, however, to be of little avail against the effects of the Mohammedan conquest.

The northeast church is still splendid in its ruins, as is the south one, too. Its floor was originally covered with slabs of white marble, with which its walls too were decorated to a height of over six feet. Brilliant mosaics and bright paintings further heightened its beauty. Indeed, still faintly to be seen in the apses of the south church are remnants of religious paintings, with which most of these Byzantine churches were decorated. With each passing year, the colors progressively become more faint or disappear as a result of exposure to the inclemency of the elements and the unkindness of humans. The subject treated in the south apse of the south church seems to have been that of the Transfiguration, with parts of the figures of the Apostles still being faintly visible. Various saints were sculptured on Corinthianized capitals of the southernmost Byzantine church of Transjordan at Aila, on the northeast side of the Gulf of Aqabah.

NITSANAH

A large part of the wealth which supported the Byzantine towns and churches of the Negev and which had brought prosperity to the Nabataean settlements and temples there before them, was derived, as we know now, from the rich caravan trade which crossed the land. Much of the merchandise of the Orient was brought overland from the port of Gerrha on the Persian Gulf to the Arabian port of Leuke Kome on the east side of the Gulf of Aqabah and then shipped or transported by caravan northward to Aila. From there it was carried to Petra, to which a direct, overland route led also from Meda'in Saleh in Arabia. And "thence to Rhinocolura (modern el-Arish in Sinai on the Mediterranean) . . . and thence to other nations," according to the Greek geographer Strabo, who wrote about the Nabataeans at the beginning of the first century A.D.

One of the places in the Negev, through which the heavy caravan traffic passed both in Nabataean and Byzantine times, was the border post of Nitsanah (Auja Hafir). Roads forked off from there to Gaza and el-Arish on the Mediterranean or to Kadesh-barnea in Sinai and to Egypt. In the Byzantine period, large numbers of pilgrims passed through Nitsanah on the way to the Holy Mountain in Sinai. Nitsanah (Nessana), and other stations like it which were located on the main caravan highways, benefited enormously from the constant movement of people and goods along them. The travelers required food and lodging and services. Tolls were exacted from each caravan.

In his *Natural History,* Pliny the Elder of the first century A.D., writing in Latin, gives a succinct description of this entire process. "Frankincense," he writes, "cannot be exported (from Arabia) except through the land of the Gebanites, and so a tax is paid to their king too. From Thomna, their capital, to Gaza is . . . sixty-five camel stages. . . . All along the road there are expenses, here for water, there for food or lodging at the halts and various tolls, so that the expenditure for each camel is 688 *denarii* as far as the Mediterranean, and then another tax is paid to the publicans of the Roman empire."

The results of excavations carried out at Nitsanah by the Colt expedition have thrown a great deal of light not only upon its history, but upon that of the entire Negev in the Nabataean and Byzantine periods. The rebuilding and enrichment of Byzantine Nitsanah, following its decline after the Roman conquest of the Nabataean kingdom, are reflected in some amazing, contemporary papyri discovered there, which have been interpreted by Naphtali Lewis. From them we learn that soldier-farmers, *limitanei,* who were settled there, grew wheat, barley, peas and grapes in the Wadi Hafir and adjacent lands, which Nitsanah commands. Their livelihood did not depend solely, however, upon the yield of their crops. They also received military pay, for which, in return, they were supposed to garrison the fortress built on top of the Nitsanah hill. A deep well was sunk through it, to assure them a safe water supply in case of attack.

Some of these *limitanei* were quite affluent, to judge from the will left behind by one of them. He bequeathed "a house of ninety-six beds" to his heirs. The size of this caravanserai or hotel is indicative of the heavy and continuous commercial and pilgrim traffic that passed through Nitsanah. It was a busy settlement, having its own potter and goldsmith. Some of its inhabitants, too, must have been engaged in the weaving of cloth, to judge from the numerous spindle whorls and loom weights found there.

The Church of Saints Sergius and Bacchus, built on the acropolis hill, next to the fortress, played an important role not only in the religious but also in the business life of the community. Its presbyter was also the chief money lender, who, according to one of the papyri, was not above charging considerably more than the legal rate of interest. Of extraordinary importance was the discovery at Nitsanah of parts of an amazing library of wide ranging scope. It was very catholic in its collection, extending from several pages of the Acts of St. George and fragments of the Fourth Gospel and a Syriac religious text to approximately a hundred pages of a Latin-Greek lexicon to Vergil. This library catered apparently to a most literate and sophisticated community. We must assume that there were comparable libraries in some of the other, important Byzantine towns in the Negev.

ABDAH

In a class of its own, both so far as location and appearance are concerned, is the Nabataean-Byzantine city of Abdah, which is spelled Eboda on the fourth century A.D. Peutinger map. If Isbeita is the most beautiful Nabataean-Byzantine town in the Negev, Abdah must be considered the most striking and important. The massive ruins of a large, Byzantine monastery and fort, the outlines of an extensive Roman camp and attached reservoir, and collapsed buildings of all kinds need to be disentangled, before the plan and periods of occupation of Abdah are understandable to the onlooker. The impressive ruins crowd the top and slopes of a large outspur, which tongues its way into a broad, once intensively cultivated valley. On the far side of this valley is the Wadi Ramliyeh, into whose banks have been thrust great, pillared cisterns. One of these is completely intact and is still in use by the Bedouins of the area. Most of the length of the Wadi Ramliyeh to the southwest is strongly and intricately terraced, with its soil being washed away in those places by the winter floods, where the erosion walls have fallen into disuse.

About eight more or less horizontal steps or benches ascend the precipitous rock face of the Abdah outspur, with all manner of structures being erected on them. Their ruins are now piled on top of each other in chaotic disorder, resulting in part from earthquakes. The steep west and south slopes are pitted with man-made caves. These represent the rear chambers of dwellings or tombs, whose pillared porticos and entrance halls made of well dressed stones have collapsed. They give the face of the outspur the appearance of a lowering, many eyed dragon, gazing wearily and balefully at the processions of the centuries on the road below it. At the very base of the hill are the fairly intact ruins of a Byzantine bath-house, by the side of which exists a deep well. That Abdah was originally Nabataean is indicated by large quantities of Nabataean potsherds on the surface, by some Nabataean inscriptions incised on rock surfaces there and by the name, itself, which reflects that of Obodas. We have previously pointed out that it is not certain just which Obodas was the one involved. Under the ruins of the monastery are the foundations of a large Nabataean temple, which was probably dedicated to him. One of the Nabataean inscriptions found to the east-southeast of the Roman camp, reads: "by the life of Obodas." Still another bore the prayer: "peace to Esau, the son of Amru!"

The latter inscription was of particular interest to us, who had found a Greek one at Khirbet Tannur in Transjordan, which bore the name of "Alexandros Amrou." Our theory that many of the Edomites who infiltrated into the Negev and became Nabataeanized there, after being pushed out of their homeland in southern Transjordan, seems to be borne out by this combination of names. One recalls in this connection the words of Genesis 25:30: "And Esau said to Jacob, feed me, I pray thee, with some of this *adom, adom* (red pottage), for I am faint. Therefore was his name called Edom."

Numerous underground tombs at Abdah were originally Nabataean, but were used again by the Byzantines. A particularly large one, with twenty-two burial niches, is located on the south slope below the walled town area. It has been called the Tomb of Obodas by the great Dominican scholars, Fathers Jaussen, Savignac and Vincent. On the west slope, below the monastery ruins, is another underground tomb of several chambers, which clearly bears the imprint of Byzantine occupation or reoccupation. They are all carved out of the natural, soft limestone rock.

Painted on one of its walls are some crude Byzantine drawings and Greek inscriptions. One picture is clearly that of St. George, equipped with spear, buckler and steed. He is represented in the act of slaying the dragon. Above him is another figure, whose identity is obscure. In his right hand, he holds a staff, which is surmounted with a cross. To judge from one of the inscriptions, he might be either St. John or St. Theodore. Were it the latter, there would be a connection with a bas-relief of St. Theodore on a Byzantine capital at Aila. A camel and its driver are drawn between the two figures. There is repeated reference in the inscriptions, which invoke divine assistance, to the name of BOETHON, the Savior. We found it incised in bold characters on a pillar in a Byzantinized cistern, located about five and a half miles northwest of Abdah, as pointed out above.

Protruding from the ceiling of one of the underground chambers at Abdah is a cartwheel-like shield, out of which triangular sections were chiseled to form a Byzantine cross. The upper corners of the room are decorated with crude reliefs of bulls, whose horns rest on the ceiling. Their features have been accentuated by paint. In one instance, where the paint is gone, it is hard to make out the head of the bull. It would be easy to explain the significance of these reliefs, if they were Nabataean in origin, as indeed they may be. Bulls were commonly associated with the Nabataean deity, Zeus-Hadad.

The centrality and importance of Abdah in every phase of history cannot be exaggerated. To judge from our finds on the slopes and tops of hills in its vicinity, it is not at all unlikely that Judaean kingdom and still earlier Abrahamitic period installations once existed on the Abdah hill. They could easily have been completely destroyed by Nabataean and Byzantine constructions over them. Whether or not that was actually the case, the fact remains that Abdah is the center of a fertile agricultural area, which was inhabited from early prehistoric times on, and which knew numerous Abrahamitic to Byzantine settlements.

It was above all a major station on the great, central highway, which led through the Negev. One of the most important routes led to Abdah from Gaza or Beersheba and then continued from it southeastward and east-southeastward via the Wadi Raman and the Wadi Siq to the Arabah. Another great travel route led more or less westward from Abdah across the watershed separating the Wadi Ramliyeh from the Wadi Hafir to Bir Hafir, and thence via Bir Birein and Bir Resisim to Nitsanah (Auja Hafir), where it joined the Way of the Wilderness of Shur through Sinai to Egypt.

Still a third track led generally southward from Abdah through the thickly settled Wadi Nefkh. It crossed the southern watershed which separates the beginnings of the Wadi Jerafi, whose terminus is the Wadi Arabah, from the easternmost branches of the Wadi el-Arish (Nahal Mizraim), which empties into the Mediterranean. Continuing southward past the Ras Raman, which towers above the western end of the Wadi Raman, it reaches first the wells of Biyar Ideid Umm Salih and then those of Biyar Ideid es-Samawi. Other tracks branching off from these wells lead eastward through the southernmost Negev to the Wadi Arabah or westward through Sinai.

Along these avenues, peaceful and martial travelers pursued their ways throughout many periods of history. Among them were pilgrims who sought quietness for contemplation and strengthening of their souls in the nearness of God. His voice could be heard in the stillness of the Southland and of Sinai. Others settled down to cultivate the soil wherever possible and build stone dwellings for themselves and their children. The conditions of the times could always be determined by the nature and number of the caravans that passed along the lines of march. When peace prevailed, they brought precious goods from far-off places in the east in exchange for the products of the west. The Negev throve during such eras, its depots bulging, its inhabitants content and creative, its soil tilled and gardens tended, its temples or synagogues and churches thronged with hosts that paid glad obeisance to the divine.

But then, at repeated intervals, the happy sounds of bustling civilization were muted or ceased altogether. Sometimes this happened suddenly, as when the Kings of the East burst upon the scene like the Four Horsemen of the Apocalypse, spreading death and destruction before them. At other times, it occurred imperceptibly, in consequence of changes introduced by Roman or Moslem rule. The end result of drastic changes, whether sudden or prolonged, was the fading or disappearance of civilization. Settlements like those of the Abrahamitic period of the twenty-first to nineteenth centuries B.C. were reduced to almost indistinguishable ruins and Nabataean-Byzantine cities such as Abdah and Isbeita collapsed into pathetic shreds of their former grandeur. The Negev, in each instance, reverted to wilderness, with only nomads and their camels to tread its paths and keep them from disappearing completely.

Aftermath

The high point of Byzantine fulfillment in the Negev was reached in the sixth century A.D. The destruction of the Church of the Holy Sepulchre in Jerusalem by the Persians shortly after the beginning of the seventh century A.D., was a portent of the desolateness and darkness that were to engulf the Negev about a century after Mohammedanism rocketed into existence. While the Christian communities there were not directly interfered with, changes affecting them adversely gradually took place. Taxes were increased, non-Moslems were discharged from public service, trade routes were diverted, commerce dwindled, agriculture declined, and the people of the land began in growing numbers to drift away and seek their livelihood elsewhere. It became thus progressively impossible to maintain the resplendent churches of the Negev in proper repair and to continue the services in them with wonted opulence.

In the end, squatters lived where bishops had presided. A few small mosques were built next to or in the ruins of several churches for prayers to Allah, centering about the person of the Prophet Mohammed. In spite of the discovery of some Arabic pottery of the thirteenth and fourteenth centuries A.D. at such places as Isbeita and elsewhere in the Negev, it may be said that on the whole a pall of abandonment enveloped it from early in the eighth century on. It is beginning now to be lifted again. The only imposing,

even though poorly built structures erected after the end of
the Byzantine period, were those on the strongly walled and
fortified Jeziret Far'un (Isle of Pharaoh), several hundred
yards off the northwest coast of the Gulf of Aqabah, opposite
Bir Tabah in Sinai. It was called the Isle of Graye by the
Crusaders. Erected perhaps originally by the Saracens on
Byzantine foundations, the buildings on this island seem to
have had no integral connection with the Negev proper.
They occupied a strategic position on the route between
Egypt and Arabia. Otherwise, the Negev once again became
the haunt of Bedouins, with history at home elsewhere.

The Care of the Dead

The sense of the past is omnipresent in the Negev. Cairns to
the dead crowd its hilltops and slopes. Ancestor worship and
concern for proper burial were a preeminent concern of the
ancients. The most striking manifestation of this was represented by the pyramids, which the Pharaohs of Egypt built
for themselves as monumental insurance policies for life
after death. To be sure, provision by the living for proper
housing of the dead was always combined with a healthy,
earthy sense of caution. Generally speaking, the graves were
located on rocky heights or inhospitable slopes that were
not suitable for agriculture anyway. Their number throughout the millennia is incalculable. Had all or even most of
them been established on cultivable soil, a large proportion
of the arable lands, upon which the living depended for
their food, would have been withdrawn from productive use.

Particularly prominent in the Negev are Byzantine burial
monuments. They can be seen silhouetted against the skyline
on numerous hills, and frequently seem to be better preserved than the stone houses which were occupied by the
living. The appearance is deceptive, however, because it is
an exceedingly rare discovery to come across an ancient grave
which was not looted long ago. It is common for several

Byzantine burials to be continued in long, rectangular, platform-like structures, that usually hug the tops of prominent hills. They measure from forty-five to sixty feet in length, fifteen to twenty feet in width and about three feet in height. On top of them, especially at their ends, are separate, circular burial cairns. Sometimes, there are long rows of these burial cairns, each one standing on a supporting base measuring from eight to twelve feet in diameter. Earlier burials, going back to Abrahamitic and prehistoric times, may often be found on the same sites. They are usually marked by stone circles, which are flush with the ground, although that may well not have been the case originally.

The fondest hope of every son of the Holy Land was to be buried in its sacred soil. Joseph had heeded Jacob's dying request to be buried "in the cave that is in the field of Machpelah, which is before Mamre, in the land of Canaan, which Abraham bought . . . for . . . a burying place" (Genesis 49:30). And when his own time approached to die, he "said unto his brethren, . . . God will surely . . . bring you up out of this land unto the land which he sware to Abraham, to Isaac and to Jacob . . . and ye shall surely carry up my bones from hence" (Genesis 50:24-25).

A Passion for Worship

The chief impression that remains with me from the examination of several hundred Byzantine hamlets, villages and cities in the Negev, is the passion for the worship of God, which seems to have possessed their inhabitants. Wherever we turned, in settlements large and small of this period, we encountered the remains of Christian sanctuaries. Sometimes, they were as comparatively intact as the still imposing church ruins of Isbeita. At other times, they were discernible only in barest outline or through isolated architectural fragments. If ever the sum of them all could be obtained, it would yield an amazing total. Whether the Byzantine Christians of the Negev were immensely pious or enormously rich or both, the fact remains that they delighted in building numerous and elaborate churches and magnificent basilicas. It is of course possible that the cost of their construction impoverished the population at large, although that seems doubtful, in view of the general prosperity of the Negev especially in the fifth and sixth centuries A.D. Be that as it may, the fact remains that no Byzantine town there seems to have been without one or more churches. At Khirbet Kuseifeh in the northern Negev, near Tell Arad, for example, as we have already seen, there are visible the overthrown column bases, broken pillars, marble chancel posts, mosaic squares and upended building blocks, some of them decorated with crosses, which belonged to two separate churches.

The Symbol of the Menorah

God was worshipped also in Byzantine synagogues in the Negev. There is reason to believe that in almost every Byzantine town, the Jewish citizens had a synagogue of their own. They formed an influential minority of the total population of the Southland. The seven-branched candelabra was as characteristic of their communities as the cross was of the Christian congregations. We have seen that Talmudic and Midrashic references attest to the presence of Jews at Byzantine Khalasah (Elusa), which was equated with Sinai itself. It is most probable, indeed, that there was a considerable number of Jews permanently resident in the Negev in Nabataean times also. They persisted in their own faith, when their Nabataean fellows were Christianized.

Indeed, it may be said that from the time of Abraham on, Hebrews and Israelites and Judaeans and Jews, as they were known in different periods, were at home in the Negev. It is not surprising, therefore, that some synagogue remains should have been unearthed at Khalasah. And it is most likely that others, in addition to those already known, will be discovered in the Negev in the course of future excavations. The magnificent mosaic floor of a Byzantine synagogue recently exposed at Nirim, close to the Gaza strip, is illustrative of what may be expected.

With the exception of a beautiful candelabra, several shofars (rams' horns) and ethrogs below it, the lion and lioness flanking the ark and the initial Aramaic inscription at the very top, the rest of the Nirim mosaic floor could have been situated in a Byzantine church, too. As a matter of fact, a sixth century A.D. mosaic floor from a church near Tell Jammeh on the Wadi Shellaleh, situated like Nirim in the northwesternmost Negev, could have been created by the same artist, so strikingly similar are they in many respects. The mosaic of the nave of the synagogue is divided into medallions by means of an arbor of winding grapevines. They rise from an amphora, which was flanked probably by two peacocks, only one of which is preserved intact. The medallions enclose representations of beasts, birds, palm trees, vases and baskets of various shapes and contents. They were faithfully or whimsically portrayed on the Nirim canvas, depending upon whether or not the artist was familiar with them.

The birds included a hen and an egg it had laid. That scene must have afforded several hours of quiet amusement to the craftsman who drew it with his tiny stone tesserae of different colors. The only animal he was obviously not familiar with was an elephant. Two of these pachyderms were drawn. He formed each of them by adding tusks, a large trunk, thick legs and a weird head to the body of a donkey. The contrast with the authentic naturalism of the bull, leopard and lion, for instance, not to mention the other animals, is most striking. There was also an outer panel, with an intricate design of flowering lotuses. It is very similar to one which frames a closely related mosaic in a Byzantine church at Beit-gubrin, just north of the Negev.

It seems certain that a Byzantine mosaic of this kind will be found some day among the ruins of the large Nabataean-Byzantine settlement at Aila. Capitals of a fine church of that period have been discovered there. It is known that the Jewish community of Aila afforded refuge to many of their co-religionists who fled Arabia to escape persecution. Mohammed finally made a special treaty with them to safeguard their rights at this important seaport. The close connections which the Jews of Aila enjoyed with their Sabaean or Himyarite brethren on the mainland of Arabia must have facilitated the traffic in the valuable goods of that land and of the far Orient.

Even in largely uninhabited districts of the Negev and Sinai, the urge to worship God manifested itself in the establishment of the simplest kind of sanctuaries. The same practice prevailed in pagan times too. Small Nabataean temples have been found at natural halting places along caravan trails through remote wildernesses. The spirit of this quest for communion with the divine has been caught in some inscriptions and rock drawings on the walls of an inconspicuous little canyon in Sinai. It is called the Wadi Umm es-Sedeir, and is but a few miles to the west-northwest of the modern Israeli seaport of Eilat on the northwest shore of the Gulf of Aqabah.

Few landscapes could be less attractive than that of Wadi Umm es-Sedeir and its surroundings. The jagged sandstone hills resting on chalk foundations, through which it hews its way, are completely covered with loose boulders and pebbles. There is nothing to relieve the naked bleakness of the scene, except in late winter and early spring. The tenderest of flowers briefly adorn the cruel surface crust then, and water cascades frenziedly for moments down the narrow, torrent bed. Yet it was there, on the opposite sides of an obscure bend in the canyon, that wayfarers pecked out inscriptions in various languages, as well as drawings of birds and beasts and religious symbols. Some of them have been so weathered by the elements that they are hardly legible. Others stand out most clearly. Among the most striking of them are two seven-branched menorahs, one of which is supported on a three-pronged base.

It is a strange and stirring sight. One seems to hear the words echoing through the stillness of this remote retreat: "Put off thy shoes from off thy feet, for the place whereon thou standest is holy ground" (Exodus 3:5; Acts 7:33). It was obvious that this had long been a sacred place, near a route of travel across Sinai leading from the head of the Gulf of Aqabah to the head of the Gulf of Suez. But why, we asked ourselves, had this particular point, so difficult of access, been chosen? Why, indeed, one could ask further, had a particular, grim, bare mountain top in Sinai been selected to be the seat of God's revelation of His Moral Law to Moses and Israel?

Six centuries and possibly more were spanned by this concentration of inscriptions and drawings in the Wadi Umm es-Sedeir. There were some carefully engraved Nabataean sentences, commemorating the dead. On one rock surface was a contemporary inscription in Greek of the name AKRABOS. It was current in the Semitic world of the times, and was commonly used by Nabataeans, Arabs and Jews, among others. On the ledge beneath it, a poor Latin scholar had laboriously spelled out in abbreviated form a familiar salutation. The first word originally appeared as VCTORA. A later hand inserted the missing letters to make it read correctly VICTORIA. The entire inscription, consisting of three words which were run together, reads: VICTORIA-AUGC, which stand for VICTORIA AUG(USTI) C(AESARI). That may be translated roughly as "Hurrah for Augustus Caesar," or "Victory to the Exalted Caesar." It was a legend which occurred on Roman coins of the Emperor

THE CROSS AND THE CANDELABRA

Domitian, which were struck in Caesaria in Palestine between 81 and A.D. 96.

Every accessible blank space on the canyon walls in this hidden nook of the Wadi Umm es-Sedeir was utilized to the full during the course of successive centuries. Sometime in the Byzantine period, a worshipful Jew made use of the remaining bit of smooth surface of the rock face next to the Latin inscription. On it, he carved a seven-branched candelabra with a tripodal base. It bore thus a resemblance to the one depicted on the mosaic floor of the synagogue at Nirim in the northwesternmost Negev. On the left side of its base is a shofar (ram's horn), with another on the right side, together with an ethrog and some other objects. The religious atmosphere of this site was further heightened by the presence on the opposite wall of the canyon of another, larger and cruder and less well preserved candelabra, which was unadorned with any other symbols.

In the candelabras and crosses and in the synagogues and churches of the Byzantine period, the Negev and Sinai found their crowning glory. Never had the Southland been more intensively cultivated or more densely inhabited. Many peoples in many ages had dwelt and prospered there whenever peace prevailed. The scintillating Nabataeans were the first to exploit the potentialities of the land to the full through the exercise of unparalleled ingenuity and energy. Kenites and Rechabites and their related clans were rooted there of old. Judaeans and Hebrew and Chalcolithic settlers left traces of their being behind them. Never in historical times had radical and permanent changes of climate placed it beyond the pale of settlement. Prehistoric peoples knew it well long before pottery was invented.

The geographical position of the Negev has always made it part of a passageway between continents. Its truest importance, however, transcends its location, physical nature and boundaries. This is no ordinary land of broken plains and naked ranges and scanty water. God walked abroad in it and divine purpose was made manifest there of old. It has always been, together with Sinai, a sanctuary of revelation and reformation, with the spirit of the Holy pervading the very atmosphere. And thus, both in the physical and the spiritual sense, the words of the Prophet may be applied to it: "And the wastes shall be builded. And the desolate land shall be tilled, whereas it lay desolate in the sight of all that passed by. And they shall say, This land that was desolate is become like the Garden of Eden" (Ezekiel 36:33-35).

INDICES

GENERAL INDEX

Numbers placed in parentheses refer to illustrations; thus 204 (fig. 44) means that illustration 44 follows text page 204.

A letter followed by a number (as in Abdah, C-5) indicates the location of the entry on the endpaper map.

Aaron, 206
abayeh, 155
Abdah, 23, 34, 48, 80, 91, 95, 198, 204 (fig. 44), 223, 226, 228, 229, 231, 235, 236, 237, 244, 249, 255, 258, 262, 265, 268, 271-276, C-5
Abigail, 127
Abishar, 104-105
Aboth, 66
Abraham (Abram), 14, 19, 21, 61-84, 94, 98, 102-107, 111, 112, 114, 120, 135, 137, 157, 171, 261, 278
Abrahamitic period, xi, 61-84, 88, 95, 97, 100-101, 108, 114, 128, 132, 149, 208, 215, 216, 260, 274
Absalom, 125
Achish, 123, 124, 125, 126
Achsah, 139-140
Acts of St. George, 271
Ad Dianam, 258
Adino, 137, 138
Admah, 72, 73, 105
adze, 26
Aegean Islands, 122
Afiqim ba-Negev, 93
Africa, 108, 119, 150, 158, 160, 196, 241, 246
Age of Abraham, 68, 69, 71, 76, 97-101, 106-107, 168, 170, 226
agriculture, 3, 5, 7, 11, 51-52, 57, 58, 74, 76, 77, 81, 84, 88, 91, 97, 100-101, 139, 142, 144, 169, 187, 197, 199, 200, 202, 210, 211, 212
Ahab, 10, 20
Aharoni, Johanon, x, 178
Ahaz, 168
Ahinoam, 127
Aila, 32, 160, 164, 228, 237, 243, 258, 269, 273, 281, E-12

Ain Aqrabbim, E-4
Ain el-Ifdan, F-6
 -Qadeis, 88, 236, B-6
 -Qattar, 258, E-5
 -Qudeirat, 63, 73, 88, 96, 112, 236, B-6
 -Wehbeh, 229, 258, E-6
Ain Fiqreh, 205
 Gedi, F-1
 Ghadyan, 36-37, 46 (fig. 5), 133, 258, E-10
 Gharandel, E-9
 Haruf, 258
 Hosb, 80, 89, 203, 204, 205, 229, 258, F-5
Ain Mishpat (see Kadesh-barnea), 73
 Mureifiq (Ain Ovdat), 83, 88, 95, 96, C-5
 Murrah, C-5
 Netifim, D-11
 Ovdat, 95, 96, C-5
 Shehabiyeh, D-5
 Shellaleh, 237
 Umm Qa'ab, D-5
 Wehbeh (Ain Yahav), 229, 258, E-6
 Yerka, 23, 24, 46 (fig. 2), E-4
Ajjul, 49
Akrabos, 282
Aksa Mosque, 250
Albright, William Foxwell, 7, 9, 30, 84, 102, 139
Alexander Jannaeus, 189, 192
Alexander the Great, 188
Alexandria, 196
Alexandros Amrou, 194, 273
Ali Baba, 54
Allat, 237
Alon, David, x
altar, 63, 83, 194-195, 225

GENERAL INDEX

Amalekites, 73, 88, 113, 114, 116, 124, 127, 128, 129, 130, 132, 133, 148, 169, 185
Amen-em-heb, 119
American Schools of Oriental Research, 217
Amman, 167, 237
Ammon, 11, 147, 172
Amorites, 73, 116
Amos, 65
amphora, 79, 280
Amraphel, 71-72, 73
Amratian, 49
Amru, 273
amulet, 46, 48
Anakim, 137
Anati, Emanuel, x
ancestor worship, 27
annihilation, 73
Antioch, 252
Antiochus IV, 188
Antipater, 191
anvils, 43, 46
Apophis, 108
apses, 265, 268, 269
Aqabah, 32, 89, 156, 160, 161, 164, 167, 168, E-12
aqueduct, 92, 211, 234
Arab, 103, 175
Arabah, 18, 32, 36, 37, 44, 45, 79, 86, 87, 121, 123, 145, 146, 153-163, 165, 170, 171, 179, 202, 203, 205, 226, 229
Arabia, 12, 15, 41, 59, 65, 89, 97, 146, 150, 158, 160, 162, 163, 165, 166, 172, 173, 193, 195, 196, 198, 208, 212, 229, 235, 237, 239, 241, 249, 252, 253, 269
Arabic, 25, 55
Arad, 18, 40, 49-53, 88, 114-115, 133, 176, 178, 180, 181
Aramaic, 172, 188, 194-195
Arba, City of, 137
architect, 174-177, 196
architecture, 251, 256
Aretas IV, 191, 192, 195
ark, 280
Ark of the Covenant, 122
Armageddon, 119
armies, 70
armor, 110, 115
Aroer, 50, 130, 131, 180, 184
arrow heads, 26
Artaxerxes, 5
artesian well, 95
artisan, 48
Aryoch, 72, 73

Asa, 171
Ascalon, 89, 108, 196
Ascent of Aqrabbim, 34
Asherah, 116
Ashtaroth-Karnaim, 11, 73, 74, 105
Asia, 119, 160
Asia Minor, 109, 153, 162, 229, 246
Asphalt Lake, 3, 49
asses, 67
Assurbanipal, 5
Assyria, 5, 119, 151
Astarte, 76 (fig. 18, 19), 117, 267
Atargatis, 196, 197
atrium, 268
Audeh ibn Jad, 155
augury, 116
Auja Hafir, 26, 29, 262-263, B-4
Aurelian, 248
Avaris, 108
axe, 3, 26
Aztec, 106

Baal, 116
Bab edh-Dhra, 84
Babylonia, 5, 19, 119, 142, 154, 187
Babylonian conquest, 132
Babylonians, xii, 116, 154, 188, 189
badge of office, 167
baksheesh, 166-167
Balaam, 10, 134
Balak, 10
baptismal font, 267
baptistry, 268
barley, 45, 144, 213, 215, 270
basalt, 4, 46 (fig. 9), 48
basilica, 250
basin, catchment, 92, 253, 266
Basin of Beersheba, 80
Basin of Rekhmeh, 78
Basutoland, 82, 84
bathhouse, 262, 272
Bayir Wells, 201
beads, 4
beaker, 57
Bedouins, 6, 11, 12, 20, 22, 23, 25, 26, 32, 48, 75, 80, 91, 108, 127, 140 (fig. 26, 27), 169-170, 177, 178, 183, 185, 187, 209, 214, 223, 228, 229, 231, 232, 234, 254, 260
beehive-shaped houses, 82
Be'er la-Hai Ro'i, 63, 104, 263
Be'er Orah, D-11
Beersheba, xi, 18, 20, 21, 39-41, 45, 47, 49, 50, 52, 56, 57, 58, 59, 64, 69, 79, 82, 86, 88, 89, 96, 114, 117, 123, 134, 138, 141, 146, 168, 175, 176,

GENERAL INDEX

177, 178, 180, 181, 189, 215, 228, 229, 237, 243, 258, 262, 265
Beersheba Basin, xi, 58, 82, 134, 140, 185
Be'er Yeruham, 140
Beit-gubrin, 281
Bela, 73
Beni Adam, 3
Beni Hassan, 104
Beq'ah, 121
Bera, 72, 73
Bered, 63, 259
Bereshit Rabba, 259
Bessemer, 36, 165
Beth-eglayim, 41, 49, 50
Bethel, 66, 67, 69
Bethlehem, 3
Beth-shan, 40, 50
Beth Yerah, 30
Beyond Jordan, 250
Bible, 30-31, 53, 68, 69, 74, 75, 135
Biq'at Yeruham, 78-84
Bir Asluj, 88, 96, C-4
  Auja, 88, 90, 96
  Birein, 64, 83, 88, 90, 96, 97-98, 100, 216, 260, B-5
  Hafir, 22, 23, 83, 88, 96, 236, 260, 265, C-5
  Ibn Odeh, D-7
  Madhkur, 235, F-7
  Maliha, E-8
  Milh, 88, 96
  Milhan, D-10
  Mishash, 88, 96, D-3
  Mitnan, 96, B-6
  Rekhmeh, 78-84, 88, 134, 140
  Reseisiyeh, 83, 88, 96, C-5
  Resisim, 260
  Tabah, 277, D-12
  Themeleh, C-4
birds, 93, 205, 240
birkeh, 201
Birsha, 72, 73
bitumen, 72
Biyar Ar'areh, 57, 88, 96, 131, E-3
  el-Mishash, 88, 96, 182, D-3
  Ideid Umm Salih, 237, 275, C-7
  Ideid es-Samawi, 237, 275, C-7
blast furnace, 36
blockhouse, 185, 233
Boethon, 204 (fig. 41)
Boethos, 224
bone, 4, 47, 48, 58, 64
Borot Qedem, 96
bowls, 27, 46
Bozrah, 42, 244, 245, 252
bracelet, 48

bread, 155
Bronze, Early, 42, 49, 59
  Middle I, 60-84, 88, 94, 98, 99
  Middle II, 95
Brook of Egypt (Wadi el-Arish), 14, 49, 149, 170, 171
bull, 274
burial, 238
  cairn, 278
  circle, 54, 278
  grounds, 216
  monument, 277
  tomb, 212, 273, 277-278
  tumuli, 34
burin, 241
burnt offering, 62
Byzantine, xii, 34, 50, 79, 80, 92, 95, 96, 97, 149, 172, 173, 178, 179, 182, 188, 207, 208, 209, 210, 215, 242, 243-284
  art, 251-252, 256
  Christianity, 249-252
  churches, 249, 250, 251, 256, 262, 265, 269, 279
  cistern, 95, 224-225, 248, 253, 262, 266, 272, 274
  cities, 34, 219, 249, 252, 257
  crosses, 208, 225, 249, 260, 268, 274
  monasteries, 256, 272, 273
  mosaic, 208, 251-252, 259, 269
  population, 256
  synagogue, 251, 279-284
  terraces, 248, 253
  theological school, 259
  trade, 252, 254, 259
  water conservation, 215-222, 248, 253
Byzantium, 246-248, 252, 253, 254

Caesarea Maratima, 189
Caesarea Phillipi, 189
cairns, 277, 278
Caleb, 20, 86, 113, 124, 129, 134, 136, 137, 139, 140
Calebites, 125, 136, 141, 143, 145, 154, 169
camel, 53, 67, 75, 93, 118, 155, 160, 181, 183, 201, 203, 210, 238, 239, 270
Canaan, 15, 18, 20, 26, 39, 49, 53, 59, 60, 61, 63, 66, 75, 86, 88, 89, 102, 103, 107, 109, 115, 117, 118, 119, 128, 132, 137, 144, 168, 172, 196, 215, 278
Canaanite, 51, 79, 110, 114, 115, 133, 139, 140, 141, 231
candelabra, 280, 283

cap, 117
Caphtor (Crete), 109
capitals, 195, 251, 268, 269
captivity, 73
caravan, 19, 59, 67, 69, 83, 89, 114, 162, 186, 187, 196, 197, 205, 207, 225-228, 233, 237, 244, 248, 259
caravanserai, 36, 173, 179, 189, 201, 203, 204, 225-228, 233, 271
carbon, 14, 29
care of the dead, 277-278
Carnaim, 73
catchment basin, 92, 221-222
cattle, 67
cave, 47, 272, 225
Cave of Machpelah, 137
chaff, 177
Chalcolithic, x, xi, 42-50, 54, 56, 57, 58, 59, 60, 61, 70, 78, 79, 80, 81, 91, 96, 157, 182, 208
Chaldees, 33
chalices, 46
chalk, 206
channel, 92, 164, 216-222, 223, 225
charcoal, 36, 164-165
chariots, 107, 153, 170
Chedorlaomer, 72, 73, 102, 105, 106
Cherethites, 125, 129, 130, 134, 141
chieftain, 103, 183
child sacrifice, 48, 61-63
Children of Israel, 27, 65, 112
  Giants, 113
  Man, 3
China, 196
Christian, 34, 156, 194, 208, 256-257
Christianity, 245, 249-252, 260
Church of St. Mary, 250
  Saints Sergius and Bacchus, 271
  the Holy Sepulcher, 250, 276
  the Nativity, 251
Cilicia, 153
circles, 54
cistern, 23, 34, 92, 94-97, 140 (fig. 21), 172 (fig. 37), 173, 174, 176, 179, 185, 204 (fig. 38, 40), 209, 210, 211, 216, 217, 222-225, 234, 248, 272
cities, 5, 10, 34, 40, 41, 112, 113, 170, 171, 178
Cities of the Decapolis, 230
Cities of the Plain, 84
City of Arba, 137
City of Copper, 44
civilization, xii, 4, 5, 7-12, 97, 210
clay figurine, 48
climate, x, 3, 7-12, 16, 42, 47, 180, 209-210
coffin, 1

coiffure, 47
coins, 8, 204, 282
Colt Expedition, 270
commerce, xii, 11, 37, 150, 151, 152, 247
conduits, 215-222
conical cap, 116-117
conservation, soil and water, 80, 215-222
Constantine I (the Great), 246-248, 250, 251
Constantinople, 246
copper, 36, 37, 41, 42-50, 58, 61, 89, 133, 134, 146, 150, 155, 158, 153-163, 167
Corinthianized capitals, 251
cornet base, 57
courtyard, 99, 179
crafts, 45, 110
crater, 40
Creed of Rechabites, 142-145
Crete, 109
crocus, 91
cross, 224, 225, 256-257, 260
crucible, 45, 164-165
Crusaders, 52, 250, 277
Ctesiphon, 244
cultivation, 77, 198, 248, 253
Cupid, 240
cupholes, 76 (fig. 16), 77-84
curbstones, 228

Daiqa, 80, 96
dam, 76 (fig. 14, 15), 79-84, 90, 92, 209, 211, 212-213, 221, 248
Damascus, 72, 192, 228, 245
Dan, 13, 72, 149
Darb es-Sultani, 228, 258
David, 20, 122-132, 135, 136, 138, 141, 146, 147, 148, 153, 168, 169, 174, 184
Dead Sea, 3, 40, 42, 49, 57, 72, 79, 84, 87, 105, 121, 135, 143, 155, 176, 179, 180, 183, 191, 192, 199
Debir, 9, 139-140
Decapolis, Cities of, 230
deer, 3
denarii, 270
density of population, 97
Derekh ha-Melekh, 33
desert, 15-16, 91, 141-145, 187
dew, 91
dhows, 163
Diodorus, 198
Dionysus, 199, 224, 225, 267
distaff, 55
dolphin, 196, 267

GENERAL INDEX

Domitian, 283
donkey, 53, 181, 183
doves, 268
draft furnace, 165
drawings, rock, 236-242
dry farming, 23, 51, 91, 95, 186
Dura, 100, 244
Dushara, 199, 224, 225, 267
dye, 152

eagle, 268
ear-handles, 54, 70
Early Bronze Age pottery, 49
earthquakes, 272
Eboda, 271-276, C-5
ebony, 248
Edom, 10-12, 15, 18, 21, 32, 44, 45,
    87, 89, 90, 117, 123, 132, 146, 148,
    153, 154, 156, 158, 159, 160, 161,
    164, 165, 166, 168, 179, 185, 197,
    201, 204, 206, 207, 228, 237, 273
Egypt, 5, 12, 15, 16, 19, 39, 46, 49, 58,
    59, 60, 63, 66, 71, 75, 92, 102, 107,
    108, 109, 111, 119, 120, 129, 133,
    146, 149, 151, 152, 153, 162, 172,
    173, 196, 229, 260
Eilat (Elath), 20, 80, 89, 281, D-12
el-Arish, 14, 49, 121, 269
el-Hosb, 206
Elam, 73
Elath, 18, 32, 65, 140 (fig. 20), 141,
    159, 160, 165, 166, 168, 172, 173,
    D-12
Eleazer, 206
elephant, 23, 280
Elijah, 20, 142, 144
Ellasar, 73
Eloth (Elath), 140, 158-159
El-paran, 73, 74
Elusa (Khalasah), 257-260
embattlements, 106
Emessa, 245
Emim, 73
engraved stone, 167-168
En-mishpat, 73, 112
eponym, 244
Eros, 240
erosion, 9, 35, 92, 93, 202
Esau, 154, 273
Esdraelon, 40
Essenes, 143, 198
et-Tabun, 1, 2, 4
et-Telah (Toloha), 172 (fig. 31), 201-
    202, 203, 204, 212, F-5
Ethiopia, 249
ethrog, 280, 283

Euphrates, 5, 11, 108, 109, 149, 171,
    244
Eusebius, 156
Evenari, Michael, 219, 220
Execration Texts, 102, 103
exile, 151
Exodus, 10, 15, 16, 44, 45, 88-89, 109,
    111-115, 118-121, 129, 142, 146,
    155, 160, 180
exploration criteria, 8-10, 37-38, 76,
    78, 96, 184
eyeballs, 28
Ezion-geber:Elath, xii, 15, 18, 31, 36,
    41, 45, 46 (fig. 10), 51, 122, 123,
    138, 140 (fig. 23), 146, 150, 152,
    153-163, 165, 168, 170, 171, 172,
    185, 186, D-12
Ezra, 187

falcon, 184
famine, 66
Far'ah, 49
farmer, 40, 48, 187
farming communities, 149
farming, dry, 23, 51, 91, 95, 186
Father of a Multitude of Nations, 76
fawn, 4
Feinan (Punon), 44-45, 50, G-6
Feldman, Jose, x
fellahin, 181, 213
fenced cities, 171
Fertile Crescent, xii, 5, 23, 52, 58, 59,
    60, 71, 76, 106, 109
fertility, 27, 46-47, 141, 196, 197, 211
Fezzan, 241
fields, 36, 45, 179, 180, 184, 185, 202,
    211-213, 215-222
fig tree, 90, 112, 144, 266
figurine, clay, 48
fire, 65, 116, 119
firstborn, 61-63
Fisher, Clarence S., 7
fishes, 267
fishhook, 163
fleet, 159, 163
flint, 1, 2, 3, 4, 26, 27, 48, 54, 57, 58,
    116, 208
flocks, 4, 23, 101, 210, 232
flood, 45
floors, 27, 30
flour, 182
flower, 91, 92, 240
flues, 36, 164-165
flute, 25
fortification, 8, 106, 107, 177, 179, 182,
    185-186, 187
fortress, xi, xii, 10, 14, 19, 37, 73, 88,

94, 95, 107, 108, 133, 138, 149, 168, 170, 171, 174, 176, 178, 179, 185, 186, 187, 208, 215, 222-225, 264, 271
fossils, 235
foundation offering, 61
foundations, 45, 81-84, 99, 215
Four Horsemen of the Apocalypse, 72, 275
Frank, Fritz, 32, 161
frankincense, 150, 162, 270
fruit trees, 36, 90
furnace, 36, 156, 164-165, 172

Gad, 155
Galilee, 1, 192, 251
game pieces, 54
Ganymede, 240
Garden of Eden, 5
Gethsemane, 250
gardens, 7, 36, 92
garrisons, 148, 173, 179
gateways, 106, 186
Gath, 123, 125
Gaza, 55, 108, 109, 121, 196, 258, 262, 270, 274, B-1
gazelle, 3, 93, 205, 209, 236 (fig. 47), 238-239, 240
Gebanites, 270
Ge-harashim, 156
Genesis, 66, 71, 75
Gerar, 41, 75, 261, 263
Gerasa (Jerash), 35, 245, 250
Gerasa (Thamilet es-Suweilmeh), 237, C-9
Gerrah, 196, 269
Gerzean, 49
Geshurites, 124, 125
Gethsemane, Garden of, 250
Gezer, 95
ghazzus, 111, 124
Ghor Basin, 79
Giants, 137
Gibeon, 95, 106
Gibraltar, 152
Gilead, 13
Gilgal, 10
Girzites, 124, 125
glaçis, 176-177
glass, 201
goats, 22, 56, 93, 181, 210, 231
goatskins, 46 (fig. 4)
goddess, 28, 46-47, 117
gods, 28, 118, 199-200, 224-225
Goiim, 73
gold, 67, 150, 158, 159, 161, 162
golden calf, 27

goldsmith, 271
Goliath, 56
Gomorrah, 72, 73, 105
Goshen, 209
Gospel, Fourth, 271
grain, 45, 48, 53, 66, 84, 181, 182, 207
grapes, 112, 137, 199, 270
grapevines, 90, 240, 280
grass, 92, 203
graves, 40
grazing, 40
Greece, 196
Greek, 172, 188, 194, 200, 224, 282
grinding quern, 27
guard tower, 106, 171
Gulf of Aqabah, 18, 32, 121, 132, 155, 156, 158, 159, 160, 228, 237, 243, 269, 277, 282, D-12
Gulf of Suez, 282

Hadad, 19, 153, 195
Hadrian's Temple of Venus, 250
Hagar, 21, 63-65, 75, 153, 259
Haila, 258
Ham, 73, 74
hamada, 15
Hamath, 14, 149
hamsin, 16, 91
handle, 47
Hapiru, 71
Harabat Atiqa, 96
Harabet Umm Dimneh, 131, 138, E-3
harbor, 152, 172
Haretath, 195, 257-258
Har Geshur, 237
harpsichord, 179
Hasmonean, 188
Hauran, 192
Havilah, 129, 133
Hazazontamar, 73
Hazor, 95, 107
headers, 140 (fig. 24), 176, 186
heartland, 66
Heber, 134
Hebrew, 165, 167-168, 171, 178, 279
Hebron, 51, 72, 88, 122, 124, 136, 137, 138, 139, E-1
Heiyani, Wadi, 87
Hellenistic, 50, 152, 178, 185, 245
herds, 23, 101, 210, 232
herem, 115
hermitage, 265
Herod Antipas, 19, 189, 191, 192, 195, 258

GENERAL INDEX 291

Herod the Great, 12, 188, 189, 191, 195, 258
Herodias, 191-192
herringbone design, 46
Hezekiah, 79, 116
Hierusalem, 258
high places, 116
highways, 108, 215, 231, 232, 243
Hillel, 66, 144, 220
Hillel, D., 220
hilltops, walled, 171, 216-222
Himyarite, 281
hippopotamus, 2
Hiram, 43, 151
historical gap, 59
historical memory, xi, 31, 64, 68, 71, 156
Hittites, 109, 125, 151, 153
Hobab, 134
Hobah, 72
Holy Land, 90, 114, 169, 187, 249, 250
Holy Mountain, 270
homo sapiens, 2
Horites, 73
Hormah, 18, 41, 86, 87, 88, 114, 115, 118, 119, 120, 128, 131, 137, 180, 215, E-3
horses, 153
Horsfield, George and Agnes, 200, 237
horse trader, 153
hotel, 271
Hotham, 184
household implements, 47
House of Rechab, 143
houses, 26-30, 45, 48, 52, 179, 199
  beehive, 76, 77, 81, 82-84, 99
  circular, 76 (fig. 13), 215, 259, 268
Howeitat, 203
Huldu, 195
human control, 12
  rights, 141-144
  sacrifice, 65
humidity, 48
hunting, 239, 240
Hyksos, 105-109

ibex, 93, 238, 239, 241
Ibrahim, 103
identification, pottery, 34
idolatry, 141
idols, 62
Idumean, 12, 154, 189, 204
images, 117
implements, 47
incantation cups, 102

incense, 162, 194, 195, 207, 255, 257
India, 150, 158, 196, 247
industrial center, xii, 44, 45, 150, 157, 162, 163, 173
Injadat Arabs, 155
inscription, 162, 166, 194-195, 197, 238, 257, 258, 267, 272-273, 274, 280, 282
invasion routes, 71
Iqfi, Wadi, 87
'Ir Nahas, 156
iron, 32, 36, 43, 133, 152, 153-163
Iron Age, 95, 132, 178
irrigation, 4, 5, 36, 201-202
Isaac, 19, 61-65, 75, 104, 117, 137, 263, 278
Isaiah, 65-66, 119, 120
Isbeita, 34, 204 (fig. 45, 46), 215, 219, 249, 264-269, 272, 276, 278, C-4
Ishmael, 63-65, 75, 153
Islam, 247, 250
islands, 158
Isle of Graye, 277
Israel, 10, 41, 49, 62, 64, 65, 88, 95, 118-119, 120, 121, 122, 124, 125, 132, 135, 137, 141-145, 146, 147, 148, 149-151, 152, 153, 168, 169, 173, 187
Israeli, xiii, 33
Israelites, 10, 15, 16, 17, 20, 44, 45, 51, 86, 87, 89, 90, 109, 110-115, 119-121, 128, 134, 140, 141, 155, 158, 228, 229, 261, 279
ivory figurines 46 (fig. 6, 7), 46-48, 58

Jacob, 19, 117-118, 137, 154, 196, 278
Jacobites, 249
Jael, 134
jar, 49, 61, 162
Jauf, 237
Jaussen, Father A., 273
Jebel Druze, 192
  el-Medhra, 91, 205, 206, E-5
  Hauran, 230
  Ideid, 237, 238
  Medhra, 172 (fig. 35), E-5
  Mene'iyeh, D-11
  Tubeiq, 237
Jebusites, 116
Jedidiah, 150
Jehoshaphat, 159, 163, 171
Jehovah-yir'eh, 62-64
Je'iel, 184
Jephuneh the Kenizzite, 137
Jerafi, Wadi, 87

GENERAL INDEX

Jerash, 35, 245, 250
Jeremiah, 19, 119, 143, 144
Jericho, 4, 10, 26-30, 46 (fig. 8), 114, 122, 133, 143
Jerome, 259
Jerusalem, xii, 15, 41, 63, 95, 102, 106, 118, 119, 122, 123, 138, 143, 150-151, 162, 167, 170, 171, 172, 186, 187, 194, 243, 246, 250, 258, 276
Jesus, 66, 144, 245, 250, 255
jewelry, 48
Jews, 188, 199, 255, 259, 279, 283
Jezebel, 20, 142
Jeziret Far'un, 277
Jezreel, 40, 126, 134
Joab, 153
Job, 10, 35, 56, 119
John the Baptist, 192
Jonadab ben-Rechab, 143
Jonathan, 126
Joram, 159
Jordan, 3, 30, 117, 121, 143, 148, 245, 250
Joseph, 19, 278
Josephus, 49
Joshua, 20, 86, 113, 137
Josiah, 118
Jotham, 140 (fig. 22), 167-168
Judaean, xi, 11, 19, 33, 34, 45, 57, 73, 79, 88, 94, 97, 106, 116, 123, 124, 125, 133, 141, 146-153, 156, 158, 161, 165, 166, 168, 171, 179, 182, 183, 185, 187, 191, 208, 215, 216, 231, 279
Judah, xii, 12, 15, 19, 41, 63, 79, 81, 95, 119, 120, 123, 129, 130, 132, 133, 134, 138, 139, 141, 146, 147, 148, 151, 154, 155, 159, 165, 168, 170, 171, 172, 174, 180, 185, 187, 188, 189, 192, 222
Justinian, 246-247, 250, 251, 253
Kadesh-barnea, 11, 16, 18, 20, 34, 41, 63-65, 73-75, 86-88, 90, 96-98, 100, 102, 105, 112-115, 119-121, 128, 138, 153, 169, 186, 206, 215, 236, 258, 261, 263, B-6
Karnak, 119
Kedesh, 134
Kenaz, 139
Kenites, 2, 45, 86, 111, 125, 131, 132, 133, 134, 137, 140, 141, 142, 143, 145, 154, 155, 169,
Kenizzites, 45, 133, 136, 137, 140, 141, 154
Kenyon, Dorothy, xiii
Kerak (Qir of Moab), 41-42, H-3

Khalasah, 34, 257-260, 261, 262, 265, 279, 280, C-3
Khayana, 108
Khiltsa, Way of, 259
khirbeh, 155, 226
Khirbet Abu Tulul, D-3
  Ar'areh, 50, 115, 131, 132, 180, 184-185, D-3
  Gharrah, x, 140 (fig. 25), 174-179, 181, D-2
  Ghazza, x, xi, 42, 179-180, E-3
  Kuseifeh, 279, E-2
  Medhbeh, 56, 180, D-3
  Mefjer, 240
  Mishash, 56, 88, 115, 131, 132, 180, 182-184, D-3
  Nahas ('Ir Nahash), 44, 155-156, G-6
  Neqb el-Hamleh, 226
  Paqu'ah, C-4
  Samra, 40, 53-56, 58, 61, 80, E-2
  Sfar, 207
  Tannur, 172 (fig. 29, 30), 194-195, 196, 197, 200, 236 (fig. 50-54), 255, 258, 267, 273
  Umm Radin, 179
  Umm Rujum, 264, C-3
kiln, 48, 55
Kilwa, 204 (fig. 42), 237, 241
King of Arad, 51, 88, 114-115, 118
King of Judah, 168
Kingdom of Israel, 90
Kings of the East, 11, 72, 73, 74, 75, 76, 101, 105, 228, 275
King's Highway, 10, 33
Kir-haresheth, 95
Kiriath-arba, 137
Kiriath-sefer (Debir), 9, 139-140
Kish, 184
Koeppel, Father Robert, 57
Kuntillah, C-9
Kurnub, 34, 76 (fig. 14), 79-80, 89, 91, 131, 138, 189, 207-210, 229, 258
Laban, 117
Lachish, 95, 108
ladle handle, 47
Lake of Galilee, 1, 30, 121
lamb, 62
Land of Goshen, 261
Land of Moriah, 63
Land of the Negev, 63
Latin, 188
Lawrence, T. E., 33, 34, 74, 261, 263
lead, 152
leaf and fruit design, 260
leaves, 197, 236 (fig. 52)

GENERAL INDEX

Lebanon, 209
lentils, 45
leopard, 280
leprosy, 168
Leuke Kome, 269
Lewis, Naphtali, 270-271
library, 271
lid, stone, 84
Life of St. Hilarion, 259
lime, 164
limestone, 4, 48
limitanei, 270-271
lion, 280
Lisan, 42
Lloyd George, 13, 14
loess, 40, 43, 47, 50
loom, 55-56, 271
loom weight, 55, 61
Lot, 72
lotus, 280

Ma'aleh Aqrabbim, 89, 206
Maccabees, 188, 189, 204
macehead, 43, 49, 61
Machaerus, 192
Machpelah, 278
Machtesh Gadol, 23, 89, 229
   Qatan, 89
   Ramon, 87, 226, 229
Madeba, 258
Madmannah, 131, 138
malachite, 44
Malichus II, 204
Mallon, Father Alexis, 57
Mamre, 278
Mampsis, 79, 89, 138, 189, 207-210, E-4
Mamshat, 79
Manasseh, 116
Manual of Discipline, 143
maps, Madeba, 258
   Peutinger, 258, 271-272
Marah, 259
marble, 269
market, 181
Masada, F-2
masons, 25
mausoleum, 40
Mecca, 199, 224
Meda'in Saleh, 196, 269
medallion, 267, 280
Megiddo, 40, 95, 106, 119
melon, 91, 206
Memphis, 104
Mene'iyeh, 36, D-11
menorah, 279-284
mercenaries, 141

merchant, 207
mermaid, 196
Mesha, 10
Mesolithic Natufian, 3
Mesopotamia, 60, 107, 108, 109, 149, 152
metallurgical crafts, 110, 134, 154, 157
metalsmith, 134
Mexico, 106
Middle Bronze I pottery, 69-70, 82
Middle Sea, 49
Midianites, 19, 46 (fig. 1)
Midrash, 279
milestones, 33, 204 (fig. 39), 227-228, 230
military draft, 171
   post, 186, 233
   rule, 170, 178
millstones, 57
Minaean, 162
minerals, 170
mines, Arabah, 37, 44, 155
   copper and iron, 32, 36, 37, 44, 133, 153-165, 197
mirage, 81
Mishrefeh, 34, 172 (fig. 36), 218, 265, C-4
Mizpah, 13
Moa, 231, 235, E-6
Moab, 10-12, 21, 41, 90, 95, 117, 148, 149, 197, 204, 207, 228
moat, 184
Mohammedan, 247, 256, 269, 276
molds, 43, 117
mollusc, 47
monasteries, 249, 256, 268, 272
money lender, 271
Monophysites, 249
monuments, 73
moon, temple, 30
Moral Law, 142-145
Moriah, 62, 63
mortar, 4, 26, 84
mosaic, Byzantine, 208
   Isbeita, 267, 269
   Khalasah, 259, 280
   Madeba, 258
   Nirim, 236 (fig. 48), 280
Moses, 2, 19, 20, 27, 34, 65, 112-114, 115, 119, 120, 129, 133, 134, 137, 143, 144, 155, 197, 206
Moslem, 199, 224, 249, 250
mosque, 276
Mosque of Omar, 83
mother-of-pearl, 48
mound, 5, 6
mounds of stone, 228-229

GENERAL INDEX

Mount Carmel, 1, 2
  Hor, 206
  Horeb, 142
  Moriah, 63
  Sinai, 27, 65, 144
  of Jehovah, 62
Mountains of Hebron, 53, 189
  Judah, 40, 176, 178
Moyet Awad, 229, 231
mud brick, 45
Multiplication of the Loaves and Fishes, 267
murals, 104, 240
Mudowerah, 81
myrrh, 162

Nabal, 127
Nabataeans, xii, 12, 34, 36, 79, 80-89, 91-95, 97, 142, 149, 154, 160, 166, 172, 173, 190-253, 269-282
nahal, 22, 129
Nahal Besor, 129
  Lavan, 79, 96
  Mizraim, 75, 79
  Mor, 95
  Nitsanah, 79, 98
nails, 163
Naples, 196
Naqb Sa'far, 89
  Sufei, 89, 206
Natairu, 257
Natayr'el, 195
Nathan, 125, 136, 150
Natufian, 3, 4, 28-30
Nazareth, 1
Neanderthal, 1
Nebo, 2
Nebuchadnezzar, 5
Negev of Caleb, 134, 136, 138, 139
  Cherethites, 134, 141
  Judah, 134, 141, 178
  Kenites, 133, 134, 136
  Yerahmeelites, 134, 141
Nehemiah, 187
Neolithic, 26-30, 230
Nessana, 26, 215, 269-271
net weights, 163
New Testament, 224
Nike, 195
Nile, 16, 104, 108, 109, 124
Nirim, 280, 283, B-2
Nitsanah, 26, 34, 215, 220, 262-263, 265, 269-271, B-4
nomads, 59, 109, 111, 227
Nubia, 108

oasis, 44, 90, 205, 237, 244

Oboda (Abdah), 258, 262, 271-276, C-5
Obodas, 192, 198, 244, 272
Oboth, 45
oil, 165
olive trees, 144, 266
Omayyad, 240
Omri, 134
Ophir, 32, 150, 152, 157-163
orchard, 36
ores, 36-37, 156, 164-165
ostraca, 162, 172
ostrich, 239
Othniel, 139-140
ox, 2, 241

Padan Aram, 117, 196
Painted House, 240
painting, 240, 269
Paleolithic, 1, 2, 30, 208, 230
Palestina Tertia, 252-253, 259
Palestine, x, 1, 2, 14, 26, 49, 58, 69, 103, 105, 108, 109, 110, 115, 121, 138, 152, 154, 160, 188, 189, 191, 245, 251
palm, 133, 200, 280
Palmer, E. H., 220
Palmyra, 171, 244, 247-248, 254
Pan, 240
papyri, 199, 260, 270
papyrus, 209
Paran, 21, 73, 153, 154
Parthia, 244, 245
path, straight, 226-228
Patriarchal Age, 103, 105, 171
Patriarchate of Antioch, 252
Patriarchate of Jerusalem, 253
Paul of Tarsus, 192
Pax Abrahamitica, 76-84, 107
Pax Romana, 107
peace, 76
peacocks, 280
pear-shaped mace, 49
peas, 270
Pelethites, 125, 141
pelican, 47
pendants, 4, 48
Peraea, 191, 192
perfumes, 248
Perrot, Jean, xi, xiii, 43, 48
Persian, 188, 247, 250, 276
  Gulf, 165, 196, 269
pestle, 26, 27, 84
Petra, 42, 89, 134, 193-194, 195, 196, 197, 199, 225, 235, 240, 244, 248, 254, 258, 269, G-7
Petrie, Sir Flinders, 7
petrified stone, 235

GENERAL INDEX 295

petroglyphs, 236-240
Peutinger map, 258, 271-272
phallic, 27
Pharaoh, 67, 102, 152, 153
Philadelphia, 50
Philistia, 49
Philistine Plain, 41, 50, 90, 108
Philistines, 110, 115, 122, 124, 125, 126, 128, 130, 141, 147, 148, 149, 172
Phoenicia, 32, 151, 152, 162, 245
pick, 26
pictographs, 241
pilgrim's progress, 66
pillars, 224-225
pin, 47
pistachio trees, 172 (fig. 33)
pit, 46, 48, 184
Plains of Moab, 57, 59
plaster lining, 48
Pliny, 162, 270
police post, 138, 173, 181
political power, 174
pomegranates, 90, 112, 144, 266
Pompeii, 239
pool, 23, 24
Potiphar, 19
potter, 48
pottery, 8-10, 32, 34-35, 43, 49, 54, 55, 57, 61, 69-70, 76, 79, 82, 102, 109, 116, 160-162, 172, 182, 183, 201-203, 207, 232, 263
precious stones, 162
prehistoric rock drawings, 241
presbyter, 271
priests, 246
Promised Land, 10, 15, 32, 44, 51, 86, 112-114, 120, 129, 148, 155, 157, 229
prophetic ideals, 141-142
Prophets, 18, 142
Prophets of Israel, 144-145
Province of Arabia, 230, 243, 244, 252
Psyche, 240
Ptolemies, 71, 188
publican, 270
public works, 174
Punon, 18, 44-45, 50, 87, 89, 121, 122, 155
Puteoli, 196, 197
pylon, 152
pyramid, 277

Qa'at en-Nefkh, 226
Qasr el-Juheniyeh, F-3
  es-Sirr, D-3
  Feifeh, 202, 203, G-4
  Muheileh, 231-232, 233, 235, D-6
  Rabbah, 236 (fig. 47), 240, 241
  Ruheibeh, 264-265
  Sfar, 207
  Siq (see Qasr Wadi Siq) E-6
  Umm el-Qeseir, 234-235, E-6
  Wadi Siq, 233-234, E-6
Qausanal, 165-166, 168
Qeseir Amra, 240
Qetsiot, 220, B-4
Qir-haresheth, 41-42, H-3
Queen of Sheba, 15, 19, 162, 186
quern, 27
Qumran, 143, 144, 199

Rabinowitz, Louis M., xiii
Rabboth Ammon, 50, 147
Rachel, 117-118, 196
Rafah, A-2
raid, 126-127
rain, xi, xii, 7, 12, 20-25, 40, 77, 92-94, 100, 138, 173, 176, 216-222
ram, 167
Rameses III, 109
Ramoth, 130, 131
Raphia, 108
Ras Raman, 275
Ras Zuweira, F-2
Rebekkah, 263
Rechab, Jonadab ben, 143-145
Rechabites, 136, 140, 141, 142-145, 198
Red Sea, 32, 121, 123, 138, 146, 150, 152, 153, 155, 157, 159, 163, 165, 169, 196
Refa'im, 26, 73
refining, 37
Rehobot, 261-264, C-4
Rekhmeh, 78-84, 91
religion of Israel, 31, 141-145
renaissance, 248
Rephidim, 129
reservoir, 92, 95, 173, 201, 210, 211, 223-225, 231, 262, 266-267, 272
resin, 163
retainers, 102, 103
Retenu, 102, 103
retreats, 249
retrograde, 167-168
revetment, 62, 74-75, 106, 176-177, 268
reward, 167
rhinoceros, 2
Rhinocolura, 269
Rhodes, 196, 197
ring, 48, 166-168
risers, 24
River of Egypt, 120, 142, 198
Road of the Sultan, 33, 228

GENERAL INDEX

roasting, copper ore, 36-37, 43-44, 164-165
rock altar, 83
  buildings, 196
  drawings, 204 (fig. 42, 43), 236-242
roads, 41, 46 (fig. 3), 186, 227-228, 258
Roman, xii, 34, 42, 79, 92, 193, 210, 243
  church, 245-251
  cities, 34
  milestones, 33, 227-228, 230
  policy, 230
  pottery, 35
  roads, 33, 42, 228
Romans, 230
Rome, 188, 254
rooms, 27, 45-48, 179, 185
ropes, 163
Rothenberg, Benno, xiii
Royal Road, 228
Ruheibeh, 34, 260-264, C-4
Ruin of Samra, 53-56
Rujm Sfar, 207
rujum, 54, 207

Sabaean, 281
Sabkhah, 117
sacred images, 117
sacrifice, 61-63, 119
Saint George, 273
  Hilarion, 259
  John, 273
  Mary, Basilica, 250
  Theodore, 273
Salameh, Demetrius, 194
salt, 248
Salt Sea, 73
Samaria, 20
sanctuary, 83
sandstone, 17, 206
sandstorm, 164
Saracens, 277
Sarah, 63-64, 75, 102, 103
Saudi Arabia, 142
Saul, 123, 124, 125, 126, 129, 132, 133, 147, 153, 184
Savignac, Father R., 273
Savior, 224, 274
scarab, 8
Scorpion Pass, 34, 89, 206, 207, E-4
sculpture, 4, 27-28, 49, 61, 102, 195
Scythopolis, 50
seal, 79, 165, 166-168, 178
Sea of Lot, 3, 121
Sea of Salt, 3, 52, 121
Sea Peoples, 90, 141
seaport, 150, 157, 162, 163, 173, 174

sea route, 158
Sedei Boqer, 224-225, 229, C-4
sedentary occupation, xii, 7, 9, 11, 14, 40, 104, 106, 108, 169
Seir, 73, 153, 154
Seir-Edom, 206
Sela, 134, 193-194
Seleucids, 71, 188, 189
Semites, 104
Semitic, 194-195, 199
Seostris (Sen Usert I), 103
serpent, 45
servants, 67
seven, 48
Shabbath, 66
shafts, 45-46
Shamah, 184
Shanan, L., 220
Shaqilath, 204
Sharuhen, 41, 49, 108
Shaveh-Kiriathim, 73
sheaves, 53, 196
Sheba, 162
Shechem, 102, 107, 122
sheep, 22, 48, 67, 93, 181, 210, 231
Sheikh Audeh ibn Jad, 155
Sheikh Sa'ad, 73
shell eyes, 28
shells, 47
Shemeber, 72, 73
shepherd, 48, 181, 203, 208
shepherdess, 22, 55
sherds (see pottery), 172
Sheshonk I, 119, 138, 152
Shihor, 124
Shiloh, 122
Shinab, 72, 73
Shinar, 73
ships, 151-152, 157-163
Shishak, 119, 138, 152
Shobek, 95, 106
Shofar, 280, 283
shrubs, 93, 213, 233
Shuhah, 138
Shuhatites, 138
Shur, 63, 75, 128, 129, 133, 261
shuttle, 56
sickle, 4
Siddim, 72, 73
sidr, 203
sieve, 177
sigillata, 201, 203
signet ring, 166-168
silk, 207
silos, 45
silver, 67, 152

GENERAL INDEX

Sinai, 11, 12, 14, 15, 18, 19, 20, 23, 49, 50, 51, 58, 61, 63, 64, 65, 69, 71, 72, 74, 75, 77, 80, 85, 86, 87, 89, 91, 97, 100, 103, 105, 109, 111-114, 120, 121, 127, 128, 129, 138, 141-145, 148, 152, 153, 158, 160, 163, 169, 170, 189, 193, 196, 197, 212, 228, 236, 259, 277, 279
Sinuhe, 101-105
Siq el-Bared, 240
Sisera, 134
Site 306, 185-186, D-4
   307, 58-59, 80, D-4
   308, 57-58
   310, 58-59, 80, D-4
   345, 97-102, 140 (fig. 28), B-5
   346, 216, 217, B-5
   367, 216-222, B-5
skull, 28
slag, 36-37, 156
slaves, 156
smelter, 36, 43-44, 45, 150, 156-158, 159-163, 164-165
Smith, George Adam, 6
smiths, 46, 48, 134
Sodom, 72, 73, 80, 89, 105, F-3
soil, 17, 33, 40, 41, 47, 80, 90-92, 174, 221-222
soldier-farmers (*limitanei*), 270
Solomon, xii, 15, 19, 20, 32, 36, 37, 43, 44, 45, 63, 106, 132, 138, 146, 148, 149, 150, 151, 152, 153, 154-157, 163, 165, 170, 171, 172, 173, 174, 178, 185, 186, 222
Sown, 12, 58, 212
Spain, 152, 247
spear, 26
spices, 150, 158, 162, 163, 195, 207, 257
spillways, 211
spindle whorls, 271
spinning, 55
spiritual values, Israel, 142
springs, 24, 25, 33, 34, 35, 36, 37, 78, 88, 93, 95, 96, 98, 106, 138, 139, 173, 201, 203, 205, 233, 237
staircase, 223-225
statuettes, 58, 117
S'tav, 91
stele, 10
Stephen of Byzantium, 244
steps, 24, 212, 222-224, 272
stibium, 104
Stone Age, 25-30
stone bowls, 27, 45, 46 (fig. 9)
storage pits, 46
store room, 45
Strabo, 199, 270

stream bed, 40
streams, 92-94
stretchers, 176, 186
stronghold, 173, 177, 185
Subeita (Isbeita) 34, 215, 219, C-4
subterranean, 45-48, 95
Succoth, 43
survey, Negev, 171
   Transjordan, x, 13, 30, 160
synagogue, 208, 251, 279-284
Syria, 14, 61, 71, 72, 74, 75, 97, 105, 108, 117, 123, 147, 148, 149, 152, 162, 171, 192, 193, 195, 196, 210, 212, 228, 244
Syriac, 271

Taanach, 40
Tablets of Law, 144
Tadmor, 171, 244
Tadmor, N. H., 220
Talmud, 14, 259, 279
talus, 268
tamarisk, 213
Targum, 259
Tariq es Sultani, 33
Tarshish, 152, 159, 163
Tarsus, 192
Tartessus, 152
teakwood, 248
Teima, 190, 237
teleilat el-anab, 92, 172 (fig. 36), 216-222, 229, 265
Teleilat Ghassul, 57, 59, 61
tell, 5, 6, 40, 50, 79
Tell Abu Hureireh, 41, 75, C-2
   Abu Matar, 43-49, 44-45, 56, 58, 61, 80, 89
   Arad, 41-42, 50-53, 56, 57, 76 (fig. 11), 88, 96, 114, 116, 132, 133, 138, 180, 279, E-2
   Ashtarah, 73
   Beit Mirsim, 9, 108, 139-140
   el-Ajjul, 41, 50, 108
   -Far'ah, 41, 49, 108, B-2
   -Kheleifeh, 32, 51, 132, 159, 160-163, 165, 185, D-12
   -Milh, 56, 88, 115, 131, 132, 180, 181-182, E-3
   Jammeh, 280
   Rekhmeh, 79-84, 91, D-4
   Sab'a, 40-41
temple, 30, 196, 197, 212, 237, 241, 244
Temple of Solomon, 63, 119, 142, 150-151, 152, 188
tent, 51, 56, 75, 131, 134, 136, 142, 169, 182, 183
Tenth Legion, 243

teraphim, 117
terra cotta statuettes, 117
terraces, 35, 52, 53, 54, 91, 92, 94, 97, 172 (fig. 32-34), 202, 211-213, 214-215, 216-222, 236 (fig. 55), 261, 265
terra sigillata, 203
tesserae, 280
textile, 56
thamileh, 22
Thamilet es-Suweilmeh, 237
Thamudic, 241
thatched roof, 82
The Desert of the Exodus, 220
The Seven Pillars of Wisdom, 33
The Wilderness of Zin, 33, 34
Thebes, 104, 119, 152
theological school, 259
Thomna, 270
Thotmes I, 109
threshing floor, 53
thunderbolt, 195
Thutmose III, 119
Tiber, 245
Tid'al, 72, 73
Tiglath-Pileser II, 151
Tigris, 244
tillu, 5
timbers, 163
Timnah, 36
tin, 152
toggle pin, 47
tolls, 187, 270
Toloha, 201, F-5
Tomb of Obodas, 273
tombs, 212, 273, 277-278
tools, 27, 29, 48, 47, 158, 207
tournette, 48
towers, 172, 222-225
trade, 76, 151-153, 163, 169, 171, 179, 181, 199, 204, 244
trade route, xii, 14, 70, 78, 155, 162, 170, 195, 201, 225-228
trail, 227-228, 234, 237
Trajan, 33, 228, 248
Transfiguration painting, 269
Transjordan, x, xii, 6, 7, 10, 11, 12, 13, 35, 49, 58, 59, 60, 71, 74, 81, 105, 108, 160, 194, 201, 204, 210, 212, 228, 237, 239, 240, 255
travel route, 14, 23, 26, 74, 78, 89, 105, 108, 138, 150, 158, 170, 234, 235, 237, 238, 248-249, 274
treaty, 163, 171
tribal life, 75
trough, 22
Tubal-Cain, 45, 134
tumuli, 34

tunnels, 45-46, 95, 106
Turkish rule, 228-229
tusk, 3
Tyre, 43, 151

Umm el-Jemal, 210
es-Sedeir, xiii, 281-283, C-11
underground chamber, 225
springs, 106
tombs, 273
village, 45-48
water, 93, 95, 100, 106, 173, 213, 231, 233
United Kingdom of Israel and Judah, 106
Ur, 33, 66
Uzziah, 168, 171-172, 173-174, 176, 177, 178, 222

Valley of Eshkol, 112
the Lebanon, 121
the Smiths, 44, 45, 134, 156-157, 207
Vergil, 271
village, 45, 60, 69, 97, 100
Vincent, Père Hugo, 7, 273
vinedresser, 174
vines, 144, 206
vineyards, 17
Vulcan, 46

Wadi Abdah, 96
 Abu Rutheh, 96
 Abyad, 79-80, 86, 96, 266
 Arabah, xii, 24, 36-37, 42, 45, 46, 50, 80, 87, 89, 91, 92, 121, 131, 133, 134, 146, 149, 154, 156-163, 164, 179, 197-198, 201, 203, 204, 205, 207, 212, 228, 231, 232, 235, 258, 275
 Ar'areh, 57, 96
 Asluj, 96, 129
 Auja, 79, 96
 Azeizi, 96
 Baqqar, 96
 Beqqarah, 96
 Besor, 129
 Dana, 44
 Dhobai, 210
 el-Arish, 14, 79, 86, 92, 121, 149, 198, 275, A-5
 -Qudeirat, 73
 Fiqreh, 86, 91, 205, 206, E-4
 Ghazzeh, (Gaza), 41, 52, B-2
 Hadhirah, 89, F-4
 Hafir, 21, 23, 96, 98, 221-222, 270
 Haleiqim, 96

GENERAL INDEX

Hathirah, 23, 89, 229, D-4
Heiyani, 87, E-8
Hismeh, 237
Iqfi, 87, D-9 and 10
Jeib, 203
Jerafi, 87, 275, C-9
Jurf, 96
Khalasah, 90, 96, 129, 260
Khalil, 138
Kurnub, 79-80, 138, 213
La'anah, 96
Luzan, 172 (fig. 33)
Mishash, 52, 58, 86, 96
Mitnan, 96
Murabba'at, 199
Murrah, 95, 206
Nafkh, 96, 275
Nitsanah, 25
Qreiq, 233
Qudeirat, 63, 96
Raman, 33, 226, 228, 229, 230, 231, 232, 235, 243, 274, 275, C and D-6
Ramliyeh, 223, 272
Ramm, 237
Raviv, 76 (fig. 17), 96, 213-215, 236 (fig. 55), 265
Rekhmeh, 78-84, 96, 209
Reseiseiyah, 96
Ruheibeh, 261, 262, 264
Sab'a, 43, 45, 47, 49, 52, 78, 79, 129, 138
Shellaleh, 52, 280
Siq, 226, 229, 231, 232, 233, 274
Sirhan, 238
Themeleh, 129
Umm es-Sedeir, xiii, 236 (fig. 49), 281-283, C-11
Zayatin, 266
wadi(s), 94-96, 210-215, 216-222
Wahabi, 142
war, 71
wasm, 225
watchtower, 185, 233, 264
water, 20-25, 33, 90-92, 100-101
 channels, 92, 217
 conservation, 92, 94, 202, 210-213, 216-222
waterhole, 88, 227, 232, 237
watershed, 52, 78, 180
waterskin, 232

waterfall, 23-24
Way of Khiltsa, 259
Way of Shur, 19, 63, 259, 261, 264, 274
Way of the Land of the Philistines, 50, 108, 189, 261
Way of the Wells, 88, 112
way station, 203, 207, 226, 238
weapons, 43, 207
weather, xii
weavers, 48, 56
weaving, 55, 76 (fig. 12), 271
weight, loom, 55, 61
 net, 163
well, 23, 33, 34, 41, 78, 83, 88, 93, 95, 98, 100, 173, 229, 260, 262
Well of Oath, 39
 Seven, 39
 the Seeing God, 63-64, 263
wheat, 53, 91, 144, 177, 183, 270
whorl, 55
wilderness, 6, 172, 187, 226
Wilderness of Paran, 21, 65, 112, 153
Wilderness of Shur, 261
Wilderness of Zin, 15, 16, 21, 33, 34, 112
winds, 17, 163-165
wine, 198, 199, 207, 259
witness mounds, 228-229
Woolley, C. Leonard, 33, 34

Yam Suph, 121
Yerahmeel, 140
Yerahmeelites, 124-125, 131, 134, 136, 140, 141
Yerka, 23, 24
yoke, 53
Yeruham, 78
Yeruham dam, 76 (fig. 15), 80-81
Yotvatah, 36

Zaanannim, 134
Zamzumim, 26
Zarethan, 43
Zeboyim, 72, 73, 105
Zeus, 188, 195, 197, 240, 274
Ziklag, 123, 125, 126, 127, 128, 129, 130, 138, 184
Zoar, 72, 73, 75, 105
Zuzim, 73

INDEX OF BIBLICAL CITATIONS

GENESIS	page	GENESIS	page
1:26	3	31:17-19, 30	118
4:22	45, 134	32:28	154
12:9	66	36:1	154
12:1-20	67	36:9, 11	154
13:1-5	67	49:30	278
13:3	67	49:31	137
13:12	84	50:13	137
14	71, 101, 228	50:24-25	278
14:4	106	EXODUS	
14:1-7	11, 73	2:15-22	132
14:5-7	74	3:1	142
14:10	72	3:5	282
14:12	72	4:22, 23	120
14:14	102	13:17	50
14:14-16	72	15:22	19, 261
16:7	19, 259, 261	15:23-26	259
16:7-14	63	17:16	129
16:14	259	19:0	142
17:4-5	61	34:30	197
17:5	104	LEVITICUS	
18:1-8	103	18:16	192
20:1	19, 63, 69, 75, 261	19:18	66
20:12	102	NUMBERS	
21:14-21	21	13:17-20	113
21:18	65	13:21	34
21:19	64	13:27-29	113
21:21	65, 153	13:29	128, 129
21:30-31	39	14:36, 37	113
22:2	63	14:45	128
22:7-8	62	20:1-5	16
22:12	61	20:23-28	206
22:14	62-64	21:1	114, 115
22:18	64	21:1-3	115
22:19	64	21:3	115
24:15-20	23	21:8-10	45
24:62	19, 104, 263	21:9	134
25:18	19	21:18	22
25:30	273	24:21	134
26:19	22	33:8	19
26:22	19, 260, 261	33:37	206
26:22-23	263	33:40	114
31:19, 34-35	196	33:42	44, 50

300

INDEX OF BIBLICAL CITATIONS

NUMBERS	page
33:43	45
34:4	207
34:4, 5	120

DEUTERONOMY	
1:2, 44	154
2:20	26
6:15	66
8:8	144
8:9	32, 44, 157
23:7	154
30:19	65
33:1	154
34:3	133

JOSHUA	
11:17	154
12:7	154
13:2-3	124
14:14	137
14:15	137
15:1-4	14, 34
15:3	207
15:4, 47	120
15:17	139
15:18, 19	139
15:21, 31	132
15:21-32	51, 178
19:8	130

JUDGES	
1:9	133
1:14-16	139
1:16	132, 133
3:9	140
4:11-23	134
5:4-5	154
9:45	6
20:1	13

I SAMUEL	
3:20	13
13:19	110
15:5-7	129, 133
17:7	56
18:7	123
25:1	153
27:8	124, 125, 128
27:10	124, 133, 134, 141
27:11	125
27:12	124
29:4	126
29:6-7	126
29:8-9	126
29:11	126
30:1-5	127
30:14	124, 129, 134, 136, 141
30:16	130
30:26	130

I SAMUEL	page
30:27-31	131
30:28	50, 184

II SAMUEL	
2:4	124
5:20-25	147
7:12-15	136
7:22	135
8:2, 14	148
8:18	141
10:19	147
12:24	150
23:8	138

I KINGS	
3:1	152
4:21, 24 (5:1, 4 in Heb. Bible)	149
4:24 (5:4 in Heb. Bible)	171
4:25 (5:5 in Heb. Bible)	149
7:45-46	43
8:65	14, 149
9:19	170-171
9:20-22	171
9:26	31, 32, 159
9:26-28	151, 152, 158
10:2	162
10:10	162
10:11, 22	152
10:22	31, 151, 171
10:28, 29	153
11:14-22	153, 154
11:15, 16	148
11:14, 17, 21-22	20
16:25-27	135
19:8-15	142
21:8	167
22:48	152, 159

II KINGS	
3:16-18	22
14:25	14
16:6	165
21:2-7, 16	116

ISAIAH	
1:11, 16, 17	62, 66
28:21	147
31:1, 3	120
34	154
35:1, 6-7	93
35:10	93
45:9	9

JEREMIAH	
10:9	152
13:19	187
33:13	187
35:2	143
35:6-7	143
35:11	142

INDEX OF BIBLICAL CITATIONS

JEREMIAH	page	I CHRONICLES	page
35:12, 13, 16, 17	143-144	2:49	132, 138
35:16-17	143	2:55	140, 142
43:6-12	19	4:11	138
49:17-22	154	4:12-14	44, 45, 134, 156
EZEKIEL		4:15	140
20:26	65	4:42-43	154
20:46-47	139	11:44	184
25:12-14	154	12:1	184
25:16	141	13:5	124
27:12, 25	152	14:16	147
36:33-35	284	II CHRONICLES	
HOSEA		2:11, 12	151
6:6	62	3:1	63
AMOS		4:17	43
1:11	154, 156	8:4	171
5:24	65	9:12	162-163
9:7	109	14:6, 7	171
OBADIAH		17:2	171
1:19, 20	139	20:36, 37	152
HABBAKUK		26:6-8	172
3:3	154	26:10	172, 174, 222
ZEPHANIAH		MATTHEW	
2:4-5	141	2:13-15	19
HAGGAI		7:12	66
2:23	167	LUKE	
PSALMS		10:17	66
63:1	90	10:25-27, 36, 37	66
107:7	227	ACTS	
126:4	93	7:33	282
126:4-6	frontispiece, 94	II CORINTHIANS	
PROVERBS		11:32-33	192
31:10-25	55-56	GALATIANS	
JOB		4:22-25	65
2:8	35	HEBREWS	
7:6	56	13:6	224
I CHRONICLES		REVELATION	
2:42	140	6:2-8	72

Map: Judah and the Negev

Regions / Bodies of Water:
- MEDITERRANEAN (SEA)
- GAZA STRIP
- DEAD SEA
- JUDAH
- NEGEV
- EGYPT
- LEBANON
- WADI GAZA
- WADI EL-ARISH

Locations (with alternate/ancient names in parentheses):

- Kerak (Qir of Moab)
- Hebron
- Ain Gedi (Engedi)
- Masada
- Ras Zuweira
- Kh. Kuseifeh
- Tell Arad
- Kh. el-Gharrah
- Kh. el-Mishash
- Kh. Jamra
- Tell Milh (HORMAH?)
- Kh. Ghazza
- Biyar el-Mishash
- Kh. Ar'areh (Aroer)
- Harabet Umm Dimneh
- Sodom
- Kh. Medinbe (Beth-Pelet?)
- Biyar Ar'areh
- Qasr es-Sirr
- Qasr el-Juheniyeh
- Kh. Abu Tulul
- Beersheba
- Bir Mishash
- Kurnub (Mampsis)
- Qasr Feijeh
- et-Telah (Toloha)
- Kh. Nahas (Ir Nahash)
- Feinan (Punon)
- Ain el-Ifdan (Fedan)
- Tell Abu Hureirah (GERAR)
- Bir Asluj 304 306
- 309 310
- Tell Rekhmeh (YERUHAM)
- WADI HATHIRAH (MAKHTESH QATAN)
- SCORPION PASS
- Ain Aqrabbim
- Ain Hosb (Eiseiba)
- Kh. Paqu'ah
- Bir Themeleh
- Ain Murrah
- Ain Umm Qa'ab
- JEBEL MEDHRA (HAR HA-HAR)
- MAKHTESH GADOD
- Ain Qattar
- Qasr Muheileh
- Khalasah (Elusa)
- Ruheibeh (Rehobot)
- Mishrefeh
- Sedei-Boqer
- Ain Mureifiq
- Abdah (Ovdat, Eboda)
- Ain Shehabiyeh
- WADI HATHIRAH
- Ain Fiqreh
- Ain Wehbeh
- Gaza
- Rafah
- Nirim
- Tell Far'aho (SHARUHEN)
- Kh. Umm Rujum
- Isbeita
- Bir Hafir
- WADI PARAN
- Auja Hafir (Nitsanah)
- Bir Birean (Be'erotayim)
- Qetsiot
- 345
- Bir Reseisiyeh (Resisim) 346
- Bir Mitnan
- 367
- Ain el-Qudeirat (Kadesh-Barnea)